Yale French Studies

NUMBER

Perecko... / Reading Georges Perec

WARREN MOTTE AND JEAN-JACQUES POUCEL	1	Editors' Preface: On Reading Georges Perec
JACQUES JOUET	4	In Brief
CLAUDE BURGELIN	9	Georges Perec, or the Spirit of Beginnings
MARCEL BÉNABOU	20	From Jewishness to the Aesthetic of Lack
SYDNEY LÉVY	36	Emergence in Georges Perec
WARREN MOTTE	56	The Work of Mourning
BERNARD MAGNÉ	72	Georges Perec on the Index
GERALD PRINCE	89	Preliminary Discussion of Women in *La vie mode d'emploi*
JACQUES ROUBAUD	99	Perecquian OULIPO
DAPHNÉ SCHNITZER	110	A Drop in Numbers: Deciphering Georges Perec's Postanalytic Narratives
JEAN-JACQUES POUCEL	127	The Arc of Reading in Georges Perec's *La clôture*
RENÉE REISE HUBERT AND JUDD D. HUBERT	156	Georges Perec's and Paolo Boni's *Métaux*
JACQUES ROUBAUD	178	Perec's 17 Extreme Experiences

Yale French Studies

Warren Motte and Jean-Jacques Poucel, *Special editors for this issue*
Alyson Waters, *Managing editor*
Editorial board: Edwin Duval (Chair), Ora Avni, R. Howard Bloch, Peter Brooks, Mark Burde, Thomas Kavanagh, Christopher L. Miller, Donia Mounsef, Susan Weiner
Editorial assistant: Scott Hiley
Editorial office: 82-90 Wall Street, Room 308
Mailing address: P.O. Box 208251, New Haven, Connecticut 06520-8251
Sales and subscription office:
Yale University Press, P.O. Box 209040
New Haven, Connecticut 06520-9040
Published twice annually by Yale University Press

Copyright © 2004 by Yale University
All rights reserved.
This book may not be reproduced, in whole or in part, in any form (beyond that copying permitted by Sections 107 and 108 of the U.S. Copyright Law and except by reviewers for the public press) without written permission from the publisher.

Designed by James J. Johnson and set in Trump Medieval Roman by The Composing Room of Michigan, Inc. Printed in the United States of America by the Vail-Ballou Press, Binghamton, N.Y.

ISSN 044-0078
ISBN for this issue 0-300-10274-7

Pierre Getzler, "G.P. in 1970, rue Vilin," 2002. Courtesy of the artist.

WARREN MOTTE AND
JEAN-JACQUES POUCEL

Editors' Preface:
On Reading Georges Perec

Not so very long ago, any serious piece of writing dealing with Georges Perec had to be accompanied by a preface, cast in more or less serious terms, arguing the legitimacy of dealing with Georges Perec in a serious manner. Undoubtedly that is no longer the case. Nevertheless, a reader might well ask why an issue of *Yale French Studies* should be devoted to Georges Perec, now, and what might be at stake therein.

Beginning to address those questions, one might suggest that it seems to be clear, now, that Perec is one of the major French writers of the twentieth century (let us not forget that four whole years yawn between that century and the present). Indeed, some of the contributors to this issue would doubtless claim that Perec is *the* French writer of that century. Now, twenty-two years have passed since Perec's death, roughly the same amount of time that Perec himself devoted to writing, in a serious manner. As the profile of his work becomes gradually more apparent, one aspect of Perec's project becomes inevitable: a will to traverse the spectrum of generic, thematic, and technical potential in order "to write everything that someone today can possibly write" (as he himself put it in 1978). If he did not actually realize that impossible goal, he was nonetheless unflaggingly faithful to it. The variety of Perec's texts is striking, and it enables them to ramify well beyond the boundaries within which tradition might have confined them. It is also important to note that as they ramify, they sketch out new horizons of possibility for literary experiments conducted in their wake.

Yet the very variety of Perec's writings may make it difficult for one to imagine them as an oeuvre, and the reader coming upon them for the first time may be hard pressed to find a path through them. Neither of those eventualities is particularly dire in itself, of course, but they each pose questions about our protocols of reading. A reader might, for instance, follow one of the four directions that Perec himself claimed to have pursued in his writing: a concern for the everyday and its details; a tendency toward confession and autobiography; an impulse toward formal innovation; and a desire to tell engaging stories. There are, however, many, many other paths that one might walk. And if the critical writing devoted to Perec in the last three decades confirms nothing else, it most certainly confirms this: just as Perec's writings are extremely various, so, too, are the readings those writings have elicited.

In Perec's case—most particularly in his case, that is—writing always returns to reading. In the first instance, the notion of legibility itself was a fascinating one for Perec, and he tested it continually, in different ways. Some of his texts (*Alphabets*, for instance) are printed "in constraint" along with their "translation," a choice that necessarily brings the question of legibility into focus for his reader. Other texts, though highly "constructed," bear few obvious traces of that construction (*La vie mode d'emploi* is undoubtedly the best example of that tactic), and can be read luxuriously, "flat out on one's bed," as Perec suggested. Perec's rethinking of the notion of legibility has important consequences, too, in terms of the contract that he establishes with his reader. While the reader's willingness to come to terms with the bold and the new remains a fundamental clause in that contract, Perec also offers his reader a broader franchise in literary creation, staging literature as an artisanal activity rather than as the product of inspiration, insisting on the collaborative relation of writer and reader, and providing his reader with the tools he or she will need in order to come to satisfactory terms with the text.

Reading Georges Perec, one can never forget for long that one is, well, *reading* Perec. His commitment to reading as a crucial human gesture can be found even in his most complex, arduous texts. It provides a remarkable coherence to his work as a whole; and it also provides coherence, we believe, to the essays in this volume. For the common thread here, just like in Perec's work, is the question of reading. Or that of rereading perhaps, since many of the contributors have been reading Perec over and over for what seems, now, like many years. In fact, some of them (Marcel Bénabou, Claude Burgelin, and Jacques Roubaud come to mind) have been reading him since well before Georges Perec became "Georges Perec." Granted that, it will not be astonishing that most of the pieces presented here are also about beginnings in one sense or another: about first gestures in writing or in reading, or about small figures that serve to generate vast imaginary landscapes, or about the way memory structures experience both lived and represented, or, more simply still and finally, about the manner in which things come to become.

We would like to express our gratitude to the authors who have contributed to this volume, as well as to the translators. We are also grateful to Ela Bienenfeld for permission to reprint poems from *Métaux*, to Pierre Getzler for sending us his drawings, and to Alyson Waters for her help in preparing the manuscript.

JACQUES JOUET

In Brief

I. THE BRIEF LIVES OF GEORGES PEREC

Everyone knows the story of the young orator who, on the day he gives his first speech, announces: "I shall be brief." He places his hand on his heart. And he dies. Life is short, and the story of the young orator is a "brief life." A "brief life" [*vie brève*] is a literary genre that obeys Jacques Roubaud's principle—life is brief and a brief form is necessary to account for this. Biographies, in general, are not "brief lives."

* * * * *

Georges Perec's life was brief.

* * * * *

Perec made his brief life as a writer more complicated by means of literary constraints. Among their other advantages, these constraints enabled him to confront and to communicate the fact that the life of his forebears had been made even briefer.

* * * * *

Georges Perec was born on 7 March 1936 in Paris and died on 3 March 1982 in Ivry—all in all a very brief journey unless we add a few of the stops he made along the way: Villard-de-Lans, Étampes, South Godstone, Chateau-d'Oex, Haifa, Sarajevo, Belgrade, Pau, Sfax, Saarbrucken—and Mabillon, Italy, or rue Vilin or Jussieu as well—Royaumont, Villeneuve-lez-Avignon, Brisbane, Ellis Island. . . .

* * * * *

The fact that in 1978 (that is, if we take into account the dates at either end of his life, +42 and −4 years) Perec published a book entitled *Je me souviens* remains tattooed in my memory.

* * * * *

La vie mode d'emploi [*Life a User's Manual*] is a novel filled with brief lives. These brief lives are circumscribed by two dates—birth and death, 1900–1975 (Percival Bartlebooth); the beginning of a career and misanthropic senility (Rémi Rorschach); a brilliant start and a violent death (the trapeze artist for whom Rorschach is the impresario). An exhaustive inventory would be, well, long.

* * * * *

Georges Perec's brief life was not as brief as, say, Kafka's, but then the average life expectancy at the beginning of the twentieth century was not the same as it is today. Georges Perec's brief life was filled with letters, games, places, letter games, word games, word-letters and word-places, as well as with private things. He made films, too. He could go from the very ordinary to the very outrageous. He needed the very ordinary to offer himself the outrageous. He needed the very outrageous to allow himself the ordinary.

* * * * *

Georges Perec is a member of the Oulipo; this fact modifies the accepted date of his birth and cancels out, to a certain extent, any date of his disappearance.

II. BRIEF LIVES, LONG LIVES

In the matter of brief lives, Pierre Larousse is a plagiarist by anticipation of Jean Queval. In the entry on Céline (Louis-Ferdinand) in the latter's *Première page, cinquième colonne* (1945), we can read a few praises of *Voyage au bout de la nuit*, a few reservations about *Mort à credit*, and then these words: "After having published this second book and fulfilled his destiny, Céline died. But an industrious prankster took hold of his name and his formula with impunity." You remember Pierre Larousse, the guy who wrote: "Bonaparte, general of the French Republic, born in Ajaccio (on the island of Corsica) on 15 August 1769, died at the Château de Saint-Cloud, near Paris, on the 18th Brumaire year VIII of the French Republic, one and indivisible."

Those are two wonderful lives, more abridged than brief, and fanciful—they rely on a cellular division of the biographical kind.

Another kind of fantasy uses addition rather than division. This would give us a "long life." Let's see what we get.

"The Long Life of Georges-Jules Perne-Verec"

In 1839, when he was eleven years old, Georges-Jules Perne-Verec left Nantes covertly as a deck hand on the *Coralie* to bring coral back to Carolina. He was caught in the nick of time by his father in Painboeuf. Not quite one hundred and eleven years later, he reappears in Paris, at the stamp market in the gardens of the Champs-Elysées, claiming not to have aged.

"He was eleven years and two months old. . . . He was wearing a jacket of gray woolen cloth with three buttons, a pair of navy blue short pants, brown shoes, and socks of blue wool.

"He raced down to the dock."

The navy and the dock will follow him forever after. This event led, much later, to the film *Les lieux d'une fugue*, from which the above quotation is taken.

In 1877, Hector Servadac (whose name is "cadavers" spelled backwards in French), wrote a rondeau using a compass. "Did he wield the compass in order to give his verses a rigorously mathematical meter?" For a time Servadac and his friends believe they are the sole survivors on earth; in fact, they are extraordinary travelers for the duration of a novel whose title could be that of Chapter XVI of its second part: "Wherein Captain Servadac and Ben-Zouf leave and return as they had left."

One hundred years later, or thereabouts, Perne-Verec, taking things to the extreme, would write the "Great Palindrome."

In 1881, he publishes *La jaganda* and in the encrypted document where the name of Ortega's assassin is revealed just as the decoder arrives—the moment the document is decoded[1] (II, 12)—to prove the innocence

---

1. It must be noted that the message has to be decoded again, since it relies in part on the false claim that there can never be, "in any language," three of the same letters in a row in one word, which would refute the existence of the French past participles *créée recréée, récréée*. . . . This is a task for Pierre Bayard.

of Joam Dacosta, Perne-Verec has Jarraiquez the decoder say: "Aha! . . . I have made a surprising observation: in this paragraph alone, all the letters of the alphabet are used! How strange!"

Even stranger, though, is the fact that the table of frequency of the letters of the message, which appears directly above this statement in the novel, invalidates this assertion, since one of the 26 letters of the French alphabet is missing.

Perne-Verec is saving this letter—the W—for his later work.

Exactly one hundred years later, in 1981, Perne-Verec composed this economical alexandrine:

w, w, w, w

Tireless anticipator of modern technologies, Perec just missed out on the world wide web.

Perne-Verec, it has always been said, greatly anticipated machine technology and the fates of the world. This is what made him decide, belatedly, to reveal the existence of Hugo Vernier—why not Pernier? you might ask—Vernier who turned out to be the most extraordinary anticipator in the entire history of French-language poetry.

In 1895 he published his *L'île à hélice* [Helix Island] for the first time, from which he made a kind of prequel in 1982 called *Ellis Island*. (You can see that it is through the medium of film that Perne-Verec readily returns in his later years to some of his youthful projects.) "What . . . I have come to question here is wandering, roaming."

Both *L'île à hélice* and *Ellis Island*, like the Abbey of Thélème, have no use for undesirables ("Here enter not. . . .") and both stand out because of their ex-territorial status: the first, Jaganda dreaming of being perennial, is mobile and detached from the United States in its utopia of fabulously wealthy people; the second is fixed and remains a short distance away from the promised land. The island just short of the United States; the island beyond.

Tired of *Extraordinary Voyages*, Perne-Verec imagined other, "infra-ordinary" ones, thinking, perhaps, of Xavier de Maistre.

He died in his 154th year.

It was important that, born in '28 (1828) he died in '82 (1982).

III. DO I REMEMBER?

Do I remember that in 1978, Georges Perec published a book called *Je me souviens*?

Do I remember that *Je me souviens* is part of a virtual set entitled *Les choses communes*?

I recall that I promised myself never to write down the least little unshared memory that would start off with the phrase "I remember . . ."

Do I remember a record of Kathleen Ferrier singing Schubert?

Do I remember, through photographs, that Georges Perec had no visible beard and no long shaggy hair?

Do I remember a time when everyone was writing "I remembers" in the newspapers?

I recall not having met Georges Perec in 1935—but he was really miniscule then.

Do I remember the blank pages at the end of Georges Perec's book entitled *Je me souviens*?

Do I remember that in 1978 Georges Perec published a book entitled *La vie mode d'emploi*?

Do I remember the thickness of the "novels" *La vie mode d'emploi*?

I recall how long and how heavy was the Oulipo's mourning when Georges Perec died.

I me souviens that in 1975 Joe Brainard published a book called *I remember*.

—Translated by Alyson Waters

CLAUDE BURGELIN

Georges Perec, or the Spirit of Beginnings

10 November 1619. A French horseman, crossing a Europe battered by terrible wars, shut up in a bedroom in faraway Germany, decides to doubt the very origin of all the knowledge he has accumulated ("nourished on letters since my childhood," [5]) and that has guided his thought and his conduct. Alone (a recluse in his "stove-heated room" [5]), and in an indisputably heroic manner, though free of any fantasy of heroism on his part, he uproots the tree of knowledge. Nothing can withstand the calm obstinacy of his project. In his own words, it is a matter of "rebuilding the house which we inhabit" after bringing down the ancient walls and framework (15).[1]

He is moved by "an excessive desire to learn to distinguish between the true and the false" (8). Why this great desire? Without a doubt because he lived during a somber moment of our history, when, to cite his near-contemporary Hamlet, "the time is out of joint." It was an era when representations of God, the place of the earth and sun, the authority of the monarchy, and the value of books and accepted wisdom were all sent reeling. Out of a passionate urgency to redraw the borders between the true and the false, the *Discourse on Method* was born, and with it a radical renewal of thought, of paths to knowledge, and of symbolic order in the West.

More than three hundred years after René Descartes, a very young and forlorn child, having lost all support and points of reference, must, in order to keep from slipping even further, reconstruct in his own way

---

1. René Descartes, *Discours de la méthode* (1637). (English translation: "Discourse on Method," trans. Elizabeth S. Haldane, in *The Philosophical Works of Descartes* [Cambridge: Cambridge University Press, 1911], vol. 1 and reprinted in René Descartes, *Discourse on the Method and Meditations on First Philosophy*, ed. David Weissman [New Haven: Yale University Press, 1996]. All page numbers refer to this edition.)

the foundations of what he can know and think, for they have collapsed in and around him. Because his world seems made up of incomprehensible and unanchored appearances, he too must reestablish fundamental distinctions between the true and the false and come to know how he thinks.

Let us recall the striking chapter in *W ou le souvenir d'enfance* that follows the blank page punctuated only by the typographical code of an ellipsis enclosed within parentheses, emblem of the mother's disappearance in Auschwitz.[2] A child is thus evoked, tormented by the ghostly image of a fragmented body, no longer able to comprehend how time and space are structured,[3] the meaning of the closest familial attachments, the value of words, the meaning of the human face,[4] or, of course, the very possibility of saying "I."[5] A child nearly mad, infinitely more lost than the horseman Descartes in his forest, a child removed from all that forms the basis of culture and the social fabric, from everything that permits the sharing of subjectivity and intimacy.

That child, and the writer who recreates him, both feel the same urgency as Descartes, the philosopher of disastrous times. How does one distinguish between the true and the false, between illusion and reality? The first part of *W ou le souvenir d'enfance* conveys the violent confusion of someone who feels deprived of a homeland ("I have no memories of childhood") and senses himself to be prisoner of a memory where some evil spirit has doggedly falsified perspectives, sowed memory-screens [*souvenirs-écrans*], and brought down the snows of amnesia.

Imre Kertész has been able to say: "I consider it a unique bit of luck and even a divine favor to have been at Auschwitz as a stigmatized Jew, and to have lived something because of my Judaism, to have seen something with my own eyes and to know once and for all and irrevocably something that I will never let go of."[6] Georges Perec did not witness that something with his own eyes; he only lived its consequences. Something had happened, but this something remained invisible under the snow of the Vercors, a truth thus marked with the possible stigmata of doubt, of the untrue, of the unreal.

---

2. Georges Perec, *W ou le souvenir d'enfance*, (Paris: Denoël, 1975). (Perec, *W or the Memory of Childhood*, trans. David Bellos [London: Collins Harvill, 1988], 61.)
3. "No beginning, no end. . . . It happened somewhere far away, but no one could have said very precisely where it was far from" (*W,* 69).
4. "Things and places had no name, or several; the people had no faces" (*W,* 69).
5. "You didn't ask for anything. . . . You didn't ask any question" (*W,* 69).
6. Quoted in *Le monde* (10 December 2002).

With simple yet masterly authority, Descartes restored the precepts of method, the foundations of thought and science, and coherence between knowledge and experience. There is something thrilling in Descartes's text, which comes from the alliance of the lucidity of his intellectual approach with the firm and reassuring energy that animates it. Observing that "all those things which fall under the cognizance of man might very likely be mutually related in the same fashion" as "those long chains of reasoning" of the geometricians, Descartes concludes plainly (and Perecquishly?) by asserting that, in relation to things still to be understood, "there can be nothing so remote that we cannot reach to it, nor so recondite that we cannot discover it. And I had not much trouble in discovering which objects it was necessary to begin with, for I already knew that it was with the most simple and those most easy to apprehend" (Descartes, 13).

One could certainly and effortlessly pursue this parallel between the precepts of method according to Descartes and Perec's manner of proceeding, including the very Perecquian last precept: "in all cases to make enumerations so complete and reviews so general that I should be certain of having omitted nothing" (13). But let us put down the looking glass that we have held up between the two before it turns into a mere rhetorical game. Of course this does permit me to state in passing that Perec's œuvre is a discourse on method endlessly reexamined, and that *Perecquism*, even in its most unbridled Rousselianism, still remains, if not a rationalism, at the very least an enterprise governed by method in its firmly held principles of clarity and rigor, and in a dynamism created by these principles alone.

The rules of method quickly led Descartes to pronounce his decisive "I think therefore I am" upon which everything was to be rebuilt. Here Perec's and Descartes's paths diverge. Without a doubt, the child from the Vercors found salvation in the reasoned acquisition of numbers, signs, and letters; in the elementary understanding of the principles of connection and intellectual articulation; and by marking out the safe territory of books. But where Descartes builds on solid foundations, Perec constantly reminds us that everything he constructs is rebuilt from a void, around an absence, upon a blank. Perec too has in mind the imagination of an architect (how else could he have conceived of *La vie mode d'emploi*?), but this constructive "I" remains an "I" between parentheses and ellipses, and surrounded by too much blank page. The evacuation or rupture of the "I" transforms the nature of the Perecquian "I think": it is constantly threatened with remaining a pure abstraction, a setting-in-motion of a method, or a mechanism that functions as if in his absence—as Perec notes sometimes with humor, sometimes with anguish, sometimes with a kind of jubilation, sometimes with anger or despair.

Still, the juxtaposition of Descartes's and Perec's inaugural gestures seems to me the most telling in the two men's need to go back and start everything over at its foundation, their only motivation an enthusiasm for thought, the certitude of reasoning, and an obstinacy to make sense.

If Perec's style and textual method are so convincing, it is because he always returns to that original gesture, to the most elementary sources of (his) knowledge and (his) thought, and to the origins of these origins: question, doubt, experience. Most of his books draw their force and their wrenching power—often in a playful and unexpected way, somewhat absurdly, close in spirit at times to Alice on the other side of the looking-glass—from this preliminary return to the starting point, to the *terminus a quo,* to the very origins of thought or infra-thought (perhaps like those Enlightenment philosophers who ceaselessly questioned and debated the origin of social phenomena—language, laws, socio-economic inequality, and so on; more surely in the image of a child troubled by a world order in which it is extremely difficult to integrate oneself). The most essential in Perec's work is its variation on a Book of Beginnings stubbornly and continually undertaken anew.

Espèces d'espaces is a book of beginnings. Starting from a playful obviousness, Perec masters a subject as perilous as our relation to spaces and their intervals: the book will be written on the page—first space, thus chapter one—and continues in a segmentation-nesting [*segmentation-emboîtement*] much like Russian Matrioshka dolls. At each stage multiple questions spring forth, weightless and dream-like but never abstract, always in relation to the ordinary of our daily life and to what Perec so aptly called the "infra-ordinary," always in a dialogue between taking the side of things [*le parti pris des choses*] and having respect for words [*le compte tenu des mots*].

Je me souviens is a book of beginnings as well—four hundred and eighty times over. Starting from the most blandly straightforward and matter-of-fact utterances "I remember . . . ," it encompasses a complex reflection on memory, its paradoxical paths, its incongruent flashes, and its feral insistence. The role of the infra-ordinary in historical consciousness originates in the return to the source here staged and rendered in a prepoetic poetry.

It was by setting his sights on the most foundational practices within the range of Oulipian potentialities that Perec went the farthest: the palindrome and the lipogram, mirrored writing and the reformulated alphabet. Remove a letter from the language—another game inspired by those of childhood—invent an alphabet game, and in so doing write that unexpected and dizzying fable about the Shoah, perhaps the only fable-fiction that the Shoah has produced and one that, by transposing the event, restores some of its most profound significance to it.

Penser/classer is a libretto of beginnings. Perec responds to Descartes's magnificent assertion—"I think therefore I am"—with a modest and groping: "I don't think but I'm searching for my words."[7] His manner of zigzagging about in order to better "refer thinking back to the unthought [*l'impensé*] on which it rests, and the classified to the unclassifiable (the unnameable, the unsayable) which it is so eager to disguise" (185) is clearly a way of keeping alive the link between thought-words [*mots-pensées*] and the vacillation, hesitation, and treacherous darkness from which they emerge.

Les lieux d'une ruse, also a libretto of constant beginnings: in its twenty or so pages, Perec succeeds in writing one of the most condensed texts about the experience on the analyst's couch while seemingly making only indirect allusions to this experience. He evokes only the context of the analysis, by relating the ritual of the sessions: the openings and closings of doors, the punctuation of time produced over the course of a psychoanalysis. By ostensibly observing only the infraordinary of the analysis and speaking only of what makes it materially possible (its platform or its base), he finds a way of getting to the essence of what was at stake for him.

Finally, it is by reproducing the book of beginnings a hundred times over that Perec causes the novel to implode (as he said), and, with *La vie mode d'emploi*, erects the most surprising novelistic edifice of the end of the last century.[8] By staging the primal gestures of narrative writing, those that nobody had ever thought of revisiting and that implicitly create the relationship between author and reader, Perec brings us to the point of achievement and vertigo in which this narrative constellation culminates.

7. Perec, *Penser/classer* (Paris: Hachette, 1985). (Perec, "Penser/Classer" in *Species of Spaces and Other Pieces*, trans. John Sturrock [London: Penguin, 1997], 198.) Translation slightly modified.

8. Perec, *La vie mode d'emploi* (Paris: Hachette, 1978). (Perec, *Life a User's Manual*, trans. David Bellos [Boston: Godine, 1987].)

The preamble throws off the reader, for it leads not to the paths of fiction but to didactic deliberations on the ins and outs of the art of jigsaw puzzling. The reader's eye, setting forth on the paths laid down for it, is drawn toward the tiny figures sketched on the page—outlines of a vague hominization, oafish bodies with rudimentary arms and legs like those in a child's drawing, representations of the different classes of puzzle pieces. This novel/world is born out of these coarse and archaic (though neatly cut) shapes.

In a near-scholarly tone, this opening proposes a user's manual for the novel almost straightforwardly. After decades of critical skirmishes and polemics over the novel's scope, its stakes, and its stages of evolution, Perec cuts short all debate by bringing his readers back to the calm and banal memories of childhood. The puzzle is the logical extension of the building games of two- to three-year olds: it permits children to erect a framework in which they can fit the dismembered cutouts of tormented forms, thus affixing them in a frame that binds and adjusts them, removing their worrisome or unsettling aspects. Furthermore, the parable of the puzzle summons up a vital truth regarding the art of the novel: though reading is certainly a solitary act, it is but one player's turn in a game played by two, in keeping with the metaphor of the trap or the hunt. Starting from this trivial realization about a game of little mystery, the entire infernal machine of the novel is set in motion.

Finally, the novel is modeled on a rudimentary architecture, reminiscent of a toddler's drawing—the house that every child has drawn and that synthesizes in one structure his or her self, body, parents, and relation to space and to others. Here the model is reduced to its simplest form, a grid of ten squares by ten squares, traversed according to methodical division and a carefully though-out plan of attack.

Thus, starting from a child's game, a child's drawing, and what they spark, the French novel attains this moment of fulfillment or this display of fireworks.

Always returning to the root of the matter can be called "radical," if we look at the root—and how appropriately—of the word. With this gesture, as much an uprooting as a foundation, Perecquian radicalism comes into contact with the spirit and mindset of a modernity whose emblems are rupture, the uphill return to the archaic in order to discover new horizons, and the contestation of the power and codes of literature. But with his serene and discreet manner of keeping off to the side, Perec avoids the traps of modernity as ideology and rupture as fetish. Perhaps in practicing the infra-ordinary of radicalism, Perec escapes mythology and megalomania. His quest intersects sundry avant-garde movements without adhering to their myths of waging war or rallying to the standard of innovation.

Modernity has required that writing become risk, adventure, a drifting away from the old parapets. In his entirely original way, Perec made that imperative his own while still preserving an astounding freshness in his writing. It is often, as it were, writing without shadow. Whereas so many writers produce an expertly staged *chiaroscuro,* or a syntax that parades as a complex branching inward toward some hidden secret, or else an electrification triggered by the vehemence of impulses, the mystery of Perec's writing is that it is without mystery or perceptible shadow. Its outlines are clear and it is of an absolute grammatical and syntactical simplicity. This is even more paradoxical when one considers how well known it is today that his writing is most often dizzyingly encoded, a product of the secret figuring and encoding whose labyrinths Bernard Magné in particular has been so capable of mapping.[9] The fabric of Perecquian writing is studded with pebbles so white that the eye of a sleuth was needed to spot them, so discrete and hidden are they in the woof and warp of the text.

It is thus paradoxical that this neo-cabalist and word-gamer often gives the precise impression that he is not playing with words. Why all these puns, anagrams, lipograms, calculations, and verbal-literary acrobatics only to attain a clear, simple, transitive language perfectly devoid of linguistic cloudiness? As if the sum of all these constraints had acted as a filter granting his language its clarity? As if some higher principle of attraction had magnetized the signifiers, like metal filings, in such a way that they reach this discursive purity? As if the guiding imperative were to allow the advent of an *écriture* constantly beginning, finding once again the clarity of first principles and elementary conjunctions? If Perec's *œuvre* is a book of beginnings, it is because in it he rediscovers the first role of the word according to Genesis, the role of separation, and foundational and creative distinction.

This book of beginnings of a thousand and one chapters is attached as if by an umbilical cord to that which unwound the thread of writing in Perec: the death of his parents and, with it, the disappearance of the child he was when with them. "I write because they left in me their

---

9. See Bernard Magné, *Perecollages 1981–1988* (Toulouse: Presses Universitaires de Mirail-Toulouse, 1989).

indelible mark, whose trace is writing. Their memory is dead in writing; writing is the memory of their death and the assertion of my life" (W, 42).

Writing means continually referring back to "the scandal of their silence and of mine" (W, 42). This book of beginnings is endlessly put back on the writing table in order to start over from the inaugural moment that binds together writing and silence, life and death, absence and affirmation. Descartes's entire plan consisted in "rejecting the quicksand and mud in order to find the rock or the clay" (Descartes, 19). With Perec there is neither rock nor clay, nor even quicksand.

By making the life of writing and the impossibility of speech indissoluble (the scandal of silence), Perec only concurs with comments made by Blanchot or others on silence as the *terra firma* and horizon of literature—especially after Auschwitz—in order to reverse the perspective. The silence exists, the scandal of History exists, but writing draws its vitality from them without ever making us forget that it is itself only a metaphor for emptiness and a substitute for mourning.

I have presented a Cartesian Perec, rationalized his projects, and intimated in which methodological continuities his books, at least a number of them, were written. But Perec can be inscribed as well in the filiation of another somewhat unexpected Cartesian, the one who brought the light of rationality and logic to the understanding of the functions of our most obscure boutique, our most resistant, intimate infra-ordinary: Sigmund Freud.

In *La vie mode d'emploi*, Perec accomplished the amazing feat of presenting hundreds of characters and stories while at the same time allowing us a tiny glimpse—in an absolutely original discourse on method—of how these characters and stories were born from his pen. Of course he owes his success to the self-imposed constraints and to borrowings and plunder from libraries as well as from the most banal textual sources. But much more decisively, he succeeded by showing us that it was by deliberately allowing himself to be guided by the elements of dream that he created his characters and their adventures.

Perec carefully meditated on dreams and had the audacity to devote his least compliant book to them, *La boutique obscure*. The nocturnal dream is that extraordinary factory of stories and characters that play their role of *trompe-l'œil* so perfectly that they are perpetually different and enigmatically other. These expressions of our power to feign, condense, and displace never cease to produce secret resemblances and troubling repetitions. Each dreamer is caught in a strange waterwheel where figures of the other and of the same tirelessly converge and separate.

Perec provided at least two user's manuals for the novelistic *summa* that is *La vie mode d'emploi*. The first can be found in his arranging things so that the jigsaw puzzle, a metaphor for the relationship between reader and author, would also become the nerve center of the narration. Jacques Roubaud has said that *La disparition* "is a novel about a disappearance, the disappearance of the letter *e*; it is thus both the story of what it recounts and the story of the constraint which creates that which is narrated."[10] One could say the same about the jigsaw puzzle *cum* instruction guide to *La vie mode d'emploi*. A first reference could be made to Freud through this link between an organizing structure and a representation that reflects and repeats it. But above all, Perec literally staged over the course of his novel both *displacement* and *condensation*—the most fundamental tools of dreaming—as techniques for narrative invention. We are reminded of W. E. Hill's henceforth infamous caricature, "which represents *simultaneously* a young and an old woman, the ear, cheek, and necklace of the young one being, respectively, an eye, the nose, and the mouth of the old one, the old woman being seen close-up in profile and the young one's bust being seen at three-quarters angle from the rear" (*Life*, 334). The puzzler and the reader must both learn to "switch [their] perception, see *otherwise*," that which has been shown with the intention of misleading him or her: "the whole labor consisting precisely in performing the *displacement* which gives the puzzle piece or the clue its *meaning*" (335).

Puzzle-solving and reading both demand that we know how to see otherwise and to perform displacements. But the work of the puzzle-solver or the reader takes place only in response to the work of the puzzle-maker or the author. We must thus change our perspective and examine the work of the author, his way of setting traps, in this case his art of making otherness out of the same. The 375,000 pieces, roughly identical but of course all very different, of those five hundred puzzles that portray again and again the same subject (a seaport), are an obvious metaphor for the workshop that produced the 375,000 stories, vignettes, characters, and silhouettes that populate *La vie mode d'em-*

---

10. Jacques Roubaud, "Mathematics in the Method of Raymond Queneau," in *Oulipo: A Primer of Potential Literature*, trans. and ed. Warren Motte (Normal, IL: Dalkey Archive Press, 1998), 86–87.

ploi. In fact, the reader, despite having his or her view monopolized by the partitioning of a hundred chapter-spaces and their spray of stories, cannot help but see the resemblances among the innumerable tales of researchers, forgers, cheaters, plagiarists, artists, inventors, athletes, criminals, nutcases, adventurers, avengers, painters, puzzle-solvers and puzzle-makers, all *mises en abyme* of the project of *La vie mode d'emploi* and its author. The book's characters are created in the image of those of *La disparition,* united in a single structure by a link that they do not see but that gives them a family tie. And Perec enables the reader to understand that, like in the unconscious logic and the superposition-interlacing [*superposition-intrication*] found in dreams, there can be unfathomed encounters, assemblages, overlapping, and reconfigurations of assassin and victim, creator and counterfeiter, inventor and cheat, liar and truth-teller. Just like Cinoc, word-killer and word-rescuer at once (eliminating obsolete words from the dictionary in order to compile them into a new one). Like Winckler, who only hates Bartlebooth so much and becomes his murderer because he bears such a strong resemblance to him. And like all those words that Perec spent his time undoing and resetting, disfiguring and reconfiguring, with the jubilation that we all know.

Condensation and displacement. We are taken back to that passion for beginnings that characterizes Perec's endeavor. Perec reveals these primitive tools, with which on any given night even the most imagination-deprived among us become gifted narrators, to be the tools that allow him to accomplish his everyday work. And following the user's manual for the life of a novelist who cultivated the image of an artisan, he obstinately puts the work back on the building block, over and over again: here again the image of a beginning.

In *The Art of the Novel,* Milan Kundera maintained that the spirit of the great novel was a spirit of continuity and complexity. Continuity: rarely has any *œuvre* inscribed itself more than Perec's in a clearly delineated and intensely thought-out filiation of writers: Stendhal, Flaubert, Verne, Roussel, Joyce, Kafka, Thomas Mann, Leiris, Queneau, and some of the best detective novelists. Complexity: not only because he was able to construct these diabolically designed textual machines, but because he continually proved, to take up Kundera's words, that "things are not as simple as you think."[11] The fables with-

---

11. Milan Kundera, *The Art of the Novel,* trans. David Bellos, revised by Linda Asher (New York: Harper and Row, 1988), 18.

out content of the island of *W* or *A Void*;[12] the deceptively simple story played out between Bartlebooth, Winckler, and Valène; all those games he plays with reversibility; a certain manner of using *trompe-l'œil* as a means of autobiographical authentication; all are there to convince us of this. But this spirit of complexity and continuity has always been supported by the very foundations of intelligence, of the power to narrate and signify—foundations that for Perec reached down into that "unsayable" which "is not buried inside writing," but "prompted it in the first place" (*W*, 42). This writer of the *after*, of how to write *after*, brings us back every time toward the before and toward the "initial place" out of which so many of his books arose.

Perec's *œuvre* is an adventure in knowledge, it is constantly reformulated and it never forgets what motivates it. It is continuously in the grasp of the absences, doubts, forgettings, and hypotheses of the ex-child of the rue Vilin and of the "homes" of Villard. This is the source of its power to surprise, its liberty of inquiry and investigation, its way of interrogating our dessert spoons and the city walls, dreams and the alphabet, home and exile, the shapes of letters and the power of numbers, absences from the world and the black holes of History. Whether he wears the mask of the painter in a long grey smock or the mask of the sleepwalker, in the cellars and mansard rooms of the rue Simon-Crubellier like on the little isle of Ellis Island, Georges Perec incarnates, in the most vigorous fashion, that spirit of free journey and fresh beginnings whose sovereign image is the recluse horseman of 1619.

—Translated by Joseph Mai

12. Georges Perec, *A Void*, trans. Gilbert Adair (New York: Harper Collins, 1995). The original French is *La disparition* (Paris: Denoël, 1969).

MARCEL BÉNABOU

From Jewishness to the Aesthetics of Lack

The posthumous legacy of Georges Perec and his works seems to me to be one of the most peculiar phenomena of contemporary literary history. Since his death in 1982, just as he was about to turn forty-six, Perec has had the rare privilege of not having to suffer that period of relative oblivion, the ordeal called "purgatory," which traditionally follows the death of an author. Better still, not only did he escape this eclipse, indeed one from which even the greats do not always escape, but he has come to know a fame that has not ceased to grow. Interest sparked by his work has only increased. Books, specialized journals, monographs, dissertations, colloquia, exhibits, and tributes of all kinds follow one upon the other, becoming ever more numerous. And this phenomenon is not limited to France or even to Europe: a November 2002 conference held at the Université Mohammed V in Rabat, Morocco, illustrated, and at the same time attempted to take stock of, this very fact.[1]

The beneficial consequence of this posthumous craze has been a deepening of the general perception of Perec's works. Until his death, critical and public interest had successively concentrated on only a few emblematic books, each considered within its own genre as being representative of one aspect of the entire body of work. Let's review them briefly. First came *Les choses* (1965, *Things*), more or less legitimately identified as a sociological document about consumer society in the 1960s; and then *La disparition* (1969, *A Void*), a lipogrammatic novel that revealed Perec to be a verbal acrobat and enthusiast of Oulipian constraints. In 1975 came the great turning point of *W ou le souvenir*

---

1. The proceedings of this colloquium were published under the title *L'œuvre de Georges Perec. Réception et mythisation*, ed. Jean-Luc Joly and Abdelfattah Kilito (Rabat: Publications de la Faculté des Lettres et des Sciences Humaines, 2002).

YFS 105, *Pereckonings: Reading Georges Perec,* ed. Warren Motte and Jean-Jacques Poucel, © 2004 by Yale University

d'enfance (*W or the Memory of Childhood*), which sustains interest as much for its autobiographical theme (the quiet pain of a childhood destroyed by war) as for its complex structure (two different texts, seemingly unrelated, which alternate from chapter to chapter). With *W*, we were apparently quite far from the putative sociological vocation of the author of *Les choses*, or from the dexterous witticisms to which *La disparition* had originally been reduced. Finally came the fascinating masterpiece *La vie mode d'emploi* (1978, *Life a User's Manual*), which Italo Calvino, who had known Perec from Oulipo, called "the last great event in the history of the novel."

And yet, ever since his death, critical attention has moved beyond these few seminal titles. The entire *oeuvre*, including its most remote recesses (crosswords, radio pieces, articles published in journals long defunct, interviews in diverse media, jokes and games of all kinds), in edition after edition, has become the subject of commentary, interpretation, and infinite glossing. It is as though the observation has finally been imposed that, despite its brutal interruption and apparent scatter, Perec's *oeuvre* forms a coherent whole. And this whole is not just a simple juxtaposition brought about randomly by editorial needs or by the inspired flights of critics. (As an Oulipian, Perec hardly believed in either chance or inspiration.) Instead, this whole results from a double project, meditated upon, ruminated over, and hewn since childhood. The first project is, as we shall see below, autobiographical. The second project aims at nothing short of a systematic charting of literature: *to write all that is possible for a person to write today, to use all the words of the French language, to fill a shelf of the Bibliothèque Nationale,* were all avowed ambitions.

The progressive realization of this double project brought about the multiform nature of his work, and so, to orient oneself within it and to grasp the internal movement that animates it, we might best follow some of the many different paths that Perec himself carefully established for his readers.[2] But it just so happens that Perec's indications are sufficiently discreet, numerous, and ambiguous to afford each reader a large part of the responsibility in choosing which path to take. The route I shall follow here gives importance to two notions, "Jewishness" and "lack," because they seem to have played a part in crafting Perec's

---

2. Here one ought to recall Paul Klee's formula, often cited by commentators, which serves as an epigraph to the "preamble" of *La vie mode d'emploi:* "The eye follows those paths that have been laid down for it in the work."

relationship to his memory and his identity. In this respect, they jointly play an important role in his life, as well as in his work. But it goes without saying that this path is only a personal reading, making no claim to any ultimate truth about the genesis of Perec's *oeuvre*. This path remains largely hypothetical and presents itself as only one of the possible "Perecquian Paths."

I. JEWISHNESS LOST

One observation seems serviceable as a point of departure: without ever pretending to be a theoretician of literature (except for his early days in the few articles written during the time of *la ligne générale*[3]), Perec consistently engaged in a critical reflection about his "work" as a writer. This reflection took place both at the margins of his works and, at times, at their very hearts. He often, and willingly, justified his work, and so Perec's authorial epitext, to use the theoretical jargon, is as vast as it is abundant. I shall begin then from the relationship that he himself established between writing and Jewishness.

On this relationship, I have elsewhere discussed two principal statements.[4] The first comes from the autobiographical part of *W:* "The idea of writing the story of my past arose almost at the same time as the idea of writing."[5] This statement takes on a certain character when cast in the light of a personal remark Perec once made in an interview: "I believe that I began to feel Jewish once I began to tell the story of my childhood."[6] What Perec lets slip in this double admission is the concomitance and quasi-equivalence that exist in his mind among three

---

3. La ligne générale was the name of a group of young students and intellectuals who wanted to create a journal with the view to refounding, or rather to founding at last a veritable Marxist aesthetics, breaking as much from the Zhdanovism of so-called "social realism" as from the spineless eclecticism that had followed it in France. The review, which wanted neither to pledge itself to the Communist Party nor to enter into open conflict with it, never appeared as such—although this fact in no way stopped the group from being active for a long time, or from publishing a few of its pieces in diverse journals, notably in *Partisans*.

4. Marcel Bénabou, "Perec et la judéité," *Cahiers Georges Perec* 1 (1984): 15–30. In English: Marcel Bénabou, "Perec's Jewishness," trans. David Bellos, *The Review of Contemporary Fiction* 13.1 (1993): 76–87.

5. Georges Perec, *W ou le souvenir d'enfance* (Paris: Denoël, 1975), 41; *W or the Memory of Childhood*, trans. David Bellos (Boston: David R. Godine, 1988), 26. Hereafter, parenthetical page references will give the French original first, followed by the English translation.

6. Perec, "Entretien avec Jean-Marie Le Sidaner," *L'arc* 76 (1979): 9. All translations from this interview are the translator's.

elements: "writing," "writing my story" (essentially the telling of "the story of my childhood"), and feeling Jewish. These three elements (the project of writing, the choice of the autobiographical axis of childhood, and the feeling of a certain relationship to a Jewish identity) form for Perec a sort of indissociable series, as though they ultimately represent but different facets of the same reality, different aspects of the same act. It is thus indispensable to ask just what this "feeling Jewish" is, for it has been claimed to be inseparable from his autobiographical project and thus from the very project of writing.

In answering this question, it is perhaps best to turn again to Perec's own declarations about how he lived this relationship to a Jewish identity, or at least about how and in what ways he was aware of it. On this subject, two statements are particularly significant. The first is found in the interview cited above from the journal *L'arc:* "I am Jewish. For a long time, this was not evident to me; there was no association with a religion, a people, a history, a language, barely even a culture" (9). The second appears in the commentary that accompanies the film *Récits d'Ellis Island* (1980, *Ellis Island*) (a commentary edited with particular care, including the choice of typography, which gives the text the look of verse): "I don't know exactly what it is to be a Jew, or what effect being a Jew has on me. There's something obvious about it, I suppose, but it's a worthless obviousness that doesn't connect me with anything. It isn't a sign of belonging, it doesn't have to do with belief, or religion, or a code of behavior, a way of life, or a language" (58, 60).[7]

It isn't particularly useful to underscore the relationship, or rather the rigorous parallelism that exists between these two, almost contemporary texts. Rather, I believe the slight differences that one can distinguish merit a brief examination. These variations first appear in the reference to *"évidence"* (obviousness): the "this was not evident to me" of the first text is amended in the second to read "There's something obvious about it, I suppose, but it's a worthless obviousness." It is as though an embryonic awareness has slipped in from one statement to the other, the first being more spontaneous and the second more literary and thought-through: *"une évidence médiocre"* ("a worthless obviousness") is nonetheless a little more, a little better than no *évidence* (obviousness) at all. Other differences are manifest in the order and

---

7. Perec, *Récits d'Ellis Island. Histoires d'errance et d'espoir,* with Robert Bober (Paris: P.O.L., 1994); *Ellis Island,* trans. Harry Mathews (New York: New Press, 1995).

choice of words used to characterize the potential content of Jewishness. We have in effect on the one hand "religion, people, history, language, culture" and on the other "belief, religion, way of life, folklore, language." In both the first and the second declarations, we find religion and language (although not exactly in the same places), whereas culture has curiously ceded its place to folklore (which is perhaps understandable, although the word "folklore" is clearly less worthy, dare I say, than the word "culture") and most strikingly the words "people" and "history" have disappeared in favor of "belief" and "way of life," which in reality just gloss the word "religion." I do not expect, of course, to draw far-reaching conclusions from these differences, but I believe that, given an author so attentive to detail and given an issue like Jewish identity, one cannot take them to be negligible. Moreover, such differences further emphasize what does not change from one declaration to the next. In both instances, Perec cannot define his personal relationship to Jewishness other than by a succession of five negations ("it isn't," "it doesn't"), in short as *the sum of a series of negations.* This is all the more remarkable because this series of negations stands in contrast to the positive relationship of Perec's collaborator, Robert Bober, to this same Jewishness.

The question posed by such remarks is why (or perhaps how) such a situation arose—for it is quite unexpected once we realize both that Perec was the child of recent Polish immigrants (only having arrived in Paris at the end of the 1920s), still culturally and linguistically close to their native Jewishness, and that his mother, being Jewish, was deported and died in a Nazi concentration camp. What was it that led him to be reduced to what could rightly be called "the degree zero of Jewishness"? Drawing on what we know about the situation of French Jews after the war, on the information contained in David Bellos's biography of Perec[8] and in the correspondence with Jacques Lederer,[9] and on Perec's own statements, we are able to glimpse an answer.

First, of course, there is the fact that, separated from his parents at a young age, Perec was never afforded the Jewish education that they might have given him. In the family of his Aunt Esther, by whom he

---

8. David Bellos, *Georges Perec: A Life in Words* (London: Harvill, 1993). Some of this work's information must nevertheless be completed, and sometimes corrected. See Bianca Lamblin, *La biographie de Georges Perec par David Bellos. Lecture critique* (Paris: Le Jardin d'Essai, 2000), as well as *Cahiers Georges Perec* 7 (2003).

9. Perec and Jacques Lederer, *Cher, très cher, admirable et charmant ami* (Paris: Flammarion, 1997).

was taken in after the war ("taken in" and not "adopted," as he himself sometimes wrote, for a legal adoption was not possible), the desire to assimilate into French culture was strong, and so Jewish identity was banished without remorse. The impact, still recent, of Sartre's *Réflexions sur la question juive* (1947) (*Anti-Semite and Jew*) must also be mentioned, for it came at just the right moment to give form to the idea that one is Jewish only through the gaze of the other. It is not surprising, then, that Perec grew to adulthood in an almost complete ignorance of Judaism. Moreover, throughout his formative years (in the middle of the 1950s and the early 1960s), he plunged himself into an environment (the group *La ligne générale*) ideologically most marked by a fascination with socialism and revolution—a fascination that would engender in Perec a permanent and passionate demand for justice, his affirmed taste for the universal.

During this period, the young Perec, who had decided to "conceal his childhood" and to "refuse his past,"[10] developed a sort of allergy to Judaism. He could accept neither its religious heritage (so clearly incompatible with his secular ideals) nor its Zionism (nationalism being incompatible with his resolute internationalism). His Jewishness thus appeared to be nothing more than a genealogical detail: the vague awareness of being Jewish because one has Jewish parents becomes the sole content of Jewishness. This position was not unique to Perec, but was more or less shared by a number of Jewish intellectuals in French society.

In the long run, however, this position was not as comfortable as it seemed. This Jewishness, of which they knew themselves to be the bearers, this minimal Jewishness, this Jewishness reduced to almost nothing, nonetheless produced real effects in their lives—effects that were incommensurable with its putative lack of substance. This almost-nothing was yet a word, a word that had the weight of a whole history; it was a name they shared with all those who continued to give it a positive content—a name, in short, that contributed to the continuing vitality among so many of a feeling of difference. Still—and perhaps this is the uniqueness of the era—the question was no longer so much about difference in relation to another, a non-Jew, as it had been at the time of *"la question juive."* The question came to be about a more muted and insistent difference that separated the so-called "as-

---

10. From an interview (5 April 1981) with Ewa Pawlikowska, *Littératures* 7 (1983): 74–75.

similated Jew" from the whole of Jewish history, and thus in a certain manner from a part of himself. Perec explicitly raises this new question: "In some way I'm estranged from myself; in some way I'm 'different,' not from others but from 'my own people'" (59, 61).

The problem of identity progressively returned for the many Jews who had believed they had shirked it. Jacques Derrida captures this particular problem of identity in his 1967 L'écriture et la différence (Writing and Difference): "Jewish would be another name for this impossibility of being oneself."[11] This doubt about one's identity and the resulting split within oneself are not without consequences. Many Jewish writers and intellectuals have felt such consequences, and for them, the sensation of not belonging, the feeling of being at odds with something that could have been but is not, the acute sense of a *lack* all become familiar themes.

The striking convergence among the following quotations should suffice to illustrate this state of being. We begin with a statement from Edmond Jabès: "I feel that I exist only outside of any belonging. That non-belonging is my very substance. . . . That non-belonging—with the availability it allows me—is also what brings me close to the very essence of Judaism and, generally, to the Jewish destiny."[12] Jabès takes up the theme again in slightly different terms: "It is indeed the impossibility of being an 'untroubled Jew,' a Jew at peace, anchored in his certainties, that has made me the kind of Jew I think I am. This may seem paradoxical, but it is precisely in that break—in that non-belonging in search of its belonging—that I am without a doubt most Jewish" (95–96, 64). Alain Finkielkraut defines his experience of Jewishness thusly: "What makes me Jewish is an acute awareness of a lack, of an active absence."[13] Ultimately, Perec says nothing but the same thing: "What I find present here are in no way landmarks or roots or relics, but their opposite: something shapeless, on the outer edge of what is sayable, something that might be called closure, or cleavage, or severance, and that in my mind is linked in a most intimate and confused way with the very fact of being a Jew" (*Ellis Island*, 56, 58).

Perec seems to have taken the same path as a postwar group of Jewish intellectuals, one that began in the comfort (at least an apparent

---

11. Jacques Derrida, *L'écriture et la différence* (Paris: 1967), 112.
12. Edmond Jabès, *Du désert au livre. Entretiens avec Marcel Cohen* (Paris: Belfond, 1980), 52–53; *From the Desert to the Book: Dialogues with Marcel Cohen*, trans. Pierre Joris (New York: Station Hill Press, 1990), 29.
13. Alain Finkielkraut, *Le juif imaginaire* (Paris: Seuil, 1983), 129.

comfort) of ignorance and refusal but ended in the uneasiness of a rupture, a non-belonging, a lack. And yet, in his works, Perec distinguishes and explains at least one aspect of this originary and multiform lack: "In fact, (being Jewish) was the mark of an absence, of a lack (the death of my parents during the war), and not of an identity, in the two senses of the word: to be oneself and to be similar to the other" ("Entretien," 9). That which makes him Jewish lies at the juncture of a double lack, of a double mourning: the mourning of a muffled memory (as History with its big "ax" [*H, hache*] has reduced the past to nothing), and the mourning of a future that has ceased to be imaginable (the Jew, similar to other Jews, that he could have been).

II. FROM A LACK TO WRITING, OR THE AESTHETICS OF LACK

How do we respond to lack? We can once again compare Perec to Jabès, who didn't hesitate to declare: "Our decision to write, to talk, springs from a lack."[14] For his part, Perec often stated how he saw his own path to writing, notably in *W*. In the publisher's insert to the book, Perec expressly identifies "the rupture" as "the initial place where the book came from." And in the body of the book itself, he specifies that he had the sensation of a split from the outset, of a breaking, a fracture, a rupture: "I was plunged into nothingness; all the threads were broken" (77, 55), he wrote in evoking his experience of parachuting. It is thus through the means of writing that he is able to confront what he has defined as a lack, "which is not a lack of something, *but an original lack upon which one must live*" (emphasis mine). And here, one can recall another, often cited declaration. Speaking of his parents, Perec affirms: "I write because they left in me their indelible mark, whose trace is writing. Their memory is dead in writing; writing is the memory of their death and the assertion of my life" (59, 42).[15] The "indelible mark" to which Perec alludes is "the lack"—the loss of his parents, but also the loss of memory.

But this is not all: the link thus established between lack and writing will also appear on another, more general level. Thus when Perec

---

14. Jabès, *Du désert au livre*, 83; *From the Desert to the Book*, 54.
15. Let us note here that this function of writing as a link to the dead can also be found among other contemporary Jewish writers. Elie Wiesel offers an example: "The act of writing is for me often nothing more than the secret or conscious desire to carve words on a tombstone." *Le chant des morts* (Paris: Seuil, 1966), 17; *Legends of Our Time* (New York: Holt, Rinehart and Winston, 1968), 10.

wants to position himself with regard to literature in general, when he wants to define the relationships between his personal *oeuvre* and this literature, he voluntarily resorts to a very significant image, as much in his books as in his statements—the missing puzzle piece, i.e., the image of a void that needs to be filled. As Bernard Magné correctly notes, "the surroundings make a hole [*trou*[16]], which must be filled by writing."[17] Writing, which speaks the lack, will try hard to fill all empty space; it will become an unrelenting inventory of objects to possess, of spaces to occupy. But writing will also engender a frenzied appetite for exhaustibility, seen at work in Perec's resorting to combinatory systems and his quest for "saturation," hallmarks of the Perecquian style.

But once the process of writing has begun, the "lack" will have only accomplished one part—albeit an important and determinative one—of its function in Perec's works. The part that follows will consist in affirming the presence of this "lack" in the products of writing itself. Perec's originality consists in his extraordinary aptitude for the literary manipulation of the lack, which he uses in all possible ways.

1. Lack as Theme

Originating as the driving force behind writing, the notion of lack quite naturally at first becomes the very theme of this writing. Insofar as it contains the echoes of Perec's prior works, *La vie mode d'emploi* furnishes the most probing examples of what one might call the massive isotopic permutations of lack,[18] this proliferation of lack in its concrete incarnations, as well as its numerous metaphorical equivalents. Magné, in a Perecquian mode, once playfully imagined "an attempt to inventory some of the words evoking lack in *La vie mode d'emploi* through the course of reading." He begins his list of finds: "cut, openwork, space, interval, elimination, sap, void, fissure, sinking, absence, perdition" (*découpe, ajour, espace, intervalle, élimination, sape, vide, fissure, naufrage, absence, perdition*) (*Perecollages*, 44). He includes in the same inventory "the series of empty rooms, the innumerable broken objects, incomplete things (from the chipped cup to the one-armed skeleton, not to mention the cards with effaced inscriptions and the books with pages

---

16. We ought to recognize the importance of the hole [*trou*] in the works of Perec, etymologically linked to his own Hebrew name, Peretz. [Trans.] See Gen. 38:29.
17. Bernard Magné, *Perecollages 1981–1988* (Toulouse-le-Mirail: Presses Universitaires du Mirail, 1989), 44.
18. See Magné, *Perecollages*, 44.

torn out), disabled characters (from Morellet, the chemist who has lost three fingers, to Dr. Kolliker, a deaf and mute man with neither arms nor legs, not to mention the neutered male cats of the household, the widows and widowers, the orphans, those left behind and those abandoned)" (*Perecollages*, 44). One can even go further and notice, with Magné, that one of the essential characters of the novel, the painter Valène (who, in the first version of the work, had the heavy responsibility of being its narrator), is strongly marked by lack—at first in his speech, for a few weeks before his death he "lost his words, left sentences hanging,"[19] and ultimately in the very structure of his name, Valène being, as if by accident, an anagram of *enleva*, "removed."

One can ask how this proliferation of the theme of lack through other terms can find its place in the book in order to serve its novelistic ends. The answer is interesting insofar as it testifies to Perec's literary know-how. Seen up close, this over-utilization of lack seems to be responsible for accentuating certain *effets de réel*. Recall here what Perec himself said about this subject in a different context in which he analyzes the techniques that make optical illusions work:

> Everything that we can immediately, naturally place on the side of life and of nature, and not on the side of art and artifice—that is to say haphazard, disorder, wear and tear [*usure*], corrosion [*patine*], dust, the somewhat dirty, accident, imperfection, irregularity—all this will be put precisely in place and staged in order to tell our stupefied and astonished eye that we are in a living and vibrant reality: a door slightly ajar, a window barely open, a curtain imperfectly pulled aside, a shutter that does not properly close all seem more "true," not so much because they are more difficult to paint due to the effects of perspective—for which the painter consequently takes on more risk—as because the slight opening of the door or window strongly invites us to believe that the house is inhabited.[20]

Let's transpose this analysis from painting to writing, as Perec himself liked to do. We arrive then at the hypothesis that, in this novel, lack plays precisely the role that wear, corrosion, and irregularity play in an optical illusion. As Magné suggests, "lack, in the unique form of wear, would thus have as its paradoxical goal the filling of the building, the assuring of a presence of real life by multiplying its traces" (45).

---

19. Perec, *La vie mode d'emploi* (Paris: Hachette, 1978): 601; *Life a User's Manual*, trans. David Bellos (Boston: David R. Godine, 1987).
20. Perec and Cuchi White, *L'oeil ébloui* (Paris: Chêne/Hachette, 1981).

2. Stage Two: Lack as Strategy

I do not believe Perec's principal originality lies in his use of lack as theme. His skillfulness in turning the lacks imposed upon him by life into the driving force of his writing, the recurrent theme of his works, and an effective means of producing real results is ultimately one he shared with other writers. Perec's uniqueness lies instead with one of his other abilities: his aptitude for transforming a *theme* into a *strategy*, in other words his talent for making what is in general a simple *object* of writing into a *generator* of writing. In the case of lack, this transformation takes many forms, of which a few, as we shall see, are particularly sophisticated. We can group them, more or less arbitrarily, under two rubrics: lack as a generator of narrative structures and lack as a generator of literary forms.

2.1 Lack as a Generator of "Narrative Structures"

It is hard not to think here of *La disparition*. The singular force of this novel is not only its being one gigantic lipogram that amputates from the French alphabet its most used letter, but also that, from one end to the other, the story speaks only of this lack. Every character, every episode obstinately turns around the unique theme of the mysterious disappearance of a letter, one which can obviously never be named, but only suggested. The lipogram is thus not simply a constraint on writing (as the Oulipians liked to give themselves), but also the generator of the story itself.

La vie mode d'emploi furnishes other examples of this use of lack as a generator of narrative structures. We notice first that the novel has only ninety-nine chapters instead of the expected one hundred: the novel "lacks" one chapter, which Perec intentionally omitted. Perec returns again and again in his statements to this lack, bringing it to our attention just because it is the bearer of special meaning.[21] But this is not all. The novel thus amputated also contains a number of incomplete stories, the unfulfilled projects that play a central role in it. The very project of Bartlebooth, around which the narration is constructed, remains unfinished. Upon his death, this moneyed man will have failed to put back together the 500 watercolor puzzles that he painted himself; he will not even have reached the end of the 439th puzzle. Recall

---

21. See Magné, *Perecollages*, 47–48.

the scene that closes the final chapter of the novel: "It is the twenty-third of June nineteen seventy-five, and it is eight o'clock in the evening. Seated at his jigsaw puzzle, Bartlebooth has just died. On the tablecloth, somewhere in the crepuscular sky of the four hundred and thirty-ninth puzzle, the black hole of the sole piece not yet filled in has the almost perfect shape of an X. But the ironical thing, which could have been foreseen long ago, is that the piece the dead man holds between his fingers is shaped like a W" (600, 497). We find incompleteness again at the end of the epilogue, in the very last lines of the novel. This time, the incompleteness is apparent in the famous painting of Valène which normally ought to have represented the entire building on rue Simon-Crubellier, "the long procession of his characters with their stories, their pasts, their legends" (292, 228). And yet, at the moment of the artist's death, this is how the painting appears: "The canvas was practically blank: a few charcoal lines had been carefully drawn, dividing it up into regular square boxes, the sketch of a cross-section of a block of flats which no figure, now, would ever come to inhabit" (602, 500). This double incompleteness, this ultimate double lack requires the reader to re-read the text in a different way and to understand differently the book that has just come to an end.

But perhaps the most original aspect of *La vie mode d'emploi* is its use of lack as one of the novel's constraints. Let us briefly review these constraints. Each chapter is subtended by forty-two elements that must necessarily figure in the chapter. These elements can be about the chapter's narrative content (position, activity, age, sex, place, time period, characters), as well as its formal traits (length, hidden allusions). These forty-two elements are grouped by two, making twenty-one pairs. Each pair is chosen from a series of lists of ten elements each, entailing twenty-one pairs of lists. This choice is determined under the constraint of a 10 × 10 Greco-Latin square[22] which allows each pair of elements to be distributed, without repetition, among the one hundred chapters, i.e.,

22. [Trans.] A "Latin square" is the representation of a set into rows and columns such that each element appears exactly once in each row and column. The set {a,b,c} yields one possible Latin square:

a	b	c
b	c	a
c	a	b

An "orthogonal Latin square" results from the overlapping of two Latin squares of the same order such that each combination of the elements of the two sets appears exactly once. Because the letters of the Greek alphabet are often used with those of the Latin al-the one hundred possible combinations.[23] And yet, among these twenty-one pairs of lists, the twentieth plays a particular role: this pair of lists brings together the categories entitled "lack" and "falsity." Unlike the other pairs of lists, the twenty-first does not directly result in narrative or formal elements. Instead, it serves only to modify the characteristic elements for each chapter that its initial regulation has established. We have thus passed from "constraint" to "metaconstraint" (a constraint that governs another constraint). In chapter thirty-six, for example, the expected combinatory game would impose the presence of a sideboard; but the intervention of "lack" in this chapter affects this element, modifying the initial program such that the expected sideboard is not present. The category "falsity" works in the same way, obliging the element it affects to be replaced by another.

Here again we must ask the question raised earlier during the consideration of lack as a theme. In the Perecquian literary strategy, what corresponds to the introduction of "lack" and "falsity" as elements that must be included in each chapter? One response, rather technical, is suggested by Perec himself. He explains on a number of occasions that such an introduction serves to break the excessive rigor of the system of constraints that he had put in place, to pervert it from within, in short, to distort its very machinery.[24] We recognize here what the Oulipians, borrowing from the physics of Epicurus (and from the pataphysics of Alfred Jarry), called the "clinamen."[25] But a second question immediately follows upon this response: why choose to introduce

---

phabet to avoid confusion, orthogonal Latin squares have also been called "Greco-Latin squares." The sets {a,b,c} and {α,β,γ} combine to form the Greco-Latin Square:

a,α	b,β	c,γ
b,γ	c,α	a,β
c,β	a,γ	b,α

In *La vie mode d'emploi*, Perec sets out with not two sets of three elements, but two sets of ten elements—twenty-one times! Since each combination yields a pair of two elements (say a,γ), twenty-one orthogonal Latin squares afford one hundred different lists of twenty-one pairs, i.e., forty-two elements for each of the one hundred chapters envisioned.

23. Perec explains these points in "Quatre figures pour *La vie mode d'emploi*," *L'arc* 76 (1979): 50–53.

24. See, for example, the statements made to Ewa Pawlikoska, *Littératures* 7 (1983): 70–71.

25. On the Perecquian use of the clinamen, see the many remarks by Magné (*Perecollages*, 45, 120, 158, 226, 537), as well as my "Les ruses du clinamen," a paper delivered at the *Colloque de Limoges* in April 1990.

the clinamen in such a form? Other processes exist in the Oulipian arsenal to loosen the stranglehold of constraints, and we can be sure that Perec had the imagination to invent even further means had he so wanted. We might guess then that the motivation we are looking for does not come only from Oulipian technique, but from properly Perecquian obsessions—and that this motivation inscribes itself in the aesthetics of lack that we are beginning to see take shape.

2.2 Lack as a Generator of Literary Forms

We encounter here the last floor of the edifice Perec built upon lack—a level that belongs uniquely to him. And it is with letters that Perec establishes himself this time, those letters with which he so often liked to play. His undertaking here continues that same thread we were able to see at work in *La disparition*. Inspired by the lipogrammatic principle introduced by amputating from the alphabet one of its elements, Perec will ultimately both systematize and diversify this principle. This simultaneous systematization and diversification allowed him to create and instantiate a series of new "poetic forms," all of which are founded upon the use of attenuated alphabets. But the rule that governs these attenuations is not always the same. We are thus dealing with multiple constrained alphabets, of which the principal examples are:

Heterogrammatic poems (as in his 1976 *Alphabets*): These poems depend upon a drastic reduction of the alphabet. Depending upon the collection, the employed alphabet can be reduced to anywhere from sixteen to eleven letters, among which are those most frequently used in French: *e, s, a, r, t, i, n, u, l, o*. But this constraint is rendered even more difficult by the supplementary constraint of the heterogram[26]: "a written utterance that does not repeat any of its letters."[27]

Les beaux présents: Perec forces himself in these occasional texts to use only the letters contained in the names of those people celebrated therein. In an epithalamium, he constructs his text solely from the letters of the names of the newly married, to whom the "beaux présents" are offered. Perec gives a lovely justification: "It is as though their marriage has made them enter together into a language shared by them alone."[28]

---

26. On this part of Perec's poetic production, see the exhaustive study by Magné and Mireille Ribière, *Les poèmes hétérogrammatiques* in *Cahiers Georges Perec* 5 (Paris: P.O.L., 1992).
27. Oulipo, *Atlas de littérature potentielle* (Paris: Gallimard, 1981), 231.
28. Perec, *Beaux présents, belles absentes* (Paris: Seuil, 1994), 55.

Les belles absentes: The beautiful absences obey a different logic, founded upon a simplified alphabet from which the letters *k, w, x, y, z* have been removed. In each verse of the poem, every letter of the reduced alphabet must appear save one. This additional absence inscribes, line by line, the concealed name of the dedicatee. Through the absent letters of the name, its presence in the poem becomes assured.

III. WHEN LESS IS MORE

What becomes evident at the end of this path is the complexity of the nebulous literary person that Perec constructed around the idea of lack, in every possible sense of the term. In doing so, Perec accomplished what is, in my eyes, one of those rare tasks that truly merits being attempted by a writer: the transforming of lack into plenitude, the replacing of the suffering imposed by history with a meticulously won joy. Along with the other Oulipians who seek their liberty as writers in the arbitrariness of the constraints they impose on themselves, Perec made lack the instrument of his fecundity. One thinks here of those lines of Raymond Queneau which Perec knew well: "From all the blows of fate, I knew how to fashion a tale. / Less is more: a consoling inversion."[29]

But we can also link this attitude to at least one of the important stages of the ideological path evoked above. For can we not consider Perec to have remained unconsciously faithful, if not to the Marxism, then at least to the Hegelianism of his youth?

I know of no better way to close than by recalling a statement often cited by commentators in which Perec presents his own way of retrospectively understanding his literary production:

> Even if what I produce seems to derive from a project long ago articulated, one which goes way back, I believe that I instead find—and justify—my way while walking: the succession of my books creates within me the sentiment, sometimes comforting, sometimes discomfiting (because it is always suspended by a "book still to come," by an incompleteness designating the unspeakable towards which the desire to write hopelessly strives), that my books travel a path, mark out a space, gropingly plot a path, describe step by step the stages of a pursuit about which I shall never know how to tell the "why" but only the "how": I vaguely feel that the books that I've written inscribe themselves within

---

29. Raymond Queneau, *Chêne et chien* in *Oeuvres complètes* I (Paris: Gallimard, 1989), 13.

and take their meaning from a general image that I have of literature, but it seems to me that I shall never be able to seize that image, for it is to me the beyond of writing, the "why I write" to which I can only respond in writing, forever deferring that instant in which, ceasing to write, this image would become visible, as though a puzzle inexorably completed.[30]

—Translated by Brian J. Reilly

---

30. Perec, "Notes sur ce que je cherche," *Le Figaro*, 8 December 1978, 1. Reprinted in: *Penser/classer* (Paris: Hachette, 1985), 9–12.

SYDNEY LÉVY

Emergence in Georges Perec

> ... that original burbling in which we can with difficulty make out what might be called the readable (what our mental activity is able to read, apprehend, understand).[1]
>
> —Georges Perec

Nearly thirty years ago, Georges Perec remarked that "for several decades now, a whole school of criticism has been laying stress on the *how* of writing: on the doing of it, on its poetics," but that "an equivalent study remains to be made ... of the efferent aspect of this production: the taking charge of the text by the reader."[2] This statement is still valid today for his own work. Encouraged to a certain extent by Perec himself and by the posthumous publication of some of his preparatory documents, in particular his *Cahiers des charges*[3] for *Life a User's Manual*,[4] we marvel at his writing exploits, at the constraints he set for himself—some simple, others quite complex, at the way he actualized them, and at the freedom they gave him to write the hundreds of stories contained in that same *Life a User's Manual*. We placed ourselves in his writing laboratory, analyzed his experiments, and traced what we read to these very experiments, verifying his combinations, detecting the exceptions he made to his rules, uncovering his implicit quotations and borrowings. In sum, we directed almost all of our attention to something that has not ceased to surprise us, the *how* of his writing. However, this is the Perec of the astute reader and critic—called by one such critic a "lecteur chevronné."[5] But there are other

---

1. Georges Perec, "Think/Classify," in *Species of Spaces and Other Pieces*, trans. and ed. John Sturrock (London: Penguin Books, 1997), 186. Translations of texts unavailable in English are my own.
2. Perec, "Reading: A Socio-physiological Outline," in *Species*, 171.
3. Perec, *Cahier des charges de La vie mode d'emploi*, ed. Hans Hartje, Bernard Magné, and Jacques Neefs (Paris: Zulma, 1993).
4. Perec, *Life a User's Manual*, trans. David Bellos (Boston: D. R. Godine, 1987).
5. Magné, "53 jours: pour lecteurs chevronnés," *Études littéraires* 23/1–2 (summer-fall 1990).

YFS 105, *Pereckonings: Reading Georges Perec*, ed. Warren Motte and Jean-Jacques Poucel, © 2004 by Yale University

readers of Perec, blissfully unaware of the manuals he invented and the bravura he displayed in following them. Those readers—and I know a number of them—have simply picked up a copy of *Life a User's Manual*, read it easily and enjoyed it thoroughly, devouring it, as Perec says "lying face down on your bed."[6] These readers are legion (witness the thousands of copies sold); but we don't hear much about them in academic circles, undoubtedly because they do not publish essays such as this one. For such readers, the breaks in continuity from chapter to chapter in *Life a User's Manual* soon disappear; something makes the chapters stick together, connecting them into a smooth, legible, and thoroughly enjoyable surface. In that novel, there is something at work that permits the reader to feel, early on, that it is perfectly natural for the stories about the inhabitants of the building to be told in bits and pieces, seemingly sprinkled throughout the nearly 600 pages of the novel. In *W or the Memory of Childhood*,[7] there is also something at work that effaces the ruptures of the alternating chapters with their different genres, stories, and style. There is something, in sum, that assures the legibility of these books, that allows us to enter their movement, to espouse their rhythm, body and mind (compare the effect of Balzac's prose to Proust's, or the autobiographical chapters to the adventure story chapters in *W*), to anticipate the next step, and to see it confirmed as though it were the only one possible.

I will follow Perec's suggestion and look at the efferent side of things, the reading of Perec. Not, however, at "the message once grasped"—not, that is, at what we *understand* when we read one of his books—but at "the actual grasping of the message . . . what happens when we read" (171). In other words, I will look at the *how* of reading,[8] at the legibility of Perec's books. Focusing on the two books just mentioned, *Life* and *W*, I will explore first what happens between the reader and the text, and then try to identify what insures that legibility from the production side. Perec talks about that legibility, but not as often or as explicitly as he does of the production side. (The only explicit text he wrote on the subject is the one from which I have been quoting, "Reading: a Socio-physiological Outline.") The reason, perhaps, is that

6. Perec, "Notes on What I'm Looking For," in *Species*, 142.
7. Perec, *W or the Memory of Childhood*, trans. David Bellos (London: Collins Harvill, 1988).
8. Paying attention to the ways this legibility is accomplished, rather than to what we understand when we read Perec, will allow me to avoid the difficult question concerning the reader's level of knowledge and the subsequent positing of an "ideal reader."

we hardly have any words or concepts for what happens in our minds when we read, and we are left pointing to these processes indirectly and metaphorically. Moreover, it is only in the assembly of disparate fragments found in several of his books, of various genres—essay, autobiography, novel, and interview—that an outline of what Perec says of that legibility becomes apparent.

The preamble to *Life a User's Manual* has been taken as a metatextual statement on the entire book, its metaphor and its writing principle.[9] It is equally, however, about the book's legibility, about what happens when we read it. In fact, the perspective of the entire first paragraph is from the efferent side of things: it is about the phenomenology of puzzle-solving, or even its "cognition,"[10] since the paragraph contains the words "to know" and "knowledge" and their derivatives—"analyze," "derive," "take on sense," "acquisition of a skill," "perceptual act" (and "teaching," which did not make it into in the English translation). This cognition is put clearly in terms of reading:

> you can look at a piece of puzzle for three whole days, you can believe that you know all there is know about its colouring and shape, and be no further than when you started. The only thing that counts is the ability to link this piece to other pieces, and in that sense the art of the jigsaw puzzle has something in common with the art of Go. The pieces *are readable, take on sense,* only when assembled; in isolation, a puzzle piece means nothing—just an impossible question, an opaque challenge. But as soon as you have succeeded, after a few minutes of trial and error, or after a prodigious half-second flash of inspiration, in fitting it into one of its neighbors, the piece disappears, ceases to exist as a piece. [xv, my emphasis]

It is almost as though Perec is talking here about the legibility not only of *Life*, composed of one hundred discrete chapters/rooms, but also of *W*, composed of chapters in alternating genres, and ruptured within these genres. Like puzzle-solving, reading these books consists, per-

---

9. See for example Magné, "Le puzzle mode d'emploi: Petite propédeutique à une lecture métatextuelle de *La vie mode d'emploi* de Georges Perec," in Magné, *Perecollages 1981–1988* (Toulouse: Presses Universitaires de Mirail-Toulouse, 1989).

10. Regarding cognition: Perec worked for a number of years in a neurophysiology lab as a *documentaliste* and he seemed to have known some of the literature on the subject. One of the entries, for example, in the otherwise false bibliography of "Experimental demonstration of the tomatotopic organization in the Soprano (*Cantatrix sopranica L.*)," (*SubStance* 29 [1981]: 45), is a false one attributed to McCullough and Pitts, the true inventors of the artificial neuron.

haps, in connecting the pieces and making them disappear as pieces. At the risk of repeating a cliché, for Perec to read, *lire*, is nothing but an anagram, accomplished through a simple inversion of two letters in *lier*, to join, to put together (both terms are in the original of the passage just quoted, but in different forms: *"lisible"*—"readable"—and *"relier"*—"to assemble"). *"Lier"* and *"relier"* refer of course to the joining of the pieces of the puzzle. If, however, one keeps in mind the often-cited homophone of pieces, the *"pièces"* (rooms) of a building, these two words also refer to the act of relating spaces or going from one space to another, whether that space is a room in a building, or a chapter in a book—or more precisely, a chapter in a book on the subject of a room in a building. There is for Perec, in fact, something much more general in the act of going from one space to another: "To live," he says at the end of his foreword to *Species of Spaces*, "is to pass from one space to another, while doing your very best not to bump yourself" (6). If to live is to go from one space to another without running into an obstacle, then *Life*, the book, is perhaps the illustration of that particularity; and the preamble, which talks about just such a joining of spaces, is its user's manual. To read, for Perec, is something akin to joining pieces or going from one room, or from one disparate chapter, to another without stumbling, without becoming aware that you are doing so; and with each passage, each discrete chapter disappears into a single and smooth continuous space. Legibility for Perec has something to do with that continuity of space, physical as well as mental.

This continuity is quite different from the way Bartlebooth, one of the main characters in *Life*, makes up a user's manual for his life and follows it to the letter: ten years to learn watercolor, 20 years to travel throughout the world painting watercolors of seaports that he sends back to one of his neighbors to make into jigsaw puzzles, 20 years to solve these puzzles (118–19). In fact, his life consists of a precise and rigid addition of years, a linear and simple development of a plot line, which leads him at the end of his life to isolation and blindness and, ironically, to an obsessive practice of that continuity, but on wood puzzles. On the other hand, the readers of *Life*, the ones without a user's manual for the book or its *Cahier des charges*, have learned quite early on, but without paying attention, without being aware of it, not to bump themselves going from chapter to chapter and to feel comfortable in its highly complex network of continuities. It probably takes only two or three transitions between chapters for them to know they are reading the same novel, quite unlike the reader of Calvino's *If on a*

Winter's Night a Traveler,[11] who continues to bump into a new novel with each new chapter. I am talking, of course, about the embedded reader who is the focus of that novel. For us, the real readers, in following the adventures of that embedded reader, "the interruption of the book becomes the continuation of the book,"[12] as Calvino says.

Moving from one space to another without realizing that you have done so is the subject of another passage from *Species of Spaces*. It describes a lived experience of continuity, the mute learning implied in the transition to a new space and the accommodation to that space. It is found just a few pages before the chapter where Perec describes what will become *Life a User's Manual,* in a section entitled "Doors" from a chapter entitled "The Apartment." Its impact lies in every one of its details:

> It is hard, obviously, to imagine a house which doesn't have a door. I saw one one day, several years ago, in Lansing, Michigan. It had been built by Frank Lloyd Wright. You began by following a gently winding path to the left of which there rose up, very gradually, with an extreme nonchalance even, a slight declivity that was oblique to start with but which slowly approached the vertical. Bit by bit, as if by chance, without thinking, without your having any right at any given moment to declare that you had remarked anything like a transition, an interruption, a passage, a break in continuity, the path became stony, that is to say that at first there was only grass, then there began to be stones in the middle of the grass, then there were a few more stones and it became like a paved, grassy walkway, while on your left, the slope of the ground began to resemble, very vaguely, a low wall, then a wall made of crazy paving. Then there appeared something like an open-work roof that was practically indissociable from the vegetation that had invaded it. In actual fact, it was already too late to know whether you were indoors or out. At the end of the path, the paving stones were set edge to edge and you found yourself in what is customarily called an entrance hall, which opened directly on to a fairly enormous room that ended in one direction on a terrace graced by a large swimming pool. The rest of the house was no less remarkable, not only for its comfort, its luxury even, but because you had the impression that it had slid on to its hillside like a cat curling itself up on a cushion. [37–38]

11. Italo Calvino, *If on a Winter's Night a Traveler . . .* , trans. Wiliam Weaver (New York: Harcourt Brace Jovanovich, 1981).
12. Calvino, "How I Wrote One of My Books," in Raymond Queneau et al., *Oulipo Laboratory: Texts from the Bibliothèque Oulipienne,* trans. Harry Mathews, Iain White, and Warren Motte, Jr. (London: Atlas, 1995), 4.

Perec's experience occurs over time. As his walk progresses, the terrain changes, slowly and almost imperceptibly: a few more stones, a little less grass in between them, a slight elevation to his left that starts to resemble very vaguely a little wall. Along with the progression of his walk and that of the terrain, there is of course a mental activity, but this activity—an awareness that a change has occurred—lags behind the physical changes ("without thinking," "it was already too late to know"). The physical transformation of the landscape and the mental accommodation to the new space are at first asynchronous. And then there is something similar to a change of phase as he realizes, quite suddenly and after the fact, that he is now inside the house. It is as though all the clues, all the progressively changing little details, came together in his mind to make something continuous, at both the physical and mental levels (appropriately, one of the changes Perec describes is the gathering and the increasing concentration of stones to make a path); and with this gathering of details in the mind comes the sudden realization that he is now in a different space.

The experience of entering that house without doors as well as the mental activities associated with it are very similar to puzzle-solving as Perec describes it in the preamble to *Life*. In both cases, the object is to join seamlessly two spaces, or to go from one space to another without opening a door, without crossing a threshold, and, of course, without bumping, physically or mentally, into something. What happens in both has to do with some kind of assembly, with putting things together. And in both, something different on the mental level comes on quite suddenly: the awareness that he is now inside the house, or the disappearance of the puzzle piece as a separate object when it finds its place in the puzzle. Perec puts these mental activities at the very heart of reading:

> To read is in the first instance to extract signifying elements from a text, to extract crumbs of meaning, something like keywords, which we identify, compare, and then find for a second time.... These keywords may be words ..., but they may also be sonorities (rhymes), page layouts, turns of phrase, typographical peculiarities.... We are dealing here with something like what information theorists call formal recognition. The seeking out of certain pertinent characteristics enables us to pass from this linear sequence of characters, spaces and punctuation marks that the text first of all is to what will become its meaning once we have located, at the different stages of our reading, a syntactical coherence, a narrative organization and what is called a "style." ["Reading," 172–73]

Reading, as Perec describes it, shares many of the characteristics of entering that house without a door: it occurs progressively (at "different stages"); it consists in gathering varied little elements into a coherence, an organization, or a style: for the house, these elements are the changing size of the stones and the increasing elevation of the terrain, and for the text they are the "crumbs of meaning" that consist in elements of form (sound, layout, typography) or of content (the words). Reading, as he describes it here, stands in sharp contrast to that "unjoined-up writing, made of separate letters unable to forge themselves into a word" or to those "dissociated, dislocated drawings whose scattered elements almost never managed to connect up" (W, 68), which Perec produced at various times in his youth. There is also a change of phase similar to the one that occurs upon entering the house or upon placing a piece in the puzzle: reading consists in going from a linear (and serial) succession of signs (letters, spaces, punctuation marks) to something that is not: a coherence or organization that is a two- or three-dimensional mental construct. The succession of signs makes a contiguous sum, while the coherence makes a continuous whole, irreducible to the sum of the elements.

Going from a linear succession, from a sum of elements, to a coherence or organization is precisely what is today called "emergence"—the name given to the notion that "the whole is more than the sum of its parts." Emergence makes its entrance in philosophy in the late nineteenth century in an attempt to account for the fact that life (note the coincidence) cannot be deduced from the matter that makes up a living organism. It is then that it acquires a precise, albeit negative, definition: "the characteristic properties of a whole cannot be deduced from the properties of the parts studied separately."[13] Perec appears to have an intimate knowledge of that concept in the first few lines of *Life a User's Manual*. The novel starts with the very recognition of form that he assigned to the reading process: invoking Gestalt theory, he calls the whole "a form, a structure" and "*un ensemble*" (translated as "pattern" or "set" in the English version, which does not account for

---

13. Anne Fagot-Largeaut, "L'émergence," in Daniel Andler, Anne Fagot-Largeaut, and Bertrand Saint-Sernin, *Philosophie des sciences*, vol. 2 (Paris: Gallimard, 2002), 1015. The chapter provides a good discussion and history of emergence. Most commentators point to John Stuart Mills' *System of Logic* (1843) to find the first expression of what will come to be known as emergence, neglecting the opening of Denis Diderot's *Le rêve de d'Alembert* in *Oeuvres philosophiques* (Paris: Garnier, 1964) where a discussion of a bee colony is put in terms already familiar to us: contiguity (the sum of the elements) and continuity (the whole) (289–95).

the action of *gathering* conveyed by the French term). "Ensemble" is also a mathematical term as in "théorie des ensembles" (set theory) where, according to the inventor of the notion, Georg Cantor, "a set is a Many which allows itself to be thought as a whole."[14] In 1967, Jacques Roubaud published a book entitled ∈ (the symbol in set theory used to signify "belongs to"), which starts with, of all things, a "User's Manual for this Book," to explain that the book is patterned on the game of Go (itself mentioned in Perec's preamble) where the poems, like the stones on the grid of the game, "entertain among each other various relationships of meaning, succession, and position."[15] In fact, Perec dates to that same year, 1967, the project of a book (which eventually became *Life A User's Manual*) in collaboration with Roubaud and another mathematician, Claude Berge, based on "Latin squares."[16] As it happens, it was also that same year that he had the experience of the house without doors during a visit to Lansing, Michigan.[17] We can assume that the notions of emergence and "ensemble" (whether mathematical or otherwise), in the context of reading, are at the origin of the novel and run deep through it. They also open the novel:

> To begin with, the art of the puzzle seems of little substance, easily exhausted, wholly dealt with by a basic introduction to Gestalt: the perceived object—we may be dealing with a perceptual act, the acquisition of a skill, a physiological system, or, as in the present case, a wooden jigsaw puzzle—is not the sum of elements to be distinguished from each other and analysed discretely, but a pattern [*ensemble*], that is to say a form, a structure: the elements' existence doesn't precede the existence of the whole [*ensemble*], it comes neither before nor after it, for the parts do not determine the pattern [*ensemble*], but the pattern [*ensemble*] determines the parts: knowledge of the pattern [*tout*] and its laws, of the set [*ensemble*] and its structure, could not possibly be derived from the discrete knowledge of the elements composing it. [xv]

Note the striking resemblance of Perec's definition of the parts/whole problem (emergence) to the classic one quoted above: "the characteristic properties of a whole cannot be deduced from the properties of the

---

14. Quoted in Rudy Rucker, *Infinity and the Mind: The Science and Philosophy of the Infinite* (Princeton: Princeton University Press, 1995), 191.
15. Jacques Roubaud, ∈ (Paris: Gallimard, 1967), 7.
16. Perec, "Quatre figures pour *La vie mode d'emploi*," *L'arc* 76 (1979): 50.
17. Paulette Perec, "Chronique de la vie de Georges Perec, 7 mars 1937–3 mars 1982," in *Portrait(s) de Georges Perec*, ed. Paulette Perec (Paris: Bibliothèque nationale de France, 2001), 73.

parts studied separately." His definition, like the classic, takes as its point of departure knowledge of the phenomenon, as opposed to the phenomenon itself, and uses technical terms such as "deduced," (*déduit*, translated as "derived"): "knowledge of the pattern [*tout*] could not . . . be derived [*déduit*] from the discrete knowledge of the elements." Also, like the classic definition, Perec's definition is cast negatively. Moreover, Perec treats emergence as a concept in its own right: the puzzle is only one of its manifestations; for the others, he cites examples, undoubtedly inspired by his work in a neurophysiology lab, from the cognitive and life sciences: perception, learning, and a physiological system.

It sounds counter-intuitive to say, as Perec does, that the whole determines the parts. However, there is no emergence if we uphold the contrary—that the parts determine the whole—since, in that case, the whole would be reducible to its parts, more precisely to the sum of its parts. In describing the reading process, it would be as though we stopped at its very first stage, when a text is made up of a "linear sequence of characters, spaces, and punctuation," analogous to Bartlebooth's life as a sequential sum of years. It is in the second stage of reading, as Perec describes it, during the formation of a coherence out of the sequential addition of parts, that the whole determines the parts, that each part takes its meaning from the whole. In the episode of the house without doors, it is only when Perec realizes that he is inside—that he has, in other words, experienced the whole—that he understands the meaning of the progressive density of the stones that make up the path. Similarly, in reading, the whole will allow us to understand the elements, whether such element consists in a word, a sound, the turn of a phrase, a layout, a little anecdote, or a curious object, such as Anne Breidel's miniature tower in *Life a User's Manual*—that "airy metal construction made out of 2,715 steel pick-up needles held together by microscopic dots of glue, two yards high, as delicate as lace, as graceful as a ballerina, and bearing at its apex 366 minute parabolic receiving dishes" (179). That tower, by itself, is nothing but a curiosity. It makes sense, however, when it is integrated into a larger network of relationships made up of widely distributed elements throughout the book and even outside it: the various obsessive behaviors we encounter, the dozens of puzzles and puzzle-like objects, the preamble to the book, which explains puzzle-making and puzzle-solving, Bartlebooth's project and all the people he solicited to help him achieve it, the writing of the book and even its reading. To sum up, then, reading for Perec is a bottom-up, top-down[18] emergent phenomenon where, from a linear succession of elements, emerges an organization, which in turn determines the elements.

Emergent properties are not spontaneous. There is something occurring at the physical level for the house without doors and at the textual level in Perec's books that establishes favorable conditions for emergent properties to appear. However, we cannot precisely trace the causes of the emergent properties at the local level. As we have seen, what we find at the local level are small elements that do not necessarily determine the whole: a progressively high concentration of stones to make a path does not necessarily make the entrance to a house, let alone a house. Also, emergent properties are irreversible: in saying—with Perec and with the classical definition of emergence—that knowledge of the whole could not be deduced from the discrete knowledge of the elements, we are also saying that we cannot establish a top-to-bottom reverse causal chain, and trace the effect to its precise source. Emergent properties are, once more, quite unlike Bartlebooth's linear and additive user's manual for his life. By the very fact that it is a manual, it functions top-down and is totally reversible: in fact, once Bartlebooth completes a jigsaw puzzle, its seams are retextured, the intact watercolor is then unglued and sent back to the seaport where it was painted, to be dipped in detergent in order to leave the paper as white as it was at the very beginning of the cycle. But we can find constraints at the local level, which explain in part—rather than determine—what happens at the global level. They explain it a posteriori, of course, just as Perec understood the little changes only after he realized he was inside the house without doors. These constraints may be theorized, as does Perec, or not, as was probably the case for the architect of the house without doors—namely, Frank Lloyd Wright. There are perhaps constraints at work that train the readers of W, for example, to know early on that they are reading the same book, even though the chapters alternate between an adventure story and an autobiographical narrative, and to know ("to gather" is probably more appropriate), that, as Perec indicates on the back cover of the French edition, what the book really says lies at "the fragile intersection" of the two.

18. Paul Harris in "The Invention of Forms: Perec's *Life a User's Manual* and a Virtual Sense of the Real," *SubStance* 74 (1994), proposes the same top-down, bottom-up determination in the writing of the book: "The strange loop of formal invention threads the bottom-up schema whereby the lists assign contents to be included and the top-down pattern of the knight's routes that distribute the textual components designated by the lists" (72).

Recent work on emergence in the areas of cognitive sciences,[19] artificial intelligence, robotics, and what has come to be known as artificial *life* (note again the coincidence[20]) is starting to lead to an understanding of how emergence is produced. By the same token, its definition starts to take on a more positive, constructive aspect: "There is emergence whenever interesting, non-centrally-controlled behavior ensues as a result of the interaction of multiple simple components within a system."[21] By "interesting" is meant something that we can distinguish as meaning and that cannot be accounted for at the level of the parts. "Non-centrally-controlled behavior" is the emergence-producing behavior I've been calling "bottom-up," as opposed to top-down or centrally-controlled behavior. And the "interactions of multiple components" are the constraints at the local level. The classic example is the ant colony, whose "interesting" behavior as a unit is

---

19. Among the first users of the notion in the cognitive sciences are Francisco Varela, Evan Thompson, and Eleanor Rosch, *L'inscription corporelle de l'esprit. Sciences cognitives et experiences humaines* (Paris: Seuil, 1989).

20. Or perhaps these are not coincidences. There are good reasons to believe that Perec's inspiration for *Life* and, as we shall see in a moment but to a lesser extent for *W*, has come in part from his work in a neurophysiology lab: aside from the "socio-*physiological*" study of reading, Perec writes a book entitled *Life a User's Manual*, the writing and, as I am hoping to demonstrate, the reading of which are based in part on the notion of emergence, itself invented to explain life; and he starts his book by explaining in some technical detail that notion, giving examples from the life and cognitive sciences. Paul Harris suggests that the conception of the book could have been patterned on "cellular prosody," as proposed by Jacques Bens, Claude Berge, and Paul Braffort (57–58). See their "Recurrent Literature" in Warren Motte, ed. *Oulipo: A Primer of Potential Literature* (University of Nebraska Press, 1986), 109–114. "Cellular prosody," Bens et. al. tell us, is itself patterned after John Conway's *Game of Life*, a computer program where cells on an infinite grid are born or die according to simple rules concerning the state of neighboring cells. Depending on the initial conditions, quite recognizable forms develop and move around the grid in sometimes quite predictable fashion. The *Game of Life*, as Harris reminds us, is cited as a prototype for work in artificial life. There is a good likelihood that Perec knew Conway's game, either through his contact with his mathematician friends (the mathematician Claude Berge's name appears as one of the authors of the article where cellular prosody is explained and as one of the persons with whom Perec conceived of the aforementioned book based on the Latin square, which was to become *Life*) or directly for having read about it. It was first introduced to the general public by Martin Gardner in a 1970 column of *Scientific American*, at the very time Perec was working in that lab. See Martin Gardner, "Mathematical Games: The Fantastic Combinations of John Conway's New Solitary Game 'Life,'" *Scientific American* 223 (October 1970): 120–23. As it happens, Gardner mentions here the game of Go that Perec invokes in his preamble to *Life*.

21. Andy Clark, *Being There: Putting Brain, Body, and World Together Again* (Cambridge: MIT Press, 1997), 108. The book is a good survey of contemporary issues raised by emergence in cognition, artificial intelligence, and artificial life.

produced by simple rules of interaction among the individual ants and not by an overall directive—some sort of program telling it what to do. My favorite example, related by Andy Clark (110-11), is about a colony of artificial termites. The question is how to program the system to make piles of wood. The centrally-controlled or top-down solution would be to designate a place where the wood is to be accumulated and to instruct each termite to seek the little chips of wood and deposit them in the predetermined space. The emergentist, non-central (i.e. bottom-up) solution consists in two rules that constrain the behavior of the termites: 1. If you have nothing in your claws and you come across a wood chip, pick it up. 2. If you have a wood chip in your claws and come across another one, deposit the chip you have in your claws. With only these two simple constraints going in recurrent loops, little mounds of wood eventually form, and those mounds are eventually merged. And, of course, the entire colony will be perceived as whole, accomplishing a single goal. The term "constraints" for the rules that the termites have to follow to build their mounds of wood is not, in this instance, forcing a Perecquian or Oulipian terminology upon those termites or those who conceived them. Among the scientists who have recently attempted to discover general laws in the production of emergent phenomena (as opposed to the nineteenth-century philosophers who named and defined them) is John H. Holland, who named the set of interactive simple rules that generate this behavior "constrained generating procedures" (cgp's).[22] He does so undoubtedly without knowing anything about Oulipo or Perec who had attempted—so I claim—to devise, in his own medium and with his own tools, a legibility-producing emergence.

Leaving the efferent side of things, I will now examine the much talked-about afferent[23] side—but only in light of what occurs on the reading side, as far as I have been able to determine it. First, since, as we have seen, the legibility that Perec is seeking does not consist in any linear addition, or in a top-down user's manual regime (both à la Bartlebooth), he has to institute a way to prevent these from happening. Second, since, as we have also seen, this legibility consists in assembling the scattered elements in a different way, there has to be something at

---

22. John H. Holland, *Emergence: From Chaos to Order* (Cambridge, Mass: Perseus books, 1998), 126–32.

23. Perec's term "efferent" (as well "afferent") is interesting in this context: both *Webster* and *Le Petit Robert* point to its use in describing the direction of impulses in the nervous system.

the local level (of course unrecognizable at the global level) that allows this assembly. In other words, the work must contain mechanisms of both disruption and assembly. This is precisely what Perec says in "La chose." This unfinished and posthumously published essay on free jazz ("La chose" being the "new thing" that was free jazz) was probably written in 1967,[24] the same year that he visited the Frank Lloyd Wright house and that he and Roubaud conceived the book that was to become *Life* (and that Roubaud published ∈). As it happens, it was also the year Perec joined the Oulipo group. In this essay, he wonders what creates the coherence of a piece of free jazz when all the while it is abandoning, even destroying, everything that used to assure it a certain coherence, such as rhythm, harmony, and melody. After drawing parallels between literary writing and free jazz, insisting on the (false) dichotomies between freedom and constraints, he makes this remark, almost at the end of the unfinished manuscript:

> One can, roughly speaking, find in a free piece two types of characteristic elements: elements that could be called "negative" whose function is to break the underlying traditional structure (by sabotaging the chorus, rupturing the rhythms), and "positive" elements, true "operators of unity," from which, it really seems to me, the piece develops. To my knowledge, there are at least two and they are two of the most famous figures of rhetoric: repetition (riff) and quotation. [63]

Let us first look at *W* in light of these negative and positive elements. The element that "breaks the underlying traditional structure" in that work is of course the alternation of two texts on apparently totally different subjects, belonging to two different genres, and set in two different type fonts. In this instance, the disruptive mechanism was quite simple to realize: Perec had already written and published serially the adventure story that becomes the anthropological study of an Olympic village turned concentration camp. He then wrote the autobiographical text, and inserted its chapters between the chapters of the unaltered adventure story. Note that this adventure story traces the effects of centrally-located or top-down commands to their paroxysm; it is also a text that is itself written top-down, with its inexorable increments, from chapter to chapter, of horror. The autobiographical text, on the other hand, gathers texts from different epochs, annotates them, revises and corrects them, and seems to be made up of fleeting and false

---

24. Perec, "La chose," *Magazine littéraire* 316 (December 1993): 55–63. In an introduction to the essay, Hans Hartje estimates the date of its writing to be 1967.

memories and their revisions, as though no filter was applied, no choice made, as though chance played an important role in their arrangement. In other words, life in this book stands on the side of an emergent bottom-up regime, while user's manuals or rigid instructions or commands are on the top-down side, confirming what Perec said in an interview concerning his memories: "I know for example that *Je me souviens* is stuffed with mistakes, therefore that my memories are false. That forms part of the opposition between life and the user's manual, between the rules of the game you set for yourself and the paroxysms of real life that submerge, that are continually undoing the work of setting in order—luckily, moreover" (*Species*, 132). There is, of course, something biographical to this opposition, in view of the lives that History, "avec sa grande hache"[25] (literally "with its great axe")[26] has taken away. The autobiographical text stands, then, in complete contrast to the adventure story, not only in its subject and genre, but in what I call its "writing regime": emergent bottom-up when Perec is telling the story of his life, and top-down when he tells a story where life is taken away. When the autobiographical chapters are inserted between the chapters of the already published adventure story, they literally tear it apart (with one exception: chapter 11, at the end of Part I, and chapter 12, at the beginning of Part II, are both autobiographical). One can, of course, say that it is the other way around, that the adventure story ruptures the autobiographical text. It doesn't really matter; either way the linearity of the entire book is broken.

As for Perec's "operators of unity," the elements that will bring the text together again in a new organization, they will have the same function and status as the elements that produce the local "interaction between multiple simple components" of our modern definition of emergence, or as Holland's cgp's. To name these rules "operators of unity" is very fitting not only for free jazz, but also for the writing-reading process, and for any system displaying emergent properties, since the fundamental characteristic of an emergence-displaying system is precisely the behavior of the whole as a unit. For example, the rules that permit termites to make wood mounds, although unrecognizable as such at the global level, could literally be considered operators of unity since their function is to make the individual termites behave as a unit

---

25. Perec, *W ou le souvenir d'enfance* (Paris: Editions Denoël, 1975; reprint, Gallimard, coll. "L'imaginaire," 1993), 13.
26. "Avec sa grande hache" makes it into English as "with a capital H," *W* (6).

whose job, as it happens, is to gather. What then are the operators of unity at work in *W*? Unlike what he did for *Life*, Perec has not left us much about the production of *W*.[27] And, as we have seen, it is extremely difficult, if not impossible, to go from the product to the rules generating it. Thanks, however, to Bernard Magné's meticulous work,[28] we can posit a hypothesis on the existence of such rules, and can arrive at a fair idea of their nature. Reading *W*, we notice certain echoes between the alternating texts, the most evident being the name of Winckler's mother: Caecilia, and Perec's mother: Cécile. Magné systematically analyzes the text to see if there are other such pairs, which he calls "sutures." He discovers that there is at least one pair linking each autobiographical chapter to a neighboring adventure story chapter. Basing ourselves on Magné's work, and with the knowledge that Perec wrote the autobiographical text after the adventure story, we can imagine the simple constraint in writing each autobiographical chapter: having determined its place between the adventure story chapters, the autobiographical chapter must contain one element from the preceding and one from the following chapters. To use the same cellular representation of the constraint as the one Perec used in the *Cahier des charges* for his instructions in writing *Life*, the constraint for *W* would look like something this:

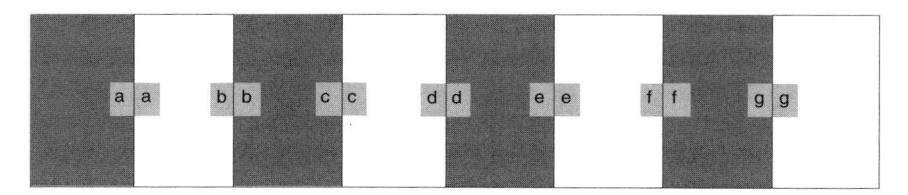

The alternating chapters are thus linked or coupled by one of the operators of unity he invoked for free jazz: repetition. The other operator he mentions in that essay, quotation, will be among those he will thoroughly exploit in *Life*, as he makes explicit in a *post-scriptum* to the book (579). Moreover, the operator of unity in *W* has the same function as the one Perec was inventing at about the same time, which he was to use for writing *Life:* the lists and their permuted combinations were

---

27. In his *La mémoire et l'oblique* (Paris: P.O.L., 1991), 128–29, Philippe Lejeune reproduces preparatory notes for the book that describe a three-part project that has clearly been abandoned.
28. Magné, "Les sutures dans *W ou le souvenir d'enfance*," *Cahiers Georges Perec 2* (*Textuel* 21, Université de Paris VII) (1988): 39–55.

to arrive at a master list of what each chapter/room was to contain, among other things. The question for *W* is basically the same: in order to enhance the possibility of making the alternating chapters not simply contiguous but continuous, a repeated element links them. This simple procedure at the local level is what makes it possible for the readers to know, after a few chapter transitions, that it is still the same book they are reading and, eventually, to know—to gather—that what the book really says is at the intersections of the chapters.

For *Life*, the disruption is also very apparent: with each chapter, the reader jumps to different apartments with different inhabitants, contents, and stories. In this case, however the disruptive mechanism had to take into account the two-dimensional surface of the front of the building as opposed to the two one-dimensional developments of the two texts in *W*. In other words, if in *W* each story line simply interrupts the other, the problem in *Life* is more difficult: a whole surface has to be disrupted. The solution Perec found is that famous constraint of the "polygraph of the moves made by a chess knight (adapted, what's more, to a board of 10 squares by 10)" (*Species*, 40), so that it touches every square on the board only once. Perec says he used it because "it would have been tedious to describe the building story by story and apartment by apartment. The succession of chapters could not have been left to chance alone" ("Quatre figures," 51). It would also have been tedious to read, because we would have had an additive inventory of what each apartment contained and the story of their inhabitants one after the other in contiguous chapters, without the very stuff of the novel, namely the immense network of relationships formed by the inhabitants of the building and their possessions, and the resulting legibility-inducing emergence. Perec had to disrupt the linearity to make room for the continuity; he had to break apart the surface in order to bring together its elements in a different way. The polygraph of the knight accomplishes that disruption in a disciplined way, without leaving the matter to chance alone.

We find *Life*'s operators of unity also in the constraints. And, as it turns out, they are almost the same constraints as in *W*: something very similar to the "sutures," but adapted to a much a larger scale and applied to chapters that are not necessarily contiguous. Let us go back to the lists Perec arrived at through the constraint of the Latin square. Looked at from the production side, the lists gave him the elements to include in each chapter, as he points out ("Quatre figures," 51) and as his critics have often repeated. But reading does not consist in reversing what the writer did—checking to see, for example, if an item from the list is included in the novel. If, however, reading is what Perec describes it to be—an emergence in our minds of some kind of organization or coherence out of a linear sequence of elements—the Latin square constraint plays a definite role in making this happen.

The constraint has been explained numerous times[29] and I will not repeat it here in detail, except for three points. First, Perec made up 42 categories to be included in each chapter, such as a body position, an activity, a style of furniture, two quotations, clothes, jewelry, a geometric shape, a kind of flower, etc. Taking as an example the first category from the "list of lists" we find in the *Cahier des charges* (42)—body position—every chapter of the book will contain, in principle only (we'll see in a moment why), a mention of a body position. Every chapter will also contain an element from the other 41 categories. Second, since each category contains ten variables (for body position, they are: kneeling, sitting, lying on the stomach, lying on the back, an arm up in the air, etc.), each one will be used, in principle, ten times. The kneeling position will be repeated in ten chapters, the standing in ten, and so on, thereby filling all the 100 chapters/rooms of the book. Third, each body position is paired with one of ten activities (painting, having an interview, consulting a map, performing an erotic act, etc.), and each of these activities will in turn be repeated in ten different chapters. Since we have ten different positions paired with ten different activities, we'll have in principle 100 unique position/activity pairs, one for each chapter of the book. In principle only, because there are 99 chapters in the book, not 100; because Perec threw a (systematic) wrench into his system in order not to be systematic; and, finally, because he did not always respect his own constraints.

What are we to make of these constraints from the reading side? First, as any uninitiated (and even a most astute) reader will tell you, these repeated elements and their 100 unique combinations go totally unnoticed when we read the actualized text. Even for what could be considered the most detectable category—the implicit quotations for each chapter—a short history of Perec criticism will confirm that only the most knowledgeable specialist of the author quoted will recognize them. These elements go unnoticed because, as Paul Harris has pointed

---

29. See Perec's own "Quatre figures," as well as two versions of that explanation that are particularly clear: Harris (62–63), and Hartje, Magné, and Neefs' introduction to Perec's *Cahier des charges*, 30–35.

out (64), they are trivial, insignificant (Perec would say "infra-ordinary")—but not unnecessary. They play no role in the deployment of any of the numerous plots in the novel and hardly any role in its main themes or in any of the wonderful subjects Perec critics have so far extracted from that novel. This is easily verified, taking at random the very first Latin square, which pairs a body position with an activity, and the very first cell (upper left hand corner of the square), which happens to be for chapter 59 (*Cahier,* 44). There, two "1's" indicate that the chapter should include a kneeling position and a painting activity. In the book, one of three characters depicted in a painting resting on Hutting's easel is kneeling (*Life,* 278). The painting activity is even more incidental: in the list of portraits Hutting has done, the last one is of a literary critic "esquissant avec brio" literary portraits of Proust's Vinteuil, Elstir, and La Berma.[30] In contrast, that very same chapter 59 explains Hutting's "protocol" for arriving at his "imaginary portraits"—a protocol not too different from the one Perec uses to arrive at his own chapters, and which I am obliquely describing here. Clearly, the kneeling position or the painting activity demanded by the constraints does not have much to do with that protocol, except as elements, among hundreds of others, that actualize it. The fact that these elements go unnoticed seems to confirm, by the way, one of the characteristics of systems displaying emergent properties: there is nothing in the actualized text that could lead the reader to the rules that actualized it. It is only with the knowledge of the rules, after the fact, that we can, as I have just done, trace the text back to the rules that generated it.

Second, the 42 categories found in each chapter give the novel a consistency, which, because of its repetition, chapter after apparently discontinuous chapter, has a muted but definite impact on the reader, even if the reader is not aware of that impact. Let us recall the house without doors: Perec experienced the gathering of stones that eventually made up a path, and the incline of the terrain that became eventually a wall, but it was only when he was inside the house that he became aware of the changes.

30. Perec, *La vie mode d'emploi* (Paris: Hachette, 1978), 354. It is really difficult to quote the English version here. Perec's original: "Le critique Molinet inaugure son cours au Collège de France en esquissant avec brio les portraits de Vinteuil, d'Elstir et de La Berma, riches mythes de l'art impressionniste dont les lecteurs de Marcel Proust n'ont pas fini de faire l'exégèse" became in the translated version: "Listing from his album Irish *mitzvahs* and lively portraits of Vinteuil, Elstir and La Berma, the critic Molinet lectures at the Collège de France on the myths of impressionist art which readers of Proust and Joyce have by no means fully elucidated yet" (*Life,* 281).

Third, the fact that any one element from the 42 categories appears in ten different chapters links those chapters in the same way that the repetition of minute details (Magné's "sutures") links the consecutive chapters in *W*. More precisely, they are assembled in a continuity. However, unlike the linked chapters in *W*, these chapters are not contiguous. The distribution of elements by the constraint of the polygraph of the knight ensured that. If we were to mark on a grid the chapters/rooms where we should encounter the kneeling position, for example, as well as the links between them, as we did for *W*, the grid would have to be 10×10 (as opposed to one line of cells for *W*). The chapters would be dispersed on that grid since, as indicated by the Latin square for that position in the *Cahier* (44), kneeling should appear in chapters 59, 58, 47, 28, 30, 94, etc. Lastly, each chapter would be linked to the nine others. It would in fact take 45 $(9 + 8 + 7 + 6 \ldots)$ links to assemble them all in a network of continuity. (It is perhaps clear that without the disruption brought about by the constraint of the knight's polygraph, those ten chapters would occupy a single row of the grid.) Each chapter, however, contains 42 of these insignificant elements, each repeated in ten different dispersed chapters, each forming a network of 45 links among the chapters in which they appear. If we want to have an idea of the entire book with all these networked chapters, we could imagine drawing the 45 links of all 42 elements on a single grid. We would have close to 1900 links in the book. We would have, in fact, a grid saturated with links, a smooth and continuous surface, a "prepared" surface, as a painter would say, ready to receive, like Valène's canvas, the "the ladles and the knives, the serving spoons and door handles, the books and newspapers, the rugs, the jugs, firedogs . . . and all around the long procession of [the novel's] characters with their stories, their pasts, their legends,"[31] ready to receive, in other words, the novel as we read it, understand it, and analyze it.

The constraints consisting in the lists of insignificant elements, in their combinations and their rules of placement in the chapters of *Life* have certainly facilitated the writing of the book. But, just as certainly, they facilitate its reading. They "instantiate the real," Paul Harris says (56). But they also imperceptibly connect the chapters over and over again. The constraints play, thus, the same role as the alabaster powder the chemist Kusser fabricated to retexture Bartlebooth's jigsaw puz-

---

31. *Life* (227–28). An entire paragraph from that chapter did not make it into English, the one starting with "Il se peindrait en train de peindre et autour de lui, sur la grande toile carrée" (*Vie*, 291).

zles, to make the original watercolors re-emerge without a trace of the discontinuities among the 750 puzzle pieces (*Life*, 21). As we read Perec's book chapter after chapter, the connections multiply exponentially to form the tissue that holds the novel together, that allows us to know, body and mind, that we are reading a single book, in spite of the jumps from chapter to chapter and in spite of the scattered plot lines. What emerges in our minds as result of these connections is almost nothing—nothing, in any case, readily identifiable—in the same way Valène's canvas is left "practically blank," as we discover in the last words of the novel (500). Now that the preparation of the canvas is complete, it is no doubt for the novelist to take over by telling stories, as opposed to filling a canvas. These stories trace movements, and are themselves part of a vast and complex web of time,[32] rather than immobile figures depicted in space. They are stories that, like Perec's definition of life, take us from one space to another without bumping ourselves. In this sense, the constraints—or Valène's blank canvas—prepared the emergence of something *like* life itself. That's undoubtedly why amateurs and experts alike devour Perec's book, lying face down on their beds.

32. For a discussion of that web of time in the novel, see my "Le temps mode d'emploi," *Littérature* 109 (1998): 98–115.

WARREN MOTTE

The Work of Mourning

Sorrow and melancholy color Georges Perec's writings from his first published works onward. In some texts, those attitudes are explicit and insistent, while in others they are more muted. Works such as *Un homme qui dort*, *W ou le souvenir d'enfance*, "La clôture," and *Récits d'Ellis Island* are clearly composed in a minor key, and present themselves to us in the first instance as lamentations. In others, like *La disparition* and *La vie mode d'emploi*, a major key dominates. Yet, in the manner of the best blues tunes, that key and the mood it connotes are continually called into question by plaintive notes and voicings, effects that serve to redirect our reading into avenues that are far darker than the ones first imagined. Undoubtedly, the sadness that Perec expresses in his work has many different objects. There is a commonality that runs through much of it however, a fundamental similarity of approach and tone that recurs with regularity throughout his writings. More organized, more structured, less anecdotal and more profound than other kinds of sorrow that Perec expresses, the phenomenon that interests me is a sustained mourning, and its object is his parents.

For the benefit of those readers who may be unfamiliar with Perec, allow me to provide a few biographical details. I shall be very brief here. Georges Perec was born in Paris in 1936. Both of his parents were Polish Jews who had come to France in the 1920s. His father enlisted in the French army, and was killed on the final day of the *drôle de guerre*, in June 1940. His mother was arrested and interned in Drancy, then deported to Auschwitz in February 1943. She did not survive, though what exactly became of her was never determined.

Many critics have read a story of personal torment in Perec's work. Philippe Lejeune, for instance, sees in Perec "an autobiographical writing of lack, of gaps, of unease."¹ It is particularly useful in Perec's case to broaden the field of what we mean by "autobiography," for his work as a whole is uncommonly shaped by the writing of the self, whether it is a question of obviously confessional texts or not. Wherever the self is placed on stage, the effect that Lejeune notes becomes apparent, as if there were something about the self itself that causes the writing to hesitate, to stutter. Let me repeat that there are, without a doubt, many objects of melancholy in Perec's writing. Moreover, I certainly do not wish to propose Perec's grief as either single or static: to the contrary, it is both multiple and constantly mobile. The sadness that Perec feels over the loss of his parents finds expression in his texts in many different ways, taking many different forms and investing many different sites. I am persuaded, however, that within such variety striking patterns of similarity exist, linking text to text in a kind of oblique narrative discourse.

I would like to begin to account for that phenomenon through a notion that Freud develops in "Mourning and Melancholia." (And I have no qualms about bringing Freud to bear in considering a writer who was analyzed by Françoise Dolto in his preteen years, by Michel de M'Uzan in his early twenties, and by J.-B. Pontalis in his mid-thirties.) In that essay, discussing "the economics of pain," Freud speaks of the "work of mourning," wherein the subject comes to terms with the reality of the loss of a loved one.² That process, Freud suggests, is a painful one, but it serves to prolong the psychic existence of the lost object in crucial ways, for if the subject were to accept the loss immediately and in the entirety of its implications, the ego would be overwhelmed. Freud insists that the work of mourning is a very gradual process, "carried out bit by bit, at great expense of time and cathectic energy," a point upon which other students of the phenomenon concur.³ He argues further that the work of mourning takes place in "piecemeal" fashion, proceeding in fits and

1. Philippe Lejeune, *La mémoire et l'oblique: Georges Perec autobiographe* (Paris: POL, 1991), 43.
2. See Freud, "Mourning and Melancholia," in *The Standard Edition of the Complete Psychological Works of Sigmund Freud*, ed. and trans. James Strachey, vol. 14 (London: Hogarth Press and The Institute of Psycho-Analysis, 1957), 244–45. See also Otto Fenichel's discussion of the work of mourning in *The Psychoanalytic Theory of Neurosis* (New York: Norton, 1945), 21, 162, 393–94, 572.
3. See, for instance, Fenichel, who speaks of "a gradual 'working through' of an affect" (162), and John Bowlby, *Attachment and Loss*, vol. 3 (New York: Basic Books, 1980), 8: "Again and again emphasis will be laid on the long duration of grief, on the difficulties of recovering from its effects, and on the adverse consequences for personality functioning that loss so often brings."

starts rather than in a continuous, uninterrupted manner. Finally, he adumbrates an end for the process, and with it a prospect of eventual recovery: "The fact is, however, that when the work of mourning is completed the ego becomes free and uninhibited again."

Freud's construct seems very cogent to me, granted what we know—or think we know—about the way people deal with intense personal loss. It is particularly apt, and useful too, when one considers Georges Perec's writing, because it offers a way of reading the kind of oblique narrative that I mentioned earlier. I would like to insist, for a moment, on both of the terms that compose it. I am convinced that a very great deal of the sorrow, regret, pain, and bewilderment that Perec expresses in his texts can be read systematically as mourning behavior, and that Perec stages such effects in utterly deliberate (if not quite programmatic) fashion. In other words, he is conscious of his mourning *as* mourning. Though I do not wish to belabor the issue of intention unduly, the consideration of consciousness is an important one. Freud distinguished between mourning and melancholia precisely on the grounds of the subject's awareness, arguing that the melancholic may be aware of *whom* he or she has lost, but unaware of *what* has been lost in him or her. "This would suggest," he argues, "that melancholia is in some way related to an object-loss which is withdrawn from consciousness, in contradistinction to mourning, in which there is nothing about the loss that is unconscious" (245). Georges Perec is the most conscious of writers. He knows all too well the places where the trauma has scarred him; and he spends a great deal of his writerly energy in making those scarifications legible to others.

In that sense (and turning now to the other term in Freud's construct), the process of grieving that Perec undertakes is very clearly organized as *work*. That is, whatever form it may take in his writing, it presents itself as effort, as labor, as toil, and as a behavior that is above all purposeful. Perec seeks an active engagement with his grief, recognizing that, if left unattended and undirected, it would threaten to cripple him. As Julia Kristeva has noted, the alternative that the death of a beloved person poses to the subject is a radical one, and one that persists in very precarious equilibrium: "loss, bereavement, and absence trigger the work of the imagination and nourish it permanently as much as they threaten it and spoil it."[4] Under the influence of his men-

---

4. Julia Kristeva, *Black Sun: Depression and Melancholia,* trans. Leon Roudiez (New York: Columbia University Press, 1989), 9.

tor Raymond Queneau, Perec came to recognize the work of the imagination *as* work, refusing the idea of artistic inspiration in favor of a vision of the artist as first and foremost an artisan, a worker. He recognized, too, that such work is productive, whether the product be a sonnet, the elaboration of a new and intricate literary constraint, or an itinerary of inquiry and reflection allowing him—however tenuously—to keep despair at bay.

From text to text, then, in different guises and according to different terms, Perec pursues the work of mourning. He proceeds in a manner that may seem disjunctive and interrupted at first glance, in fits and starts, a "piecemeal" project as it were. The tone in which it is articulated remains largely consonant throughout, however—a meiotic tone in which less is said in order to mean more.[5] I should mention here that I invoke the term "meiosis" in its rhetorical sense, for in the lexicon of medicine it means something quite different and inapposite, defined by the OED as "the state of a disease in which symptoms begin to abate." Whatever else one might think of it, it is important not to be too sanguine about Perec's work of mourning. Clearly, it is an undertaking that remains very much in process in his writing up to the moment of his own death. It presents no recognizable prospect of the kind of full recovery that Freud postulated at its hypothetical endpoint; nor does the "cure" hold the promise of anything other than a provisional and fragile—but nonetheless vital—psychic balance.

Before I turn to specific instances in Perec, I would like to suggest another way to conceive Freud's term, imagining for the moment "work" not as a behavior, but rather as the product of that behavior. In such a perspective, one might usefully think of "the work of mourning" in Perec as the work itself, the oeuvre, the individual work of literature and also the body of writing as a whole. Certain texts—*W ou le souvenir d'enfance*, to name the most obvious one—can be considered productively in such a light as elaborate and carefully constructed memorials. When for instance Perec states in *W* that "My mother has no grave,"[6] that painfully laconic utterance takes its place in a variety of textual isotopies. Chief among them is a metaliterary discourse which suggests that one of Perec's purposes in *W* is precisely to construct a site of remembrance and mourning for his mother, a grave, a

5. See Lejeune on the emotive function of understatement in Perec (21).
6. Georges Perec, *W ou le souvenir d'enfance* (Paris: Denoël, 1975), 57; *W or the Memory of Childhood*, trans. David Bellos (Boston: Godine, 1988), 41. Henceforth, first page references are to the French original, second to the English translation.

tomb, in his writing. And I am persuaded, too, that it is legitimate to view Perec's oeuvre as a whole in a similar manner. I do not mean that such a reading of Perec's work should exclude others, but only that it constitutes a vitally important and inevitable facet of a body of writing that is as remarkably multidimensional as any of which I am aware.

In what follows then, I shall try to read the notion of "work" doubly, both as activity and as product, vexing the one against the other in order to find their points of mutual complementarity. Having argued that there are many sites of mourning in Perec's writings, and that the expression of his grief is multiple and various, sometimes obvious and sometimes far more covert, I have chosen to focus upon four sites. Taken first individually and then considered together, they seem to me representative of the different shapes that mourning adopts in Perec, both in terms of the way that work is carried out and in terms of the kind of works in which it results.

The first and most readily apparent field of mourning in Perec I would like to point toward is in *W ou le souvenir d'enfance*. Many of his readers, myself included, have commented upon that text as a discourse of lack wherein Perec grapples with the articulation of concerns that remain, for him, largely unsayable.[7] *W* is a hybrid text in which chapters of fiction alternate with chapters of autobiography, approaching the problem of catastrophe from different angles; at times one mode of literary expression clearly tries to express what the other just as clearly cannot. As Perec describes it, the fundamental problem devolves upon the problem of memory. His autobiographical narrative begins thus:

> I have no childhood memories. Up to my twelfth year or thereabouts, my story comes to barely a couple of lines: I lost my father at four, my mother at six; I spent the war in various boarding houses at Villard-de-Lans. In 1945, my father's sister and her husband adopted me.
>
> For years, I took comfort in such an absence of history: its objective crispness, its apparent obviousness, its innocence protected me; but what did they protect me from, if not precisely from my history, the story of my living, my real story, my own story, which presumably was neither crisp nor objective, nor apparently obvious, nor obviously innocent?
>
> "I have no childhood memories": I made this assertion with confi-

---

7. See for example Marcel Bénabou, "Perec et la judéité," *Cahiers Georges Perec* 1 (1985): 24–29, on the notion of lack, and the portion of Lejeune's *La mémoire et l'oblique* entitled "Dire l'indicible" (13–57).

dence, with almost a kind of defiance. It was nobody's business to press me on this question. It was not a set topic on my syllabus. I was excused: a different history, History with a capital H, had answered the question in my stead: the war, the camps. [13, 6]

The first thing that should be noted about this passage is the immediate and unconditional denial of the kind of project that the title of the text implicitly announces. That is, having erected a horizon of readerly expectation based on the notion of memory—and memories—Perec very deliberately devastates that horizon in the first sentence of his autobiographical narrative. He erects in its place the beginning of an amnesic memoir where what is memorialized is precisely the lack of any reliable connection with the past. In the French original, his play on the ideas of "story" and "history" (the French word *histoire* can mean either) is particularly pungent, erecting tensive relations between the two, and suggesting that a story of personal catastrophe is rendered largely moot by the far broader and perhaps more compelling context of historical catastrophe in which it takes shape. The sort of negative narration that Perec launches here will characterize the rest of *W*, if in different ways and in varying degree. It will be characterized, too, by an extreme recursivity, an effect that Perec deploys with some ostentation in the first sentence of the final paragraph I quoted, where he rereads—and indeed rewrites—the inaugural sentence of his autobiographical narrative. That technique serves many purposes in *W*, but most interestingly it materializes and inscribes upon the page the kinds of gestures that real anamnesis requires, that is, looking back, recalling, and reconsidering.

Whenever Perec does look back, however, he fails to find what most people take as a matter of course and fundamental entitlement: *his* story. "My childhood," he states, "belongs to those things which I don't know much about" (21, 12). Among all of the memories that an adult might expect to retain from childhood, Perec seeks most urgently for some trace of his parents, some recollection that corresponds to lived experience, something upon which he can now rely. Faced with the absence of such memories, he turns toward invention, imagining emblematic situations, couching them in the conditional and the hypothetical, even suggesting to his reader upon one occasion that they "are not entirely implausible" (22, 13). In short, he turns to writing:

> I write: I write because we lived together, because I was one amongst them, a shadow amongst their shadows, a body close to their bodies. I

write because they left in me their indelible mark, whose trace is writing. Their memory is dead in writing; writing is the memory of their death and the assertion of my life. [59, 42]

He is aware—painfully and preternaturally so—that the writing of the thing is not the thing itself, and that the gap of representation cannot be bridged. Perec defines himself as a writer, though: that's what he is, and more importantly still, that's what he does. In other terms, having come squarely up against the interdict that amnesia places on the telling of his "own story," he turns to his *work*. He postulates for that work the kind of organic connection with his parents that his memory cannot provide to him, a "trace" that allows him to say, at the very least, that his parents once were, that they are now no longer, and that they deserve some kind of memorial, however artificial and constructed it might be.

The most eloquent site of such a memorial in *W ou le souvenir d'enfance* is undoubtedly the page in the very middle of the text that separates the first part of *W* from the second. It is framed by empty pages, and it is itself empty, apart from an ellipsis enclosed in parentheses (85, 61). If the alternation of chapters were to be respected, a chapter of the autobiographical narrative should be placed there; and coming after a passage of that narrative where Perec saw his mother for the final time, one might expect that it would provide information about her death. As I mentioned earlier, however, Perec has never been able to find any such information; and what he puts in its place, escaping from language as it does and suspended as it is, clearly points toward something that remains well beyond language—and perhaps beyond thought, too.

Recognizing the importance of that moment, I would like to consider another one to which less critical attention has been paid, and in which Perec's work of mourning may be still more unmistakable. In the tenth chapter of *W*, Perec discusses a photograph of himself and his mother in some detail. Among the remarks he offers is the following one: "I have fair hair with a very pretty forelock (of all my missing memories, that is perhaps the one I most dearly wish I had: my mother doing my hair, and making that cunning curl)" (70, 49). Gazing at the photograph, Perec sees material evidence of the way his memory has failed him. For the photo tells him incontrovertibly that he was *there*, with his mother, in precisely the kind of intimate setting he was forced to imagine in other circumstances; yet he recalls nothing of the scene. The possibility that this failure to remember might be a refusal to remember—and thus a betrayal—haunts him. Working though that nexus of problems, quite literally in this instance on the page, he recasts it in another form, admitting that the memory is "missing," and creating for it a privileged status within the devastated register of erasure that *W* constructs. This one would be *the* one, Perec tells us. It would be the perfect image of parent-child intimacy. The contact of body to body that one takes for granted in such a relationship is performed here as a fundamental drama. The gesture at its center is capitally important. Perec's mother arranges his curl perfectly, both by virtue of the fact that she was an exemplary mother and also because (as he mentions elsewhere in *W*) she was a hairdresser: that was her other job, her *work*, in life.

His work, right now, is to remember that moment, a moment that must have occurred, even if he is forced to resort to the hypothetical mode in order to give it shape. The fact that Perec places the evocation of this most important missing memory in parentheses is typical of the meiotic strategy upon which he relies throughout *W ou le souvenir d'enfance*, where less always means more. It may be usefully compared to the ellipsis in parentheses in the middle of the book, but here language has not abdicated—or not quite. What is crucially at issue is the parental touch, the act that emblematizes and guarantees everything else that Perec longs to recall in a past with which he is so bleakly out of touch. Metaphorically then, it figures the kind of contact with the past that eludes him. Moreover, it suggests the sort of contact that he seeks in the telling of his story, for stories are always told to an audience, however virtual. Yet as touching as his story may be, it is clear from the way Perec works through it that he deems that last sort of contact to be hypothetical, just like the others.

The second site of mourning that I would like to visit spans several of Perec's works, and first becomes apparent in *Un homme qui dort*. Toward the end of that text, which is surely the most melancholy and introspective of Perec's fictional works, the narrator (a version of Perec himself in deliberately transparent disguise) gazes at his face in the mirror: "What secrets do you expect to find in your cracked mirror? And what truth in your face? This slightly swollen moon-shaped face, already somewhat puffy, these eyebrows which meet in the middle, that tiny scar over your lip."[8] Among the details that the narrator offers as

---

8. *Un homme qui dort* (1967), second ed. (Paris: Union Générale d'Éditions, 1976), 168; *A Man Asleep*, trans. Andrew Leak (Boston: Godine, 1990), 214.

he reads his own face, it is the scar that interests me the most, for I believe that it is the best example of the sort of legible scarifications that I mentioned earlier. Earlier in the novel, the narrator alludes to Antonello de Messine's *Le condottiere*, "the unbelievably energetic portrait of a Renaissance man with a tiny scar above his upper lip, on the left, that is to say to his left, your right" (116–17, 187). The coincidence of the scars, and (more obviously still) the deliberate repetition of the phrase "unbelievably energetic" in the narrator's account of his own face (168, 214) suggest both the importance of the scar in the semiotics of the self and the kind of totemic identification that the narrator invests in the Condottiere. Extratextual evidence confirms that Perec shares his narrator's fascination with the Condottiere, for that figure returns frequently in works such as *Espèces d'espaces, W ou le souvenir d'enfance*, and *La vie mode d'emploi*. Moreover, Perec mentions in *W* that he himself has a scar on his left upper lip. He speaks about it at some length in that text, remarking that he received it in boarding school during the war at the hands of another boy who attacked him with a ski pole. "For reasons that have not been properly elucidated," says Perec, "this scar seems to have been of cardinal importance for me: it became a personal mark, a distinguishing feature" (141, 108). He adds that though he wears a beard, he shaves his upper lip so as not to hide his scar. Further, he points out that Jacques Speisser, the lone actor in the film version of *Un homme qui dort*, also has a scar on his upper lip, "almost identical to mine: it was pure coincidence, but it was, for me, secretly, a determining factor" (143, 109).

Reading this ramifying network of signs, it gradually becomes apparent that Perec reads the scar as the material trace of personal catastrophe. He received it shortly after he was orphaned, and the injustice of the incident with the ski pole is the very emblem of the sort of arbitrary, unmerited punishment that he suffered since the death of his parents, a suffering that continues to impede his efforts to come to terms with his life as he writes *Un homme qui dort*. In such a perspective, it is the token of the fact that (as his narrator puts it) "you don't know how to live, that you will never know" (27, 140).[9] His scar is the mate-

---

9. Perec's scar also plays an important role in a broader pattern of signs and structures in his work that are marked, usually by emptiness or incompletion, in their lower left-hand corners, a consideration that several of his readers have pointed out. See for instance Bernard Magné, "Le puzzle, mode d'emploi," *Texte* 1 (1982): 84–86; Warren Motte, "Embellir les lettres," *Cahiers Georges Perec* 1 (1985): 110–11; and Ewa Pawlikowska, "La colle bleue de Gaspard Winckler," *Littératures* 7 (1983): 80–82.

rial testimony that something is dreadfully wrong with the individual who is marked by it, the trace of what Jonathan Cohen has termed the "basic neurotic reaction," that is, "a psychological reaction that is simultaneously a moral reaction: namely a deep conviction of badness and defect."[10] It is moreover the only unchanging, constantly recognizable trait in a face that dramatically eludes its bearer. When the narrator of *Un homme qui dort* ponders his face more deeply, he often sees nothing more than a bovine parody of a human face: "Sometimes, you look like a cow" (169, 215). Yet even in those moments, the scar remains.

That Perec should choose to display his scar so openly—on his face and in his writings—is extremely eloquent; and it may legitimately be interpreted as an effort to make his work of mourning visible. If the scar does indeed incarnate the kind of "truth" that the protagonist of *Un homme qui dort* looks for in his face, that truth is a very difficult one. It is imbricated in a narrative that is both local and general in its dimensions, interweaving personal and historical holocaust. The implications of that narrative are dire ones for the person who feels bound by it, and those bonds are made stronger still by virtue of the fact that the story itself is a formative one. In other words, while Perec may feel that his scar and the story that it tells describe him in important ways, he may also feel, more tellingly still, that it has determined who he is. Thus Perec may be even more deeply committed to that story than it might at first seem; and that notion may help to explain some of his more pronounced and elaborate mourning behavior. As Cohen puts it, in a tone of understatement that rivals Perec's own, "It appears to be far more difficult than we have realized to give up anything we think we know for certain, especially when it has been learned under early, adverse circumstances" (202).

In *La disparition*, it is the individual, precombinatory letter that serves as the principal locus of mourning. The absence, the *disappearance* of the letter E from the alphabet provides the novel with both theme and structure—and that consideration holds true on the level of anecdote as well as on a far more sober and compelling discursive level. Thus, Perec mentions a hospital ward with twenty-six beds, all of them occupied with the exception of one; a collection of twenty-six in-folio volumes where the fifth volume is missing; a horse race with twenty-

---

10. Jonathan Cohen, *Apart from Freud: Notes for a Rational Psychoanalysis* (San Francisco: City Lights, 2001), 4.

six entrants, one being scratched; and twenty-six boxes, with the fifth being absent. Thus, too, the novel's chapters are numbered from one to twenty-six, but there is no fifth chapter; and its parts are numbered from one to six (like the sequence of vowels and the semivowel Y), but there is no second part.

The characters in *La disparition* turn around this conceit without being able to understand it or—still less—to articulate it, and they are consequently benighted by it. They recognize only that something is lacking, and that this very lack is deeply threatening to them: "I cannot avoid . . . a void! Who? What? That's for you to find out! 'It' is a void. It's today my turn to march toward mortality, towards that fatal hour . . . towards omission and annihilation."[11] When characters upon rare occasion do manage to grope their way to the fundamental truth that organizes their world, they are rewarded by death. Ottavio Ottaviani, for instance, recognizes the lipogrammatic character of a manuscript, remarking that it has no letter A; but before he can add that it likewise has no E, he falls to the ground and dies (297, 272). Olga Mavrokhordatos expires with a single, potently lacunary word on her lips: "Maldiction" (213, 195). And the novel itself ends in a generalized death that encompasses both the fictional world that it has constructed and the generative constraint that has allowed it to come to be. Let me quote that ending here, in my literal (if alas not lipogrammatic) translation:

> death,
> death with bronze fingers,
> death with numb fingers,
> death where the inscription is engulfed,
> death which forever guarantees the immaculation of an
> Album that a histrion one day thought to scribble on,
> death tells us the end of the novel. [*La disparition*, 305]

We might well have suspected such an ending, granted the title of the novel, for the French *disparition* means both "disappearance" and (by euphemism, but nonetheless clearly) "death." Moreover, if the absence of a sign is always the sign of an absence, one might expect the letter E to signify beyond what is immediately apparent on the page. For my part, I am persuaded that the E serves Perec as the *literal* enfiguration of his parents; that its absence is the one essential and in-

---

11. Perec, *La disparition* (Paris: Denoël, 1969), 55; *A Void*, trans. Gilbert Adair (London: Harvill, 1994), 39.

escapable reality of *La disparition*, just as the absence of his parents is the one essential and inescapable reality for Perec; and that the consequences it dictates in the fictional world of the novel are metaphorically descriptive of his parents' fate—and eventually, too, of the fate Perec foresees for himself. It is possible to read such analogical relations strictly within the boundaries of the evidence the novel offers, but one can also call upon other moments in Perec's work to confirm them. The dedication of *W ou le souvenir d'enfance*, for example, reads "for E," and the fact that the letter E is phonetically identical in French to the tonic pronoun *eux* ("them") suggests that Perec means the "them" who stand—in their absence, of course—at the center of that text. And when Perec refers, in an interview dating from 1979, to "the disappearance [*la disparition*] of my parents during the war,"[12] it is not by chance that he quotes the title of the book that, up until that time, had afforded him the most literary notoriety.

In that light, the kind of achievement that writing a three-hundred page novel without the letter E represents deserves to be reconsidered. It is not merely an astonishing feat of literary acrobatics (as some readers greeted and dismissed it shortly after its publication), though the virtuosity it puts on display is undeniable. It can be viewed simultaneously as the result of extremely hard and resourceful work, and as the working through of a variety of exceedingly difficult problems, both technical and existential. How might one write at all without the letter E, the most frequently-used letter in the alphabet, the beginning and the end of *écriture?* Granted the constraint he has imposed upon himself, Perec cannot say "mère," "père," "parents," "famille," "eux." In other terms, those are words that are quite literally impossible in the lexicon he has chosen to use. Nor can he write his own name, in which that letter occurs four times, without doing it a violence which leaves it beyond recognition. One might reflect on the implications of that sort of ablation for the self designated by that name, the same self that proposes to bring this impossible piece of work to fruition.

As daunting as those obstacles are, however, they are less fearsome than the climate of incipient doom that pervades *La disparition*, and which must be read, too, as part of Perec's work of mourning. When Olga cries "Maldiction," her misspoken utterance speaks in fact directly and precisely to an issue that haunts the novel from beginning to end. Variously referred to as a "damnation," a "law," a "talion," there

---

12. "Entretien: Perec/Jean-Marie Le Sidaner," *L'arc* 76 (1979): 9.

is a death sentence hanging over each of its characters. It becomes clear moreover that, more than anything else, this is a family matter, a question of inheritance, "this horror that's blighting my family," as one character puts it (289, 265). Freud remarks that people who suffer severely from grief must often grapple with a "delusional expectation of punishment" (244), and upon first consideration one might suggest that Perec is projecting such an expectation into his novel. But I think that things are far more complex than that. Perec is far more canny than that, and his awareness of what he has undertaken in *La disparition* is far more trenchant than that. For he has taken that topos and turned it to his own advantage here. He has taken a talion and turned it into his own kind of law. He works through his task, following the dictates of that law to the letter—but it is in fact the *letter* that he has chosen. The significance that he invests in that letter is his own, and he can clearly claim it as such. The same is patently true of the novel to which that absent letter gives form—and the same is true also of his grief.

The fourth and final instance of mourning in Perec that I have chosen deals with words and their fate, in a strange fable of language whose hero is Albert Cinoc. One of the most appealing characters in all of Perec's fiction, Cinoc occupies a small but nevertheless vital space in that most spacious of novels, *La vie mode d'emploi*. When we come upon him there, he is clearly not expecting visitors: "Cinoc is in his kitchen. He is a dry, thin old man dressed in a dingy-green flannel waistcoat."[13] Cinoc's profession is a very unusual one: "As he said himself, he was a 'word-killer': he worked at keeping Larousse dictionaries up to date. But whilst other compilers sought out new words and meanings, his job was to make room for them by eliminating all the words and meanings that had fallen into disuse" (361, 287–88). His vocation becomes his avocation, but in reverse as it were. Increasingly fascinated by the words that he "kills," Cinoc begins to read old literary works in order to find words that have fallen out of lexical currency, in order one day to write a dictionary of forgotten words. "In ten years he gathered more than eight thousand of them, which contain, obscurely, the trace of a story it has now become almost impossible to hand on" (363, 290).

As Marcel Bénabou has pointed out, Cinoc resembles Perec in several ways. Like Perec, Cinoc is of Polish Jewish origin; other people are uncertain how to pronounce his name, a name whose orthography

---

13. Perec, *La vie mode d'emploi* (Paris: Hachette, 1978), 359; *Life a User's Manual*, trans. David Bellos (Boston: Godine, 1987), 286.

changed many times during his family's long journey from Cracow to Paris; lastly, Cinoc is deeply devoted to words (Bénabou, 26). Both the name and the word serve Perec as sites of mourning, in ways that are analogous and mutually illuminative. Cinoc's neighbors wonder (singly and in an impromptu neighborhood conciliabule) how to pronounce his name; and Perec offers a catalogue of their efforts, twenty variations ranging from "sinos" to "shinoch" to "chinots." Though Perec's own name was perhaps not as badly misused as Cinoc's, a fundamental similarity remains: both are "foreign" names, not easily reconciled with standard French onomastic practice. As such, they both mark their bearers in important ways. The history of the spelling of Cinoc's name is likewise vexed. From the original "Kleinhof" it went through a variety of permutations as four generations of Cinoc's family migrated through Europe; Cinoc himself is unable to reconstruct that history in any satisfactory way. In *W ou le souvenir d'enfance,* Perec remarks that his own family name underwent a similar transformation, for strictly similar reasons (as did his mother's maiden name, too), and that other people always misspell it as either "Perrec" or "Pérec" (51–52, 35–36).[14]

We commonly take the name as something profoundly embedded in personal identity; and the history of a name can tell us much about the history of a family. In Cinoc's case, and in Perec's, the name describes an itinerary through place and time and a process of considerable transformation. Through his description of what Bénabou calls Cinoc's "onomastic adventures" (30), Perec is constructing a parable of his own experience, and that of the family to which he once belonged. Though his tone is reasonably lighthearted on the surface, the tale it tells by implication and analogy is a far more somber one.[15] For the name is not given, once and for all; contrary to what we often assume, it is subject to change due to circumstances that may seem largely arbitrary, circumstances well beyond the control of the individual who bears it. Names, even those with which we are supposedly intimate, may elude us in pernicious ways. Perec remarks in *W ou le souvenir d'enfance,* for example, that he made no less than three errors in transcribing his mother's maiden name before finally getting it right (55, 38). The dismal truth that strikes him there, a truth he returns to in a

14. The edition of *Un homme qui dort* that I use offers a particularly egregious example of that phenomenon, giving the author's name on the cover as "Pérec."

15. Bénabou sees in the account of Cinoc's name a "heavy-handed caricature" of Perec's experience with his own name (30).

very different manner through the mediation of Cinoc, is that one can become estranged from one's name—and estranged too from one's family, from one's history, from one's "own story."

In a similar manner, as words fall into desuetude, they take with them small portions of the memory of language. Considered in that perspective, the work to which Cinoc devotes himself, in both its vocational and its avocational dimensions, is strongly suggestive of the kind of work that Perec himself carries out. In both cases, one gesture gives rise to—and enables—another. Cinoc eliminates words from the lexicon, yet that very act, performed over many years, causes him to engage upon his project of lexical archaeology. The former involves systematic and deliberate forgetting, the latter an equally systematic and deliberate remembering. Moreover, as Perec stages his account of Cinoc's work in the pages of *La vie mode d'emploi*, he recapitulates Cinoc's gestures in significant ways. Perec offers examples of the words Cinoc "kills," in effect recalling them and inscribing that process of recollection in his novel, a process he offers to share with his reader. Similarly, when he turns toward the dictionary of forgotten words that Cinoc is preparing, he provides three pages of such words, accompanied by their definitions, hauling them up out of linguistic amnesia and inviting us to savor them in remotivated form, as fully reinfranchised linguistic signs.

What intrigues Cinoc most about those words is the lost narrative whose trace they contain, or, as Perec puts it in the passage I quoted earlier, "the trace of a story it has now become almost impossible to hand on." Perec is likewise devoted to a lost narrative, to a story that is almost impossible to tell. He mourns for that story just as he mourns for the people that inhabited it: his mother, his father, and indeed the self that he imagines to have been his own. Perec works through that mourning in the telling of other stories, stories that may bear the trace of the one that has been lost. He deploys many different strategies of mourning, testing each in turn, hoping to find one that will work, yet recognizing throughout that none of them will work—if by "work" one means something that will ease the pain of separation for good. It is in a sense the writing of mourning, the *work* of the work, that allows meaning to come forth, even—especially, perhaps—when that meaning bears only a fragile resemblance to the incomparable and perfectly abundant meaning that has been lost.

Philippe Lejeune suggests that Perec's writing has a "convivial" character to it, arguing that "there is a place for me in each of his texts, a place for me to do something" (41). His insight is an important one, I believe, since it neatly articulates a feeling that is widespread among Perec's readers. I for one have benefited from Perec's writerly hospitality, in focusing much of my own work upon his over the years. Granted that, I am tempted to invoke one more site of mourning, among the very many that I have not mentioned. Perhaps a part of our experience in reading Perec, now, is bound up in a kind of mourning for him. Not a mourning for the man, I hasten to add, but rather a mourning for the writer, for both the written and the unwritten. Reading Perec elicits that mourning and allows us to come to terms with it. It may quite possibly allow us to come to terms with other kinds of mourning, too. Those terms must remain provisional, however, and they must be renegotiated continually. For in the final analysis, it's really not a question of completion, either in Perec's case or in ours. Freud must have known that, despite what he suggests about mourning's end, because he concludes his essay on this note: "As we already know, the interdependence of the complicated problems of the mind forces us to break off every enquiry before it is completed—till the outcome of some other enquiry can come to its assistance" (258). For my part, I shall suspend my discussion of this last site of mourning right here, proposing it as a prolegomenon to a broader conversation, whose assistance will be most welcome.

BERNARD MAGNÉ

Georges Perec on the Index[1]

According to Gérard Genette, the peritext corresponds to the group of messages situated "around the text and ... within the same volume ... and sometimes elements inserted into the interstices of the text."[2] It is composed of the following elements: the author's name, title, the jacket copy, dedications, epigraphs, preface, subheading, and notes.[3] My original intention here was to show how in his writing, Georges Perec enriches the peritext, giving it a role that goes well beyond its usual functions in order to make it into one of the text's major constituents, a place of scriptural maneuvers that contribute to the construction of meaning. But I quickly realized that such a project exceeds the framework of a simple article and I lowered my expectations; so it is not the Perecquian peritext that I will study, but only one of its components: indexes.[4]

1. "I ADORE INDEXES"

Perec proclaims it. "I adore indexes. In the *Encyclopédie de la Pléiade*, it's what I prefer to read," he declares to Jacqueline Piatier,[5] when *La vie mode d'emploi* is published.[6] An attraction that practice confirms:

   1. I dedicate this article to Mireille Ribière and Dominique Bertelli. Their work in preparing the two volume *Georges Perec: Entretiens et conférences* (Paris: Joseph K., 2003) was of constant help to me. [All translations of citations are the translator's unless otherwise noted. When other translations are used, page numbers refer to the French edition, followed by the English.]
   2. Gérard Genette, *Paratexts,* trans. Jane E. Lewis (Cambridge: Cambridge University Press, 1997), 4–5.
   3. I am establishing this list from the work's table of contents.
   4. They do not figure in Genette's list, which is, we shall soon see, not innocent.
   5. "Un livre pour jouer avec," remarks compiled by Jacqueline Piatier, *Le monde*, 28 September 1978.
   6. Georges Perec, *La vie mode d'emploi* (Paris: Hachette, 1978); *Life a User's Manual,* trans. David Bellos (Boston: Godine, 1987).

YFS 105, *Pereckonings: Reading Georges Perec,* ed. Warren Motte and Jean-Jacques Poucel, © 2004 by Yale University

five of Perec's works contain an index. *Quel petit vélo à guidon chromé au fond de la cour?*[7] (1966) is followed by "INDEX of flowers and rhetorical ornaments and, more precisely metabolian and parataxi that the author believes to have identified in the text just read." *La boutique obscure* (1973) proposes, after the 124th and last dream description, an alphabetical list without a generic title that is entitled "*Repères* (points of reference) and Repairs." *Espèces d'espaces*[8] (1974) offers its reader, before the table of contents, the "repertoire of some of the words used in this volume." *Je me souviens* (1978) contains an "Index" and, finally, *La vie mode d'emploi* (1978) places one at the beginning of "Appended Documents," just before the "Chronological Reference Points," and the "Reminder of Some of the Stories Told in This Volume."

These five indexes do not have the same pragmatic status. Belonging to stories about autobiographical events (dreams, memories) or to an essay presenting itself as the "journal of a user of space," that is, to nonfiction, the indexes of *La boutique obscure, Espèces d'espaces,* and *Je me souviens* do not contain anything, in principle, that truly surprises. Their presence is certainly not required by some vague generic rule, and it is not unusual, or, even less so, scandalous.[9] The same cannot be said, however, for the indexes of *Quel petit vélo* and of *La vie mode d'emploi,* which concern two texts whose subtitles explicitly claim their loyalty to fiction: *Quel petit vélo* defines itself as an "epic story in prose form"[10] and *La vie mode d'emploi* as "novels."[11] Yet it is certainly not common practice for an author of fiction to accompany his text with an index, normally present only in scholarly reprints of a

---

7. Perec, *Quel petit vélo à guidon chromé au fond de la cour?* (Paris: Denoël, 1966); in *Three by Perec,* trans. Ian Monk (London: Harvill Press, 1996).

8. Perec, *Espèces d'espaces* (Paris: Galilée, 1974); *Species of Spaces and Other Pieces,* trans. John Sturrock (London: Penguin, 1999).

9. In the peritext of *La boutique obscure,* it is not the index that held our attention, but the table of contents and the flyleaves. For the table of contents, see Wilfrid Mazzorato, "Peut-on entrer dans *La boutique obscure* sans se heurter à la table?," *Le cabinet d'amateur* 2 (1993): 31–36; for the flyleaves, see Daphné Schnitzer, W ou le souvenir d'enfance *de Georges Perec, un texte et son entour* (Doctoral thesis, Université de Toulouse-le-Mirail, 2000), 331–38. For *Espèces d'espaces,* we shall note only that Perec deliberately opted for nonexhaustiveness when composing his repertoire.

10. The complete subtitle, right after the generic indication, states specifically: "embellished with versified ornaments quoted from the best authors by the author of *how to provide service to one's friends* (work awarded prizes by diverse Military Academies)."

11. The surprising plural had been inopportunely eliminated in the first Livre de Poche edition. The second fortunately re-established it.

work.[12] It is significant that in *Seuils,* Genette, who is interested primarily in literary texts, does not mention, as we have seen, indexes as possible constituents of a peritext. In fiction, the presence of an index is very transgressive, as, for example, is the index of *House of Leaves* by Mark Z. Danielewski, a novel that completely changes traditional pagination by multiplying unusual motifs: annexes, typographical games, diverse collages, etc.[13] It is to these two atypical indexes—those of *Quel petit vélo* and *La vie mode d'emploi*—that I will direct my attention, treating each separately, since each obeys a different strategy.

2. AN INDEX FOR LAUGHS

The index of *Quel petit vélo* is openly parodic and deceptive, and as such perfectly in tune with the novel it accompanies: it is to a scientific index what the "epic story in prose form" is to a true epic.[14] It notably disregards two fundamental demands of the genre: exhaustiveness and accuracy.

First surprise for the reader: this index breaks off inexplicably after 164 entries at the letter P, on the word "psittacism," immediately followed by an "etc., etc., etc." Perec warns readers of *Espèces d'espaces* against using "etc." in descriptions (71), yet here are three "etc." in a list, where their presence is even less acceptable than it would be in a description. A description is incapable of exhausting reality, while it is perfectly and technically possible for the author of a given text to establish a complete list of the stylistic figures to which he resorted, and even more reasonable to establish the list of those he "believes to have identified."[15]

Incomplete in its entries, the index of *Quel petit vélo* is very often imprecise in its references. A number of them, in effect, substitute diverse and unusual procedures that are massively deceptive in regard to the indispensable page numbers:

---

12. See, for example, the indexes of the Pléiade editions that Perec, we have seen, quite particularly appreciates.
13. Mark Z. Danielewski, *House of Leaves* (New York: John Hawkins & Associates, Inc., 2000). The French translation appeared in 2002 (Paris: Denoël, 2002).
14. For a detailed study of the index of *Quel petit vélo,* see Laurent Thyssen, *Stratégie de la textualisation du paratexte dans* Quel petit vélo à guidon chromé au fond de la cour? *de Georges Perec,* master's thesis (Toulouse: University of Toulouse-Le Mirail, 1985).
15. Moreover, this is what Perec pretends to have done: "I constructed a tale, then I listed *all* the rhetorical figures that I had employed in it in an index at the end of the book." ("La maison des romans," remarks compiled by Jean-Jacques Brochier, in *Le magazine littéraire* 141 [October 1978], my emphasis.) Things are evidently far from being so simple!

—enigmatic question marks: "Antanagoge?";
—provocative approximations: "Antithesis, here and there," "Asyndeton, maybe," "Parentheses, many";
—appreciations that are as subjective as they are eccentric: "Epistrophe, I've got nothing against it," "Homeoptote, no interest at all";
—acknowledgments of absence: "Swiss idioms [*Helvétisme*], aren't any," "Hispanicisms, aren't any either,"[16] sometimes tinged with regret: "Bunny rabbiticisms [*Jeannotisme*], I'm afraid not";
—tautological cross-references: "Hysterology, see Hysteron-proteron," "Hysteron-proteron, see Hystero-proton," "Hystero-proton, see Hysterology";
—disconnected cross-references: "Hypozeugma, see Mesozeugma," "Mesozeugma, see Zeugma." Because the index breaks off, as we have seen, after, "Psittacism," it is evidently useless to look for the entry "Zeugma,"[17] just as it is useless for Henri Pollack and his buddies to look for Kara . . . in the train loaded with soldiers, and they end up getting off empty-handed: "everyone returned home. And never again did we hear speak of this awkward customer."[18]

To complete our analysis of this index, let us also note that its structural deceptiveness was further increased for certain readers when the text was reprinted, by a concurrent inconvenience that the author had obviously not foreseen. A month after Perec's death, at the beginning of April 1982, the publisher Denoël put a reprint of *Quel petit vélo* on sale with illustrations by Avoine. This new presentation evidently modified the page layout and therefore the pagination. But the text of the index itself remained unchanged and scrupulously refers to pages of the original edition! Thus, in this instance, the entire index is transformed into a delirious machine. Things return

---

16. Here Perec breaches another canonic function of the index: the "non plus" [not either], by referring to the preceding entry "Swiss idioms," introduces a syntagmatic relationship in a list whose function is, in principle, purely paradigmatic. It is, in a way, the opposite of the Jakobsonian poetic function. The latter, as we know, projects the paradigmatic function upon the syntagmatic, whereas here it is the specific concatenation of the syntagma that happens to perturb the paradigmatic. This manner of combining into a syntagma the successive elements of a list reappears in the writing of *La vie mode d'emploi*. For example, in chapter XXXIII, the succession of constraints "coat," "patchwork," "wool," and "brown" produces the following description: "a bonnet of thick brown wool all pieced together with colored patches sometimes made of different fabrics" (198).

17. Note also a reference to this phantom figure beginning with the entry "Addition," "*Adjonction.*"

18. These are the last words of the novel.

(more or less) to normal with the subsequent editions in the Folio collection.[19]

This editorial misadventure reveals the lack of focus surrounding this rather peculiar index. Even when it furnishes precise and exact references, it must be handled extremely delicately; its entries do not, in effect, correspond to the words of the text—it would be easy to point out the diverse occurrences—but rather to technical terms designating figures even more difficult to identify and to locate since their names remain essentially and totally opaque to the nonspecialized reader. To understand them demands a systematic recourse to one, indeed many, reference books on rhetoric, a technical vocabulary that does not escape from a certain polysemy that in fact contains, to the eyes of some, its perverse charm. It is totally revealing that of the 164 terms of the index of *Quel petit vélo*, 36 do not figure in the index of Bernard Dupriez's *Dictionary of Literary Devices*.[20] Far from offering a convenient tool for understanding the story, the Perecquian index constitutes above all an opaque space, largely enigmatic, transforming the reader into a specialist of hermeneutics.[21] It is not a means to locate, it is an invitation to search. Perhaps we should take this list for what it undoubtedly is, a type of enumerative poem whose signifiers are finally less important than its radical strangeness. It is similar to the list of fish in *Twenty Thousand Leagues Under the Sea*, from which Perec admits deriving a "childlike pleasure" in itemizing,[22] a pleasure that he will later try to resurrect in the reader of *La vie mode d'emploi* with, for example, Madame Moreau's tool catalogue.

---

19. In order to establish the index of the edition of *Quel petit vélo* in the volume of *Romans et récits* of the collection "Pochothèque," I used a typescript where Perec mentions, and then lists in the margins, almost all the figures taken up in the index. Despite the change in pagination, the references are rigorously true to those of the original edition.

20. Bernard Dupriez, *Gradus. Les procédés littéraires, dictionnaire* (Paris: Union générale d'édition, 1984). Others present spelling differences: Perec names "cacemphate," "labdacisme," "parachème" what Dupriez calls "kakemphaton," "lambdacisme" and "paréchème."

21. There are not only semantic difficulties. Perec also takes liberties with the strictly alphabetic order: "antypophore" precedes "antiphrase," which precedes "antiparastase."

22. "When, in *Twenty Thousand Leagues Under the Sea*, Jules Verne enumerates the names of fish for four pages, I feel like I'm reading a poem" says Perec in "J'ai fait imploser le roman," remarks compiled by Gilles Costaz, in *Galerie des arts* 184 (October 1978). In his various interviews, Perec quotes this example many times, which is manifestly one of his preferred.

3. AN INDEX FOR READING

First among the "appended documents" that follow the epilogue of *La vie mode d'emploi*, the index is also the longest: 3,093 entries[23] that occupy 69 two-column pages in the original edition! And it is, by the same token, the index that Perec most often explained in the numerous interviews that followed the novel's publication, even if these explanations, as always with Perec, are (voluntarily?) incomplete and deficient.[24] From a pragmatic point of view, the index of *La vie mode d'emploi* guarantees at least four functions, whose importance and evidence are of unequal value.

The first, on which Perec insists the most often, consists of using the index as a sort of hypertextual tool before the term existed, one that permits a nonlinear reading of the novel. "Ultimately, my dream would be that the readers play with the book, that they take advantage of the index, that they reconstruct, by wandering through the chapters, the scattered stories, that they see how all the persona are attached to one another and all relate, in one way or another, to Bartlebooth; that they grasp how it all moves about, how the puzzle is constructed."[25] And to illustrate this arborescent reading, Perec most often quotes the example of Mademoiselle Crespi: "The story of Mlle. Crespi is not told. There is one short chapter on her. While sleeping, she has a dream. In fact, her whole story is very important in the book. She had been good for most people. She knew everyone quite well and you cannot reconstruct her story but by bits and pieces, by reassembling all the passages where she appears."[26] With the index of *La vie mode d'emploi*, Perec accomplishes what existed in the initial stages of a project for *L'arbre:* "It's the description, as precise as possible, of family trees, paternal, maternal and adoptive. As its name indicates, it's a book in the form of a tree, following a non-linear development, conceived a little like programmed teaching manuals, difficult to read one page after the other, but across which it will be possible to relocate (helping oneself with an index that will not be a supplement, but a veritable and essential part

---

23. Perec claims that there are 5,000 of them in "Je ne veux pas en finir avec la littérature," Pierre Lartigue, *L'humanité* (2 October 1978), but he exaggerates! In his study (*Les mots méandres*, typescript, nd, 13), Christophe Libert has listed 3,093.
24. See note 30 below.
25. "La maison des romans," *op. cit.* We find in the various interviews a good half dozen similar remarks.
26. Remarks compiled by Gabriel Simony, *Jungle* 6 (June 1981).

of the book) many incessantly intersecting stories."[27] In *La vie mode d'emploi* also, the index is "a veritable and essential part of the book" even if, as accustomed as we are these days to narrative discontinuities, we may also read the novel without particular difficulty "one page after the other," corresponding thus, it is well understood, to a normal reading. From *L'arbre* to *La vie mode d'emploi*, the index, as a tool for locating, changed its status despite everything, as its place within the volume suggests, for it is listed among the "appended documents." Still, it did acquire some original functions.

4. AN INDEX FOR PLAYING

Abandoning the spectacular provocations specific to the index in *Quel petit vélo*, the one in *La vie mode d'emploi* is presented in a standard manner: alphabetical order, typographical codes (small capitals for the anthroponyms, lower-case for toponyms, italics for the titles), page references, everything appears normal. If a very attentive reading permits locating the system's many discrepancies, these seem to stem from the traditional and unavoidable misprints in a text of this scale.[28] In short, the index offers apparently all that a text of a scientific nature guarantees. It has, we shall soon see, an incontestable ludic dimension. Many entries furnish, in effect, solutions to certain riddles evoked in the novel. In chapter LXXXV appears "an old gentleman everyone called The Russian because he wore a fur cap all year round. He was a soft-

---

27. "Lettre à Maurice Nadeau" (7 July 7 1969), in *Je suis né* (Paris: Seuil 1990), 53–54. Regarding this abandoned project, see Régine Robin, "Un projet autobiographique inédit de Georges Perec: *L'arbre*," *Le cabinet d'amateur* 1 (1993): 5–23.

28. Three examples found in the first edition: "Boa Dai" in lower case, whereas it concerns the last Vietnamese Emperor; "Betroth" placed after "BYSTANDER"; "BOSSISM (Helena)" referenced on page 586 while this French artist is mentioned on page 589. If they are of a different nature than those encountered in *Quel petit vélo*, the problems the index of *La vie mode d'emploi* posed at the time of its re-editions are no less arduous. For the second edition of the Livre de poche and for the edition in the *Pochothèque* collection, the index was updated to take the new pagination into account. As well, I proposed corrections each time the original presented obvious errors (like those I mentioned above) or oversights. But we know that with Perec, the notion of "obvious errors" must be considered with the greatest distrust. See my article "Le viol du bourdon" in *Le cabinet d'amateur* 3 (1994): 75–88. The alphabetization also underwent modifications, since it heretofore obeys the programming norms, for which, notably, the space between two words is taken into consideration: "*A la dure*, de Mark Twain" is found from this point on categorized before "Aachen." For more details on this complicated subject that I am merely pointing out, see my correspondence with Alain Chevrier in "Georges Perec et le renouveau des contraintes," *Formules* 6 (2002): 99–107.

hearted man from Alsace, a former army veteran, who spent his spare time sending in solutions to all the little competitions published in newspapers. He solved riddles with disconcerting ease ... history catch-questions ... 'word-chain' puzzles ... arithmetical problems ... anagrams" (508, 415). Each of the enumerated categories is followed by examples, some of which contain an immediate solution, for example, "the anagrams

>STREET = TESTER
>ATHENS = HASTEN
>ABSOLUTE = OUSTABLE."

Others remain enigmatic but sometimes find their solutions in the index. For example, the two questions "Who was John Leland's friend?" and "Who was Sheraton?" are answered in the entries "LELAND" and "SHERATON" where we learn that John Leland was an "English erudite from the XVIth century, a friend of Thomas Wyatt," and Thomas Sheraton an "English cabinetmaker (1750–1805)."

It is to this type of function that Perec alludes in his discussion with Alain Hervé: "Incidentally, you left little games for the reader throughout the story?—Yes, they are riddles to solve and several solutions are offered in the index at the end of the book."[29] Except that the naïveté of the answer hides mechanisms sometimes a bit more perverse. Such as the example illustrating the category "mathematical problems": *"Prudence is 24 years of age. She is twice as old as her husband was when she was as old as her husband is. How old is her husband?"* (509, 415). Conditioned by what he or she discovered thanks to the entries "LELAND" and "SHERATON," the reader consults the entry "Prudence" only to learn there that she is a "young 24-year-old woman," something he or she already knew. This time the proper noun indexed is worthless; it is an incidental and unusual entry at the letter M that will furnish the solution: *Mari* (Husband): "Prudence's husband, 18-year-old young man."

If we look at them a little closer, the solutions proposed by the entries "LELAND" and "SHERATON" are not totally devoid of ambiguity. By mentioning the name of Thomas Wyatt, the entry "LELAND" does not content itself with bringing forth the answer to a "historical conundrum"; it triggers a new index entry: "WYATT (Thomas), English poet and diplomat, friend of John Leland, 1503–1542" which on the one

---

29. See "La vie: régle du jeu," ed. Alain Hervé, *Le sauvage* 60 (1978).

hand refers to a page 508 where we find the "historical conundrum" but evidently without the least occurrence of Wyatt. At this precise point, the index dysfunctions, ceasing to refer to a lexical item in order to point out a sole referent; on the other hand, between the two entries "LELAND" AND "WYATT" a game of crossed references begins that recalls quite evidently the manner in which certain deceptive entries function in the index of *Quel petit vélo*.

The entry "SHERATON" signals two occurrences for the name of the English cabinetmaker. The first refers to the "historical conundrum" (*colle historique*) which corresponds to the answer we can consider exact since the existence of the English cabinetmaker is historically attested. But the second appears in another chapter (LXXXVII) and in a totally different context for designating without any ambiguity the famous hotel chain, since there is talk about "the formidable thrust of the two new giants of the hotel business: Holiday Inn and Sheraton." All that remains is to know if the hotel group owes its name to the English cabinetmaker; the index would seem to indicate just that, since it contains a sole entry. This fragile certitude is quickly put into question because the second page indication is followed by a question mark[30] that recalls, yet again, those abundantly provided in the index of *Quel petit vélo*. In the opposite case, it is a new dysfunction that we witness, since a sole index entry then corresponds to two homonyms referring to two distinct referents.

5. AN INDEX FOR GUESSING

The apparently simple ludic function of the index therefore does not eliminate trickery. Therein we recognize a very Perecquian maneuver about which Perec remains totally mute.

We know that *La vie mode d'emploi* contains a very important programmed intertext, each chapter containing, according to the theoretical model, two quotes and one allusion, the former borrowed from two

---

30. This question mark inopportunely disappeared in the second edition of the Livre de poche edition, and was not reinstated in the *Pochothèque* edition, whose proofreaders, moreover, in an excess of zeal, eliminated the second page indication. A double page and a question mark remain, on the other hand, in the English translation by David Bellos. My colleague and friend Warren Motte, whom I questioned about the origin of the hotel chain's name, indicated to me that the name comes from the neon sign found on the first building bought in 1937 in Springfield (Massachusetts) by the group's founders, Ernest Henderson and Robert Moore. But this sign is "of uncertain origins"! Perec thus prudently maintained this incertitude.

lists of ten authors, the latter from a list of ten works. These quotes and allusions never appear as such in the novel. On the other hand, Perec signaled their existence both in the peritext (or the post-scriptum) and in the authorial epitext, where he even furnishes the details about borrowings from two authors: Queneau and Flaubert.[31] Of course, these revelations hide as much as they reveal: the post-scriptum cheerfully mixes the quoted authors (and the authors of works to which Perec alluded), forgets some of them, adds on others that are "outside of the plan," and omits several authors who only come to light through the efforts, discoveries, and enthusiasm of a particularly perspicacious reader.[32] The authorial epitext as it relates to Queneau and Flaubert contains a good number of lacunae, about which we will prudently

---

31. Perec, "Emprunts à Queneau," *Les amis de Valentin Brû* 13–14 (1980): 42–45; and "Emprunts à Flaubert," *L'arc* 76 (1979): 49–50.

32. The use of the singular is intentional: the reader in question, to whom we owe the already ancient invention of the "diagonale" of the Compendium, is Dominique Bertelli who at this point in Perecquian studies may be considered the best specialist of the intertext in *La vie mode d'emploi*. He is preparing *Le catalogue*, a tentative inventory of implicit citations in *La vie mode d'emploi*. While waiting for this global study, to examine the novel's intertext we must turn to some scattered efforts concerning subsets of that intertext. Here is a list of Bertelli's contributions to date:

—Concerning the quotations of James Joyce: "transPhormERr/ECrire. Approche du texte signé Perec," Doctoral thesis, University of Toulouse-Le Mirail, 1992.

—Concerning the quotations of Jules Verne: "Une bibliothèque d'éducation et de recréation. Les impli-citations des *Voyages extraordinaires* de Jules Verne dans *La vie mode d'emploi*," *Le cabinet d'amateur* 5 (1997).

—Concerning the quotations of Guillaume Apollinaire: "La farce cachée des choses: du songe d'Ursule au tombeau de Vibescu," *Le cabinet d'amateur* (1998).

—Concerning the quotations of Sterne (and some others): "Les tombeaux de Cyrla. Mémoire forclose et inscription du sujet chez Georges Perec," in Andrée Chauvin et Mongi Madini, eds., *Sémiotique et inscription du sujet* (Besançon: Presses Universitaires de Franche-Comté), forthcoming.

—Concerning the quotations of: "Petite revue d'un scrutateur (les impli-citations d'Italo Calvino dans *La vie mode d'emploi*," see *Le cabinet d'amateur* (1998).

—Concerning some quotations not programmed in *La vie mode d'emploi*: "Hors programme," *Formules* 6 (2002).

And Bernard Magné's:

—"Petite croisière préliminaire à une reconnaissance de l'archipel Butor dans *La vie mode d'emploi*," in *Perecollages* (Toulouse: Presses universitaires du Mirail, 1989), 99–112.

—"Perec lecteur de Roussel," *ibid.*, 113–132.

—"Emprunts à Queneau (bis)," *ibid.*, 133–152.

For a theoretical approach to this intertext, see Bertelli, "Du bon usage de l'intertextualité perecquienne (la vie dans les livres)," *Le cabinet d'amateur* 2 (Fall 1993), and Magné, "Éléments pour une pragmatique de l'intertextualité perecquienne," in *Texte(s) et intertext(s)*, ed. Éric Le Calvez and Marie-Claude Canova-Green (Amsterdam-Atlanta: Rodopi, 1997).

avoid asking questions regarding indebtedness to forgetfulness and to concealment.[33]

However, even incomplete, the information furnished by the postscriptum and the epitext is explicit and therefore immediately accessible to the reader. Others are implicit and demand a veritable decryption. This is the case notably for what I call the "connotative metatextual." Certain enunciations that refer denotatively to the diagetical universe of the novel have, moreover, connotative signifiers that refer to textual mechanisms, and in particular, in the precise case that interests us, to the existence of implicit quotes, for example, in chapter XXVII, when Emilio Grifalconi, coming across the draft of a love letter written by his wife Laetizia to an unknown recipient, thinks "that she must have copied the passage out of some novelette" (161 French, 121 English). The narrator's comment does not only inform the reader about Emilio's confidence in Laetizia; it also suggests, in an indirect manner, that this letter, quoted at length in the novel, could very well have been "copied," but by Perec and not Laetizia. In reality, Perec did borrow from the correspondence of Flaubert, contenting himself with transforming into the feminine an entire passage of an inflamed missive from Flaubert to Louise Colet.[34] If it does not stem *stricto sensu* from this metatextual strategy, the index of *La vie mode d'emploi* participates nevertheless in a manner totally specific to the indirect revelation of implicit quotes thanks to what I will call "biographical coincidences." For instance, the following entry: "ARCONATI (Julio), Italian composer, 1828–1905" appears exactly like another: "MOZART (Léopold), German composer, 1719–1787." But if the former figures in any worthwhile directory of composers, any attempt to look there first is in vain. We will find it, on the other hand, by attentively reading . . . chapter IX of the *Château des Carpathes* by Jules Verne, where is mentioned "*Orlando*, the chef-d'œuvre of the maestro Arconati." That maestro, deprived of a first name by Jules Verne, received, in the index, the Italianized one of the author of *Château des Carpathes*. So this is not the only hint of a borrowing. As a simple glance at the entry "VERNE (Jules), 1828–1905" con-

---

33. Concerning the question of hoaxes in the epitext, see Bertelli, "Des lieux d'une ruse," *L'œuvre de Georges Perec. Réception et mythisation*. Actes du colloque international de Rabat, ed. Jean-Luc Joly and Abdelfattah Kilito (Rabat: Publications de la Faculté des Lettres et des Sciences Humaines, 2002).

34. For more details about the metatextuel strategy, I refer the reader to my recent clarifications, "Le métatextuel revisité" (consultable at *http://www.cabinetperec.org*), where references to my past works on the question may also be found.

firms, the dates are exactly the same as those of the fictive composer. The index of *La vie mode d'emploi* reiterates these biographical coincidences on three occasions: once for another borrowing from Jules Verne regarding the character of Aronnax, protagonist-narrator of *Twenty Thousand Leagues Under the Sea:* "ARONNAX (Pierre), French naturalist, 1828–1905."[35]; once with the entry "MONTALESCOT (L.N.), French painter, 1877–1933"[36] for a borrowing from Raymond Roussel, author mentioned in the index ("ROUSSEL [Raymond] 1877–1933"); once with the entry "PELLERIN, French romantic painter, 1821–1880" for a borrowing from Flaubert, mentioned in the index ("FLAUBERT [Gustave], French novelist, 1821–1880"). In "Emprûnts à Flaubert" ("Borrowings from Flaubert"), Perec clearly indicates this name's origin: "In the back of Madame Marcia's boutique, the painting entitled *La vénitienne* is the one that Pellerin (whose name appears elsewhere in the chapter) envisions making of the Marshall's wife . . . ; the description is taken word for word, but in the present tense instead of the conditional mode" (50). Yet he is careful not to signal the biographical coincidence of the index, entrusting his reader to discover it.

These four biographical coincidences indisputably constitute an allusive, indirect system of implicit quotes that Perec hid in his novel. And like all Perecquian systems, it contains its clinamen. In effect, there exists in the index a fifth biographic coincidence between a French author, "JARRY (Alfred), French writer, 1873–1907" and another character: "FALSTEN (William), American draftsman, 1873–1907." Now, despite all the research, it is impossible to find in the work of Jarry the smallest trace of a William Falsten, draftsman or not. This time, the hint is misleading since, as Bertelli has shown, William Falsten is in all likelihood borrowed from Jules Verne's novel *Le chancellor*, where Falsten's destiny presents many Perecquian traits by anticipation.[37] This being said, such a borrowing does nothing to clarify the coincidence between the dates and Jarry, which remains totally opaque to this day. So here is a deceptive mechanism carefully elaborated and forever metatextualized by the detour in one of Gaspard Winckler's tricks:

35. The comment about Aronnax in chapter 60 does not constitute a programmed quote, but rather a simple borrowing outside of the program. To learn everything about the Vernian intertext in *La vie mode d'emploi,* see the article by Bertelli cited above.
36. Louise and Norbert Montalescot are two characters in *Impressions d'Afrique.* Louise perfected a drawing machine. For Perec's borrowings from Raymond Roussel, see my article cited above.
37. See Bertelli, "Une bibliothèque d'éducation et de recréation. Les impli-citations des *Voyages extraordinaires* de Jules Verne dans *La vie mode d'emploi,*" cited above.

The blue glue Gaspard Winckler used sometimes spread a little, outside the edge of the intercalated white sheet of paper which provided the border of the puzzle, making an almost imperceptible bluish fringe. For several years, Bartlebooth used that fringe as a kind of guarantee: if two pieces which seemed to fit together perfectly had fringes which did not match, he held back from slotting them in; on the one hand he was tempted, if their bluish fringes were perfectly continuous, to juxtapose pieces which at first sight should never have been associated with each other, and it often turned out a little later that they did in fact go together. It was only when this habit had been acquired and had grown sufficiently engrained that it would be unpleasant to give it up that Bartlebooth realized that these "happy chances" could themselves perfectly well be booby traps, and that the puzzle-maker had allowed this tiny trace to serve as a clue—or rather, as a bait—on a hundred jigsaws or so only in order to mislead him more later on. [417 French, 336 English]

6. A TYPOGRAPHICAL *TROMPE-L'ŒIL*

To mislead the reader: the index of *La vie mode d'emploi* contributes to that goal in yet another manner (and this is its third function), thanks to a veritable typographical *trompe-l'œil*. I have already suggested that the typography of the entries depends on their nature: small capitals in roman for the anthroponyms, lower-case in roman for the toponyms or the anthroponyms corresponding to explicitly fictive characters (for example, "Athos, an Alexandre Dumas persona"), lower-case in italics for the titles. So, in this system that thus distinguished by typography the names of "imaginary" characters—Aramis, Arlequin, Babar, Javert, etc.—others, all characters in Perec's novel, are mentioned in small capitals, the same typographical code as the personae recognized by history. Therefore no difference at all between "BEREAUX (Marie, spouse of Juste Gratiolet), 1852–1888" and "BERG (Alban), Austrian composer, 1885–1935," or between "GOMES (Estevao), XVIth century Portuguese navigator," "GOMOKU (Fujiwara), Japanese business man" and "GONDERIC, king of the *Burgundies*"!

In the same manner, recourse to italics signals indistinctly real works and imaginary works internal to the diegesis of the novel. In literature, nothing distinguishes "*châtiments, Les,* poems by Victor Hugo" and "*châtiment d'Hitler, Le,* essay (unfinished) by Mr. Echard." In painting, no difference between "*Comtesse de Berlingue aux yeux rouges,* portrait by F. Hutting" and "*déjeuner sur l'herbe, Le,* by Manet." In music, "*Concerto à la mémoire d'un ange,* by Alban Berg" and "*Crossed Words*, musical work by Svend Grundtvig," are put on the same plane. For cinema "*Citizen Kane*, film by O. Welles" has the same form as "*Hardi, les gars!*, film with Olivia Norvell." The index is thus a privileged space of what Perec calls a "pseudo erudition," or even better a "*savoir-fiction*":

> The text is not a producer of knowledge, but a producer of fiction, of fiction of knowledge, of *savoir-fiction*. When I say that I would like my texts to be informed by contemporary thought like the novels of Jules Verne were by the science of his era, that means that I would like it to play a part in the elaboration of my fictive texts, not as the truth, but as material, or machinery, of the imagination. [*L'arc* 76, 4]

"Machinery": we see clearly all that the word owes to trickery and to dissimulation. In this complex game between fiction and reality, the index of *La vie mode d'emploi* is not, in the end, a reassuring place. It happens that these reference points turn into markers that lead the reader astray into a space mined by the undecidable, which will itself become the subject of *Un cabinet d'amateur*, where the "pleasure of making believe" rests for the most part upon an indiscernible mixture of true and false.

7. THE INCLUSION OF THE PERITEXT

Now I shall turn to another distinction put in question by the fourth function of the *La vie mode d'emploi*'s index. This time, that which is contested is no longer, in the encyclopedic universe, the distinction between true and false but, in the concrete space of the volume, the limit between the text and its surroundings, such as the following entries found in the first edition of the Livre de poche:

> "*Album d'images de la villa Harris*, Emmanuel Hocquard, 703"
> "BELLETTO (René), 703"
> "*Histoire cent*, by Jacques Establet, 703"
> "*Journal, I*, by Charles Juliet, 703"
> "*Livre d'histoire (extraits)*, by René Belletto, 703"
> "*Monument à F.B.*, by Roger-Jean Ségalat, 703"
> "PEREC (Georges), . . . , 703."
> "*Travers*, by Renaud Camus and Tony Duparc, 703"

These entries loyally reproduce those of the original edition by Hachette-POL. But the conscientious reader of the first edition from Livre de poche must surrender to the evidence: in the volume he has before his eyes, page 703 (unnumbered) contains one sole note at the bottom of the page:

IMPRIMÉ EN FRANCE PAR BRAUDARD ET TAUPIN
Usine de La Flèche (Sarthe).
LIBRAIRIE GÉNÉRALE FRANÇAISE-6, rue Pierre-Sarrazin-75006 Paris.
ISBN: 2-253-02390-6

What happened? The first Livre de poche edition is the photographic reproduction (in a slightly shortened format) of the original Hachette-POL edition whose pagination had been retained. But all specific references to the collection Hachette-POL have disappeared from it, notably those which, on page 703 (unnumbered) listed the other volumes in the collection:

In the same collection

René Belletto: *Livre d'histoire*
Jacques Establet: *Histoire cent*
Emmanuel Hocquard: *Album d'images de la villa Harris*
Charles Juliet: *Journal I*
Roger-Jean Ségalat: *Monument à F.B*
Georges Perec: *Je me souviens*
Renaud Camus et Tony Duparc, *Travers*
Bertrand Visage: *Chercher le monstre*.[38]

More discreetly, but of an identical nature, two entries refer back to a page 3, where we would search vainly for them in the Livre de poche: "OTCHAKOVSKY-LAURENS (Paul), 3" and a sub-entry of the entry "Paris," "Rue de Galliera, 3," the page 3 of the original edition containing the note: "Series directed by Paul Otchakovsky-Laurens" and the address of the publisher "4, rue de Galliéra 75116 Paris."

By reproducing the index of the Hachette-POL edition just like it was, the editors of the Livre de poche fell right into one of the traps set by Perec: loyal to a standard conception of the index, they did not suspect that it also concerned the peritext, contesting the material limits traditionally assigned to fiction and shattering the architecture of the volume.[39] In brief, by their own blindness and without wanting to, but

---

38. Bertrand Visage's book is not referred to in the index.
39. With this departure beyond the space of the text corresponds the overstepping of the chronological limits of the diegesis that ends on 15 August 1975 with the death of Valène. The index mentions, for example, the death of Queneau (1976) and that of Claude François (1978). Concerning this point, see Jean-François Chassay's "Le jeu des coïncidences dans *La vie mode d'emploi* de Georges Perec," *Le castor astral* (1992): 59–60.

with remarkable efficacy, they underscored the ultimate Perecquian maneuver allowed by the index: the surrounding and eventual capturing of the peritext by the authorial text.[40]

8. TOWARD THE UNDECIDABLE

If, once again, we recall Perec's definition of writing as the hesitation between mask and mark,[41] we must then admit that the Perecquian indexes, and in particular those of *Quel petit vélo* and of *La vie mode d'emploi*, participate fully in this writing, and in fact constitute one of its essential mechanisms. But between the parody of 1966 and the apparently imperturbable seriousness of 1978, Perec's choices changed. Considering these indexes diachronically, it seems to me that they demonstrate an evolution toward a pragmatics of the undecidable, in which the distinction between true and false becomes more and more difficult, and ambiguity takes on more and more importance. This change seems even more revealing to me when we find its equivalent in another group of texts also characterized by traps and parody: pastiches of scientific articles.[42] Composed in 1974, "Experimental demonstration of the tomatotopic organization in the Soprano (*Cantatrix sopranica L.*)" is openly presented as a joyous hoax impossible to take seriously even for an instant. In 1977, the article "Roussel and Venice," written in collaboration with Harry Mathews and published in an edition of *L'arc* dedicated to Raymond Roussel, offers on the contrary such apparent guarantees of seriousness that one researcher from Nice allowed himself to be duped by certain references. In regards to the 1980 article inserted into the exhibit catalogue of the Pompidou

---

40. In fact, they replaced a subversion (calling the limits of the text into question) with a simple reception (references to pages practically empty). It is important to note that the index also contains entries referring to the peritext, epigraphs, and certainly postscriptum. But they are more traditional. Nonetheless, the entry "*Je me souviens*, de Georges Perec, 6" refers back to the rubric "Du même auteur" ("By the same author"), which was also eliminated in the Livre de poche reprint, and is similar to the mechanism that I just evoked. At the request of the editors, all of the entries referring to the original editorial plate were eliminated from the index in the following reprints: Hachette, Livre de poche 2, Pochothèque.

41. "Once again the snares of writing were set. Once again I was like a child playing hide-and-seek, who doesn't know what he fears or wants more: to stay hidden, or to be found." *W ou le souvenir d'enfance* (Paris: Denoël, 1975), 14; *W or The Memory of Childhood*, trans. David Bellos (Boston: Godine, 1988), 7.

42. Perec, *Cantatrix sopranica L. et autres écrits scientifiques* (Paris: Seuil, 1991). Concerning these pastiches and the different strategies of reception that they suppose, see Magné, "La cantatrice et le papillon," in *Perecollages*, 193–206.

Center, "Maps and Figures of the Earth," Perec is apparently delighted by its mystifying effect:

> The last fake that I made, no one identified it [*laughter*]. It's in a catalogue on cartography. . . . I wrote a text on cartography that I did not sign and where I appear in tiny letters at the end, as translator. I appear in the index [of the catalogue, as a contributor]. People leafing through the index said to themselves: "Well, what's he doing in this catalogue?," they search but they don't find . . . Right there, that is the height of fakery. No one even knows that it's a fake."[43]

How better to conclude than with this defense of falsehood, one that stages, precisely, an index reading?

—Translated by Peter Consenstein

---

43. "For the article about Roussel in *L'arc*, we received a letter from someone . . .—who was doing a Master's thesis about Roussel in Nice—who saw [the reference to] *Les écrivains français et la tentation du fascisme* and went to the library to look for it. They told him that it didn't exist [*laughter*]." (Interview with Bernard Pous, unpublished).

GERALD PRINCE

Preliminary Discussion of Women in *La vie mode d'emploi*

Yes, it could begin this way, in a space that Perec did not quite describe. It will be a rather tidy square cellar, with a cylindrical Chinese dresser, a bunch of artificial flowers, a battered copper tray, and a torn copy of *Racine et Shakespeare* in the background. The left-hand wall is lined with a sheet of zinc to guard against moisture. A cracked mirror hangs on the right-hand wall. In the middle of the room, a little girl who appears to be no older than nine or ten is sitting on a black, brown, and beige Moroccan rug, next to a glass of orange soda. She is the youngest (human) female at 11 Rue Simon-Crubellier—except perhaps for the Réol baby, whose sex will forever remain unspecified—and she extends the range of ages attributed to female characters in *La vie mode d'emploi*, a range almost as wide as that of male characters and stretching from thirteen (Isabelle Gratiolet) to eighty-three (Madame Moreau).

The girl, who is wearing a white cotton shirt, a red tie, a red skirt, and an old Mickey Mouse watch, looks very pretty: blue eyes, pink complexion, a perfectly oval face. She has blonde hair, like a number of women in the novel (Elizabeth de Beaumont, Elzbieta Orlowska, Ingeborg Stanley) and, unlike Olivia Rorschash, Madame Nochère, or Anne Breidel, she is not pudgy. Whereas Perec often represents objects and spaces with remarkable—even exhausting—precision (think of the Altamonts' cellar, the catalogue issued by Madame Moreau's company, or the list of some of the things found on the stairs over the years), he spends little time depicting his characters, as if things mattered more than humans and the building more than its tenants. Indeed, he usually endows these characters with stereotypical features. Olivia Rorschash, for example, is a very small, curly-haired, chubby woman. Elzbieta Orlowska is majestically tall; she has thick blonde hair, very pale skin, and dark blue eyes. Geneviève Foulerot's clear eyes, long

YFS 105, *Pereckonings: Reading Georges Perec,* ed. Warren Motte and Jean-Jacques Poucel, © 2004 by Yale University

black hair, and madonna-like face make her a good choice for playing Gabriella Vanzi in a TV adaptation of Pirandello's "In the Abyss." As for Marguerite, she was nineteen when she met Gaspard Winckler and quietly attractive with her freckles, slightly followed cheeks, and gray-blue eyes. Of Adèle Plassaert we learn that she is "about forty, small, dry, thin-lipped;"[1] of Lise Berger—also about forty—we know only that "her chubbiness verges quite distinctly on corpulence, not to say obesity" (292). One character description proves (relatively) long and detailed, that of Bartlebooth at the end of the novel, seated at his jigsaw puzzle: "He is a thin, old man, almost fleshless, with a bald head, a waxy complexion, blank eyes. . . . [H]is head is very slightly tipped back, his mouth is half open, and his right hand grips the armrest of his chair whilst his left hand, lying on the table in a not very natural way, in not far short of a contorted position, holds between thumb and index finger the very last piece of the puzzle" (495). But Bartlebooth has just died.

The name of the girl could well be Xenia, featuring the only initial left unused for any of the females (not the males) in La vie mode d'emploi.[2] Like so many other elements of Perec's novel, naming no doubt required considerable deliberation, given Percival Bartlebooth, Gaspard Winckler, and Serge Valène, the possible origins and pronunciations of Cinoc, the careful fabrication of Célestine Durand-Taillefer, the Cratylic dimension of Araña, LeBran-Chastel, or Dodécaca, the awkwardness of Gilbert Berger, the hesitant gender of Noëlle Trévins, the anagrammatic quality of Celia Crespi, the social connotations of Altamont and Nochère, the spelling of Appenzzell and that of "Hortense" (always written in quotations marks), the familiar look of Paul Hébert, Hermann Fugger, Jeanne Moulin, Olivia Norvell, Ethel Rogers, Marthe Lehameau, or Léonie Prouillot, the functional, Ionesco-like pli-

---

1. Georges Perec, *Life A User's Manual*, trans. David Bellos (Boston: David R. Godine, 1987), 248. All references are to this edition.

2. On names in the text, see Bernard Magné, *Georges Perec* (Paris: Nathan, 1999), 95ff. This paper has also exploited David Bellos, *Georges Perec une vie dans les mots* (Paris: Seuil, 1994); Jacques-Denis Bertharion, *Poétique de Georges Perec, ". . . une trace, une marque ou quelques signes"* (Saint-Genouph: Librairie Nizet, 1998); Claude Burgelin, *Georges Perec* (Paris: Seuil, 1988); Jean-François Chassay, *Le jeu des coïncidences dans* La vie mode d'emploi *de Georges Perec* (Bègles: Castor Astral, 1992); Warren Motte, *The Poetics of Experiment: A Study of the Work of Georges Perec* (Lexington, KY: French Forum Publishers, 1984); Georges Perec, *Cahier des charges de* La vie mode d'emploi, ed. Hans Hartje, Bernard Magné, and Jacques Neefs (Paris: CNRS/Zulma, 1993); as well as three collections of articles devoted to Perec's work: *L'arc 76* (1979); *Cahiers Georges Perec* 1 (1985); and *Parcours Perec: colloque de Londres—mars 1988*, ed. Mireille Ribière (Lyon: Presses Universitaires de Lyon, 1990).

ancy of Riri, the wink conveyed by Marcel-Emile Burnachs, the purely homonymic link between Raymond and René Albin and the quasi-homonymic link between Hutting and Huffing, the comic character of Jean Bonnot, Dr. Gémat-Lallès (Thomas), Eleuthère de Grandair, and Madeleine Proust, the colorfulness of White-Man-Runs-Him, Rain-in-the-Face, Seen-by-Her-Nation, or Four Times, the incongruity of Grégoire Simpson (no more English than Perec is Breton), the appropriateness of Faye Dolorès and Sunny Phillips, the foreignness of Mahmoud, Nieto, Slutton, Smautf, Orlowska, Lichtenfeld, etc.

Perhaps the most striking onomastic trait of the novel is its affection for name changes and pseudonyms. Remarkably many of the humans in *La vie mode d'emploi*—from historical figures to fictional beings—acquire more than one appellation. The art critic Charles-Albert Beyssandre, who uses at least seven other names, holds the record, followed by Rémi Rorschash. Arnold Flexner, Lino Margay, and Guido Mandetta, whose real identity is still unknown, also shine. Women prove almost as onomastically rich. For instance, Ingeborg Stanley can boast of five different names and Elizabeth de Beaumont adopts several aliases. Olivia Rorschash, née Norvell, has had four other husbands and, presumably, as many other designations. Grace Twinker (the famous Twinkie), who became Grace Slaughter upon her fifth wedding, may even rival Rémi Rorschash. Because of marriage, a sizable number of female characters change names, which may not only reinforce the themes of performance, transformation, and disguise so prominent in Perec's book but may also underline the lack of autonomy of women and the instability of their (social) condition.

Xenia is not playing a board game. She is not doing a puzzle. She is not talking on the telephone. In *La vie mode d'emploi* one finds comparatively few references to the modern media and the instruments symbolizing their power: records, record players, and tape recorders, television sets (surprisingly so, perhaps, since Henry Fresnel starred in *I Am the Cookie*, Rorschash is a TV producer, and the novel takes place on June 23, 1975 at around 8 p.m.), radios (in spite of Serge Valène and Léon Marcia), computers, telephones. As for games and puzzles, their fascination extends well beyond Bartlebooth or Winckler. Chess, bridge, go, craps, roulette, backgammon get their due. Lord Ashtray is so fond of crossword puzzles that Barton O'Brien, of the *Auckland Gazette and Hemisphere*, devises special grids for him. The hamster Polonius plays dominoes once a week. Female characters, however, do not completely match the dedication and prowess of their male counterparts. If Hélène Brodin, like her husband Antoine, is a professional gambler and if Véronique Altamont likes puzzles and helps Bartlebooth when he loses his sight, Madame Moreau's nurse does not seem to excel at word problems, Flora Champigny falls asleep while waiting to be taught to play *belote*, and the puzzle in Madame de Beaumont's drawing room is far from having been solved.

Similarly, women show less of the collector's drive than men. In 1858, Lady Forthright had a fine collection of watches and clockwork toys; but does it compare with James Sherwood's *unica* or Lord Ashtray's eleven thousand ties, eight hundred and thirteen walking sticks, and two hundred and eighteen Indian horsecloths? In 1975, Isabelle Gratiolet is not as serious as her rival Rémi Plassaert in amassing promotional blotters; and Madame Marcia only owns eight animated watches, in contrast with the forty-two owned by an American watchmaker. But then she is not "a collector in the slightest" (323).

More generally, of the nearly three dozen characters who suffer from emotional or mental imbalance, obsessions, compulsions, depressions, manias, one third at most are female and that includes—apart from Anne Breidel (bulimia), Berthe Danglars (libidinal kinkiness), Adèle Plassaert (monstrous avarice), Clara Marcia (neurotic relation to furniture), Olivia Norvell (insatiable thirst for trips around the world), or Véronique Altamont (excessive concern with family history)—Madame Albin's and Dodéca's owner's with their senility, "Hortense" (who used to be Sam Horton), and Isabelle Gratiolet, who may simply have some imagination.

While waiting for two of her cousins, Xenia is looking at the picture of Simone de Beauvoir on Georgia Perez's *Mondes et labeurs féminins* (*Woman's Work and Woman's World*) and doodling in a blue notebook. Most of the familial and archetypal women roles—wife, lover, or object of desire; mother, grandmother, daughter, and mother-in-law (though not stepmother or radiant mother-to-be); sister, cousin, aunt—find a place in Perec's novel but they are generally left unexplored. There are few adulterous affairs and, as is the case with male characters, few passionate attachments and unrequited loves.[3] There are also few examinations of sib relations: of Anne and Béatrice Breidel's interaction, for example, we are just told that the latter has tried everything

---

3. There is, of course, the triangle constituted by Emilio Grifalconi, his wife Laetizia, and Paul Hébert. But note that Emilio thinks that an unfinished draft of one of Laetizia's replies to Paul must be copied from some novelette (actually, it is copied from one of Flaubert's letters to Louise Colet).

to help control her sister's binge eating (177). One role does get more attention. The novel contains numerous mothers or mother figures, some of whom conform to well-known patterns (Madame Echard, Alice Fresnel, Geneviève Foulerot) and some of whom (like Louise Réol) seem even more unremarkable. Yet the relatively large proportion of women who (contrary to Elzbieta Orlowska) fail in motherly terms, from Ewa Ericsson and Véronique Lambert to Blanche Altamont and Véra de Beaumont, deserves to be noted. Not that male characters fare much better as parents: they do not, as the cases of Boubaker and M. Criolat make clear. But Gaspard Winckler's own mother may well have been derelict. After placing him, at age twelve, with M. Gouttman, she loses contact with him, remarries, and settles in Cairo.

The jobs performed by women in La vie mode d'emploi—from cook, magician, and missionary to merchant, actor, and CEO—are impressively diverse, too, though, once again, less so than the jobs associated with men. Predictably, no doubt, since the latter make up a strong majority of humans in Perec's world. If there are no prostitutes, concierges, belly dancers, or ecdysiasts among the males, there are no gangsters, ideologues, (airplane) pilots, soldiers, detectives, or puzzle-makers among the females. Compared to men (Kusser, Wehsal, Morellet, Loorens, Hébert), few women seem attracted by "scientific" enterprises. Anne Breidel, who discovered her vocation at age nine, has a promising future as an engineer; Martine Nochère is finishing medical school; and one of the (fictional) Trévins sisters discovers a method for splitting enzymes. The same goes for scholarly endeavors. Beside Odile Trévins, the self-taught historian who published an authoritative edition of the *Danorum Regum Heroumque Historia*, and (perhaps) Béatrice Breidel, who placed first in Greek in the *Concours général*, or Clara Marcia, no woman in the novel even comes close to David Marcia, Fernand de Beaumont, Monsieur Jérôme, Cinoc, or Marcel Bénabou. Last but certainly not least, though gender does not appreciably affect number in the area of artistic undertakings, its role proves potent nonetheless. The novel contains material for several *Künstlerromanen* and inordinately many of its characters (inordinately outside of Paris) are or have been artists. Moreover, while it may be postmodern in that the very quantity of artists (and art works) represented tends to make them unexceptional, the novel remains attached to a certain modernist (or romantic) view of artists and their superiority: the puzzle maker, after all, gets the better of the puzzle solver. Now, among the female characters, Vera de Beaumont, a great operatic and classical singer, introduces Parisians to the vocal music of the Vienna School; Gertrude, who prepares monochromatic dinners for Madame Moreau, undoubtedly shows genius as a cook; and Marguerite Winckler (like Georges Perec?) is a superb miniaturist. But one hardly finds any other female painter (cf. Valène, Hutting, Vladislav, Foulerot) or any female architect, interior decorator, photographer, composer. The women tend to be "performing" rather than "creative" artists: television, theater, or movie actor; ballet dancer, belly dancer, club dancer; opera singer, cabaret singer and pop singer; pianist, accordionist, keyboardist, saxophonist.

Only in the area of "creative" writing (fiction, in particular), an area less frequented by the characters than painting or acting, do females rival and arguably surpass males. Granted, no more than two of the thirty writers listed in the postscript (579) and no more than fifteen percent of those mentioned in the entire novel are women.[4] Still, of all the "actual" male characters, only Rorschash, who published a largely autobiographical novel in 1932 (and his memoirs in 1974), can possibly be called a writer. Arnold Flexner, the one-time lover of Vera Orlova and author of several detective stories, is probably long dead. In any case, he engages in no diegetic action. Sam Horton has at least one (autobiographical and unpublished) narrative to his credit but it was finished after his sex change. As for Gilbert Berger and his two young classmates, they have written only four of six episodes of a serialized novel and do not quite know how to proceed. On the other hand, apart from Véronique Altamont, who is preparing a history of her childhood, and from the woman who composes (or, more often, copies) the "metaphysical poems" that her twelve-year-old son is supposed to improvise, there are two diegetic female novelists: Ursula Sobieski, an American doing research on James Sherwood for her next book, and Madame Trévins, author of *The Lives of the Trévins Sisters*, which every publisher turned down. The small number of writers, the proportion of women among them, and the fact that most—not to say all—are failures, frauds, or incurably tied to the representation of real life need not lead one to draw the obvious conclusions.

Xenia is nibbling on a *petit-beurre*, one of those small, flat, and crisp cakes made from sweetened and buttery dough. At 11 Rue Simon-Crubellier (before the Altamont's reception or in their cellar, after the

---

4. Agatha Christie and Unica Zürn appear in the postscript. The text also refers to several other female writers: Germaine Acremant, Jane Austen, Harriet Beecher Stowe, Gyp, Eugénie de Guérin, Anna de Noailles, Mme de Lafayette, Mlle de Scudéry, Lady Murasaki, and the comtesse de Ségur.

birthday party in the phantom apartment on the third floor, with the menus devised by Gertrude for Madame Moreau) the quantity, variousness, and sophistication of comestibles can provoke both surprise and delight. Furthermore, beyond the obvious part it plays in Henry Fresnel's successful career, Dr. Dinteville's culinary ambitions, or Anne Breidel's neurosis, food has a role in such disparate contexts as Bartlebooth's border crossings, Monsieur Jérôme's dissertation defense, Sven Ericsson's hunt for Elizabeth de Beaumont, and the artistic performances at Hutting's "Tuesdays." Yet flavors are rarely described and, except for Anne Breidel or the enormously corpulent man in the London pub, characters do not eat a lot in *La vie mode d'emploi*. As evidenced by Gertrude's monochromatic meals as well as the widely held view—shared by Henry Fleury—that the color of foods conditions their tasting, flavor is far from everything. In fact, unlike sight (or hearing, to some extent), taste matters little in Perec's novel. Touch may matter even less. It is true that, for Bartlebooth the puzzle solver, it plays almost as great a role as sight and that, when he goes blind, it allows him to pursue his ill-fated project with Véronique Altamont's help. Nevertheless, we find no kneading in the book (massaging, yes: Anne Breidel), no pottery crafting, no sculpting, molding, or fashioning with the hand. Indeed, we should note that the most valued arts (puzzle making with its jigsaws; painting with its brushes and regardless of what Hutting might argue; writing also, with its many tools) do not imply or presuppose bodily contact; and we should further note that, in the entire book, there are fewer than two dozen references to perceptions associated with the sense of touch. Smell too scarcely makes any impression, save in the Breidel affair where Elizabeth's perfume could help in tracking her down. In other words, the novel pays little attention to those senses and sensations which, rather than allowing for distance, separation, control, and stable boundaries, not only imply variable borders, closeness, contiguity, intermixing, but are also explicitly linked to the natural (remember that Vladislav "would sit in tepid mud to get back in touch with Mother Nature" [481]) and connote intimacy.

This bias in favor of distance and against intimacy manifests itself in the technical choices governing the text, from the privileging of external focalization and the avoidance of inside views to the paradoxical propensity for telling instead of showing. Descriptions abound in *La vie mode d'emploi*. Scenes do not, and the book hardly contains any dialogue. The fondness for irony, parody, pastiche, and "quotations, some of them slightly adapted" (579) like the paucity of metaphors (as opposed to similes); the equal weight given to actual characters in the diegesis and to mere representations of humans on various diegetic objects (cf. the index); the fragmentation of the text into a thousand and one pieces, a thousand and one distinct story lines, and the consequent lack of sustained narrativity all work to foreground artifice and discourage prolonged emotion.[5]

The same bias also emerges in the novel's thematic preferences and neglects. Some of the latter—for instance, the almost total lack of interest in politics or in religious experience—may not be significant for our concerns here. Others may be simple corollaries of particular themes and techniques (or authorial dispositions). Given the rejection of inside views, for example, and given Perec's well-known aversion for psychology in fiction—"Je déteste ce qu'on appelle la 'psychologie' surtout dans le roman" ["I detest what is called 'psychology' especially in the novel"][6]—emotions are named rather than examined, contoured rather than probed.[7] Similarly, the text's preoccupation with art, artifice, and artifacts (partly) explains the absence of rural, rustic, or uncultivated settings, just as the author's distaste for the procedures and props of naturalism results in his discretion with regard to personal spaces, private parts, and excretory functions. Perec—it is well known—aspired to write a kind of adventure novel for adolescent boys (à la Verne or Dumas, not Mac Orlan or Dekobra); and *La vie mode d'emploi* links sewage and slues with blindness (361) and favors dryness over moisture, neatness instead of squalor, the firm more than the soft, the fully clothed and not the half naked.

Still, as these last comments more than suggest, such expected preferences and neglects also frequently pertain to the text's view of women. Symptomatically, though death intervenes at crucial points in the novel and though the mental health of many characters proves fragile at best, their physical health is seldom evoked (Bartlebooth becomes blind; Wehsal has rotting teeth and Mme Albin false ones; headaches, stomachaches, arthritis, or kidney stones are used for comic effect). In general, the body—that is, one of the traditional constitutors or markers of the sexes—is scarcely a textual concern.

---

5. Perec was, not unjustifiably, accused of coldness and *La vie mode d'emploi* was compared by François Nourrissier to a colossal iceberg. See Bellos, *Georges Perec une vie dans les mots*, 663.

6. Perec, speaking in Warsaw on 5 April 1981. Quoted in Bellos, *Georges Perec une vie dans les mots*, 591. The translation is mine.

7. Nor are they rendered metonymically, à la Hemingway.

Sexuality itself is not ignored. The text contains numerous references to erotica: books for "Adults Only," pornographic prints and playing cards, lubricious watches, salacious magazines. It also records many sexual inclinations and activities, from the homosexuality of Olivia Norvell's second husband, of Timothy Clawbonny, or of the "distinctly butch contralto" in Henri Fresnel's troupe (255) and the "heterosexual copulation between two members of the human species, both adult, [in] the so-called 'missionary' position" (322), to fetishism, bestiality, pedophilia, and necrophilia. Furthermore, even if the range of their practices seems narrower than that of men, women—as the love life of Vera Orlova and the obscene questions of Elzbieta Orlowska's mother-in-law can attest—are not necessarily more chaste. In fact, like in *The Magic Mountain*, life itself is compared to "a woman on her back, with swollen, close-set breasts, a smooth, soft, fat belly between protruding hips, with slender arms, plump thighs, and half-closed eyes, who in her grandiose and taunting provocation demands our most ardent fervour" (446). Nonetheless, it should be mentioned that Valène and Bartlebooth are bachelors, that Winckler remains a widower for the last thirty years of his life, and that Smautf has forgotten why, on August 10, 1939, in Takaungu, Kenya, he wrote "Do you want . . . me?" in his notebook (347).[8] It should likewise be mentioned that, although the porn trade may be more desirable than the priesthood (229), the most explicit diegetic sex scene takes place in a conjugal setting, between Philippe and Caroline Marquiseaux (134). Finally, it should be mentioned that the best orgasm appears to be the one experienced by a man of about thirty in the servants' quarters, "on his bed, stark naked, prone, amidst five inflatable dolls, lying full length on top of one of them and cuddling two others in his arms" (261).

That last element, like many others, helps to underscore the constructedness of gender. Resemblance, appearance, clothes, surgery, grammar, convention make the man or the woman. On stage or in life, some females can look or act like males and vice versa. Hélène Brodin, for instance, successfully disguises herself as a boy in order to avenge her husband; in Henri Fresnel's troupe of tumblers, one of the dwarves who do a female Siamese-twin act, complete with songs, banjo, and castanets, is actually a man; and at the *Villa d'Ouest*, the famous transvestite "Belle de May" (Olivier-Jérôme Nicolin) can turn into Charles

---

8. The French is probably more evocative (in "English"): "Voulez-vous . . . moi?" See Perec, *La vie mode d'emploi* (Paris: Livre de poche, 1993), 430.

Trenet (!) "with three flutters of her eyelids" (294). There are also women—like "Hortense"—who once were men and other characters—like the Réol baby—who may be male or female.[9] Naturally, novelists frequently exploit gender interchangeability. Underneath Adélaïde, in *The Lives of the Trévins Sisters,* lies Morellet; behind Odile lies Léon Marcia; behind Roseline loom the figures of Bartlebooth and Olivia Norvell.

Yet the text does point to one possibly foundational distinction between men and women: genital organs, which can be destroyed by death and the passage of time (or modified by surgery), may constitute an essential marker of identity (272). Besides, as has been repeatedly emphasized, females in *La vie mode d'emploi* simply do not have the prominence of males and do not participate in as many activities. Nor do they exhibit quite the same determination or the same inventiveness and creativity. These differences, which perhaps sketch a tension between biological sex and cultural gender (or between life and a manual), cannot convincingly be attributed to the novelist's concern with plausibility or to his pointed endorsement of a political ideology. Rather, they suggest that he (also) recognizes a view of woman as "the same though different," as Eve, as Xenia, as copy. Of course, Perec himself is a champion at copy. But maybe a not altogether happy one.

---

9. Following French convention, Perec uses the masculine generically: "faiseur de puzzle," "poseur de puzzle," and so on. See, for example, *La vie mode d'emploi,* 18.

JACQUES ROUBAUD

Perecquian OULIPO

1 It is well known that the *Ouvroir de Littérature Potentielle* [Workshop of Potential Literature], otherwise known as the OULIPO, was founded by François Le Lionnais (FLL) in 1960, with the collaboration of mathematicians, including Claude Berge (CB), and writers, including Raymond Queneau (RQ).
   1 1 This introduction to the Oulipo marks a departure from the norm. The Oulipo has always taken pains to link RQ with FLL when presenting and delineating the history of the *Ouvroir*. But now that Le Lionnais has virtually receded into anonymity and his role is nearly forgotten, of the two names many people only retain that of Queneau
      1 1 1 if they don't fancy that it was Perec who created the Oulipo
         1 1 1 1 which has been known to happen.
   1 2 I have unilaterally decided that whenever I am asked to speak about the origin of the Oulipo, I shall present it in the above manner. This is a personal decision, one that does not implicate the entire *Ouvroir*
      1 2 1 of which I have been a member since 1966.
   1 3 In what follows, I will explain my rationale for this change.
2 For the purposes of this essay, I will divide the history of the Oulipo into three periods:
   A-the pre-Perecquian Oulipo
   B-the Perecquian Oulipo
   C-the post-Perecquian Oulipo
3 Also in the interest of this essay, I will situate the end of period A—initiated in the founding act—and the beginning of period B in 1969, the year Georges Perec (GP) published *La disparition*, his lipogrammatic novel in E. The Oulipo's decisive, or culminating moment occurs in 1978 (with the publication of *La vie mode d'emploi* (**vme**)). Pe-

riod C begins at that moment and stretches to the present (end of 2002).

    3 1 I will almost exclusively focus on periods A and B.

A - *The Pre-Perecquian Oulipo*

4 The work of the Oulipo, its goals, its desires, and its efforts are generally understood as the research, the discovery, and the invention of **constraints** for the composition of literary texts. The realization of constraints is thus the production of examples, exercises, and Oulipian works, by Oulipians (members of the Oulipo) or non-Oulipians. The latter are either authors contemporaneous with the Oulipo who borrow constraints from the *Ouvroir* (or invent them of their own accord) or authors that predate the founding of the Oulipo who, drawing on Oulipian matter, reveal themselves to be copiers of the Oulipo, thereby earning the name **PLANTs** (PLAgiarists by ANTicipation of the Oulipo). The purpose of the Oulipo is, in this sense, *literary composition under constraint(s)*. An *Oulipian author* is one who *writes under constraint*.

5 This description is not false; but it is incomplete. *Writing under constraint* is not the primary aim of the Oulipo; it is merely one of the strategies employed to attain its goal, which is inscribed in the group's very name: **Potentiality**.

    5 1 **Potentiality** must not only be sought in literature, the Oulipo's declared field of experiment. Other workshops, of the **Ou-X-po** families

        5 1 1 "**x**" being any activity worthy of potentializing, like painting, music, comics, psychology, archery, cooking, mathematics, etc.

    5 2 have embarked on such experiments. The Oulipo therefore naturally takes its place within the framework of the **IUP** (Institute of Universal Potentiality), as foreseen by its President-Founder (FLL)

        5 2 1 which, according to some, would be nothing other than the inductive limit of the **ou-ou. . . . . . X po-po.**

        5 2 2 The announcement of the **IUP**, according to others, might be cryptically inscribed in the now famous, mildly pre-Oulipian phrase: "**dousk'lipu**(they reckon)**donktan**."

6 Besides, the word "constraint" does not even appear in the name Oulipo.

7 The first properly Oulipian work [*ouvrage oulipien*] *par excellence*, claimed as such by the Oulipo, is a work that exhibits **potentiality** in all its force: the *Cent mille milliards de poèmes* (**cmmp**) by Raymond

Queneau. Its constraint is rather elementary, but its **potentiality** is spectacular.

8 The **cmmp** is a work of propaganda in favor of **potentiality,** much more than it is praise by way of example for writing under constraint.

9 *Period A* of Oulipian history may be summarized as follows: it is essentially programmatic; above all, Oulipian work from this period pursues constraint. **Potentiality,** only truly operative in the **cmmp,** is not really central to the group's preoccupations between 1960 and 1969. The **cmmp** argue notably in its favor. Yet, **potentiality** is virtually absent from the President-Founder's first two *manifestos,* as it is from the group's minutes, reproduced in Jacques Bens's (JB) book

9 1 and hardly more present, again (in terms of a highlighted, foundational goal), in the first work collectively signed by the Oulipo, *La littérature potentielle* (1973),

9 1 1 a collection of previously published essays.

9 2 It is not until quite late, in his *Third Manifesto*

9 2 1 on which I amply draw here

9 3 that FLL corrects this regrettable imbalance in exposing the ends and means of the Oulipo.

10 It is true that several of the constraints provided by the Oulipo during these years, like the famous constraint known as S + 7, hold a strong sway over the grounds of potentiality, but many years had to pass for that aspect to be revealed. For a long time these constraints slumbered like caterpillars before molting into butterflies.

10 1 The same is true of the *"poem of a single letter"* by FLL, about which it would seem at first sight paradoxical to claim the great potentiality that Harry Mathews's (HM) reading of the poem has begun to reveal.

10 2 An even more striking example is the great discovery, by Jean Queval (JQ), of the **ALVA** (**AL**exandrine of **VA**riable Length); which does not even seem to have been identified as a new constraint upon its introduction to the *Ouvroir.*

11 And that's not all. In his **cmmp,** it seems clear to me that RQ casts potentiality in the service of composition, but not of literature. That book is not, in the sense understood by FLL, an Oulipian work [*œuvre oulipienne*].

B - *Perecquian Oulipo*

12 In the life of the Oulipo, certain moments, called **Moments Oulipiens, or M.OUL**s, leave particularly indelible marks. Each Oulipian

keeps a certain number of these moments under wraps in his memorial bag of tricks.

12 1 A collection of **M.OUL**s is currently being prepared and will, in 2004, lead to the publication of a carefully thought out volume.

13 An Oulipian Moment:

> **One day, Georges Perec**

Georges Perec, one day, read us a fragment of his work-in-progress. We listened, imparting the signs of our undivided attention, a play of eyebrows and nodding heads intended to assure him of the intense concentration with which we sought to identify the constraint at hand.

— Well? said he.

— (no reply).

— Well? he insisted. It's really rather simple.

Allow me to cast a charitable veil over the hypotheses ventured by X., Y., or Z.

We acquiesced.

He had read the beginning of *La disparition.*

14 *La disparition* marks the beginning of the **Perecquian Oulipo.**

15 Why? Allow me to list the following characteristics:

(i) It is an ***Œuvre Oulipienne*, O.OUL**, not merely a ***Composition Oulipienne*, or C.OUL**

15 1 that book has always been and still is mostly seen as a **C.OUL**, and, by that token, cited as an exploit in the realization of a constraint. The constraint, to be sure, is the *figure in the carpet* of the novel; but to see only that is to overlook *the beast in the jungle* also dissimulated there, a weave in the depths of the *possible world of language* funded by the lipogram.

(ii) The constraint of *La disparition* is not a new one. The Oulipian character of the work rests on an *Oulipian principle*, one that only came to light in the wake of precisely this example: the lipogram in E disappears the E from the written language, and that disappearance generates the story. In this sense, the composition is radically different from previous uses of constraint.

16 In subsequent years, the **Perecquian Oulipo** flourished, with the Oulipian Perec as inventor and model. It is impossible to catalogue all the characteristics that constitute that Perec here; I limit this list to:

(iii) The invention of the ***Auteur Oulipien*, the A.OUL:** an author who casts constraint in the service of all of his activities as a writer, in his C.OUL, like in his O.OUL, as well as in his non-Oulipian writings—

which is more difficult, but no less essential. Perec was the first **A.OUL**. The **A.OUL** intercedes in the world as **A.OUL,** in that capacity; he responds as **A.OUL** to the social endeavor, regardless of whether his service is private or public.

(iv) By constituting itself as a literary group anchored by **A.OUL**s, the **Perecquian Oulipo** transformed the Oulipo into a *collective work*, in the fullest sense of that term, above and beyond the exploration-construction-organization of the potentially unlimited field of constraints.

(v) The birth of the **Perecquian Oulipo** revealed the **potentiality** of the Oulipo.

17 I will add one last characteristic to the Perecquian Oulipo, an essential one that surfaced with one of Perec's other great Oulipian books, *La vie mode d'emploi.*

(vi) One of the **A.OUL**s' goals—perhaps also central to the Oulipo itself, which can, in a way, be considered an **A.OUL** in its own right,

> 17 1 all the while also being a non-**OUL O.** [*œuvre*] by Queneau; an unwritten and non-Oulipian novel by that author

18 is, and will be, the composition of a **CH.OUL**, or *Chef d'Œuvre Oulipien.* Let me explain.

19 A family of Plagiarists of the Oulipo, the *Rhétoriqueurs,* dubbed "Grands" by pleonasm and redundancy,

> 19 1 be it Villon, or the "gros Georges" (Chastellain), Crétin (Guillaume) or Marot (father and son), Octavien de Saint-Gelais, André de la Vigne, the brothers Destrées, Jean Lemaire de Belges and Jean Bouchet, and even others still. . . .

20 were, in the fifteenth and beginning of the sixteenth century, the disciples and assiduous copycats of the Oulipo. In fact, the *Rhétoriqueurs* borrowed from the Oulipo their conception of literature: they consider themselves craftsmen of language and fashioned themselves as *"facteurs"* (crafters): that is to say, as artisans, joiners, or cobblers of the word. What's more, any self-respecting *Rhétoriqueur*

> 20 1 I am audaciously generalizing here, unduly, undoubtedly, but no matter

21 must compose, as a bona fide worker, an accomplished master-companion and fantabulous *"facteur"* of the French language, that which can be called a "chef-d'œuvre," in which he unfolds the entire panoply of his inventions, the vast array of his art's resources.

> 21 1 Another family of language "*facteurs*" entitled to the status of Oulipian PLANTs is that of the Troubadours

2 1 1 1 who also fashion themselves as "laborers" of language, as "blacksmiths," or, sometimes more arrogantly, as "goldsmiths" of the word.

2 2 It just so happened that I was studying one of these "chefs-d'œuvre," *Les lunettes des Princes* by Jean Meschinot

2 2 1 which, by virtue of its *Litanies de la vièrge*, a poem that may be read in many ways—an added charm and reason to dwell on it—, is one of the precursors to our mentor's *'Cent mille milliards de poèmes'*

2 3 at the very moment that GP undertook the composition of **vme.** The blinding evidence blinded me: the completion of his project would be a *Chef-d'Œuvre Oulipien,* a **CH.OUL,** regardless of whatever else it might have been, including, for example, a novel of novels.

2 3 1 And, it has become precisely that; one that remains to this day unsurpassed.

2 3 1 1 The *Cahier des charges* of the VME manifestly proves this point.

2 3 1 1 1 The *Rhétoriqueurs'* different "chefs-d'œuvre" share common characteristics. Consequently, we may discuss each individual work as a "chef-d'œuvre of rhetoric." The *"facteur"* takes pains, while elaborating a full bodied poetics

2 3 1 1 1 which might include prose

2 3 1 1 2 to demonstrate his mastery of the tools of his trade. He varies strophe forms and meters; he composes ballads, *chants-royaux,* and rondeaux; he demonstrates all sorts of variations on rhymes: he adds the icing, he casts the spin, etc . . .

2 3 1 1 3 In sum, no holds are barred, including procedures and constraints deployed by earlier *Rhétoriqueurs.*

2 3 1 1 4 That's how he signals that he belongs to the Family of *Rhétorique.*

2 3 1 1 5 And also why VME really is, on both accounts, a *Chef-d'œuvre Oulipien,* a true **CH.OUL.**

(i) Not only are there three principal Oulipian constraints—constraints that the *Cahier des charges'* editors term the book's program:
  – the orthogonal bi-square of order 10
  – the polygraphy of the knight
  – the pseudo-*quenine* of order 10

(ii) but they were provided to him, upon request, by members of the Oulipo.

(iii) He uses numerous other Oulipian constraints, locally, as "tools."

JACQUES ROUBAUD 105

(iv) The work's contribution to Oulipian production is again strengthened by its strategic use of the "clinamen"

(v) and its generous dose of citations lifted from texts written by every member of the Oulipo.

24 It is indeed clear that the Perecquian Oulipo differs in essential ways from the pre-Perecquian Oulipo, all the while prolonging it, of course. However, a recent **Oulipian moment** starkly reminded me of the distance separating the Oulipian Queneau and the Oulipian Perec.

25 In the Pléiade's *Album Queneau,* I read the following note, undoubtedly taken from the unpublished part of RQ's *Journal:*
"At the OuLiPo, Roubaud read an elegant Christmas tale and, once again, Perec delivered a monstrous work, a performance equal to his palindrome."

26 In the same note of his *Journal,* RQ adds:
"Among my preoccupations is the risk young writers run because of the OuLiPo."

27 At first—I know not how—, a bittersweet smile drew itself upon my lips. It occurred to me that Queneau's approbatory benevolence (evinced at the time in the publication of the *Bibliothèque Oulipienne,* of which I retained an excellent memory) betrayed a kind of distracted indifference, at least with regard to me;

27 1 Christmas is not once mentioned in the tale cited.

28 I remembered a remark one of the "founders" made to me one day. I think it was Jacques Bens: "'The Oulipo', you know, was primarily François's (Le Lionnais) brainchild; Queneau went along out of friendship, but it wasn't really essential for him."

29 Meanwhile, as I thought it over, the incident got under my skin and I set out on a partial, but painful, revision of my admiration for Queneau, at least in respect to what concerns the Oulipo. What has been revealed of his *Journal* abundantly demonstrates that Queneau was a misanthrope, and therefore nasty at times. Personally, I have never had any reason to bemoan his behavior, with the exception of the incident above (upon which I came only a short time ago); much to the contrary, and I have said so.

29 1 I admire the novelist, especially his tetralogy: *Un rude hiver, Pierrot mon ami, Loin de Rueil,* and *Le dimanche de la vie*

29 2 the poet even more: *L'explication des métaphores,* the second part of *Morale élémentaire;* and innumerable other poems.

29 3 etc. etc. etc.

29 4 My revisionism applies solely to his role in the Oulipo.

30 I have thus decided, for my part, to modify my presentation of the Oulipo's founding, as illustrated at the beginning of this exposition.

30 1 I am uncertain of being able to convince my little comrades from the Oulipo of the merits of this revision. Consider, for example, these fragments of a recent e-mail exchange with Paul Fournel (PF).

30 2
From: Paul Fournel <paulfournel@yahoo.fr>
To: Jacques Roubaud <jacquesroubaud@noos.fr>
Date: Monday November 4 2002 12:38
Dear Jacques,
I would like to give this quip to Europe. What do you think?
Thanks,
Paul

30 3 Here now is the start of PF's text.
QUENEAU AND THE OULIPO
Two important texts about Queneau have just been published: the first biography, by Lécureur; and, the preface to the Pléïade, by Godard. Both share the particularity of entirely sidestepping the Oulipo. This prompts me to evoke the following personal memories. May readers forgive me.
I used to drive my blue 850 Fiat on the quays of the Seine between the *route de la Reine,* in Boulogne, and the *rue Sébastien Bottin,* in the seventh *arrondissement.* Raymond Queneau seated at my side, big and bad; he filled the little car up and would hold his hat on his knees for fear of denting it against the ragtop. This is how I would often accompany him back to his Gallimard office after the Oulipo meetings, normally held at the home of President Le Lionnais. That's when he spoke to me about the importance he attributed to the Oulipo. He never launched into long-winded discourse, but rather commented on small concrete points, enumerated tasks to accomplish, suggested readings, and discretely alluded to the talents of our Oulipian friends which he enjoyed pointing out to me, lest I overlook them. For each one of us, he had a particular admiration and fondness, but never expressed it directly. One had to detect it based on often mysterious signs, just as one also had to divine the secret advice he issued to one or another of us.

. . . .

30 4 I immediately answered:
dear Paul

. . . .

I have a small concern about the beginning. When the "Pléiade" first appeared, Godard and I participated in Pascale

Casanova's radio program. While it is true that he has done his work conscientiously, it is also true that, for Godard, Queneau is markedly inferior to Céline (his specialty). Perhaps someday somebody will explain that RQ's rendering of spoken French has nothing to do with the "concierge's French" (in its ancient meaning: fink, snitch, etc.) written by that piece of trash Céline.

. . . .

Ok.

That said, I believe the Oulipo today need not take shelter behind Queneau. What the Oulipo has done with FLL's brilliant idea greatly surpasses what Queneau could have thought of it. And there is another reason: I am attaching herewith a passage from the speech I gave at a memorial for Perec sponsored by the Italian Oulipo, L'OPLEPO, in Capri, last Saturday.

"I will conclude with a recent Oulipian moment, one that resonates with a much earlier episode in the life of the Oulipo, one that perplexed me; and, it would not have failed to surprise GP, I believe (and that's putting it lightly).

30 5 And so, in my reply to PF, I pursued what I have already related here about the Pléïade album, about my Tale, about GP and the "young Oulipians"; I will add only this:

30 6 as for GP's poem, 'monstrous' or not, I am not alone in thinking that its stakes far exceed mere 'performance'."

30 7 I signed off by sharing with PF my intention of henceforth attributing the Oulipo's invention principally to FLL.

30 8
From: Paul Fournel <paulfournel@yahoo.fr>
To: Jacques Roubaud <jacquesroubaud@noos.fr>
Date: Monday November 4 2002 16:14
Subject: Re:
I have not read the texts you mention. They do sound entirely surprising and may support the Quenellian indifference you're positing. But on that score, I think you are two steps ahead of both Godard and Lécureur. Can we, in the name of what you're revealing, allow them to erase the Oulipo? For, if they erase it from the work of RQ, that would mean that they erase it all the more from everyone else. Is there not a strategic danger in dissociating RQ and the Oulipo right now? Am I wrong to link them?

30 9 I responded to PF that what he was saying was right, of course, and that what I was saying reflected a rather partial point of view . . .

C - *The Post-Perecquian Oulipo*

31 As stated, I shall be brief. The **Oulipian moment** when GP presented *La disparition* occurred at a relatively peculiar time in the history of the Oulipo. After the effervescent invention of the Oulipo as an idea, after the enthusiasm born of recognizing the project's originality, the originality of the **cmmp** and **S + 7** (to cite just these two examples), there was a marked decline, felt specifically in the waning of the taking of *Minutes* at the meetings, a task initially undertaken by Jacques Bens (JB). The result was the **Crisis of 66,** about which the **A.O.** (*Anciens Oulipiens*) (the founding members of the Group) spoke very little (or not at all) to the "newcomers"

31 1 among whom, in 1966, to be precise, I figured; quickly followed by GP.

32 It would be rather tempting to see the **Perecquian Oulipo**—or, more exactly, the concomitant decision to enlarge the *Ouvroir*—as the solution to that crisis. I don't know if this hypothesis is sound. However, it does not account for the most original aspects of the "*Ouvroir*'s second life," most of which must be almost exclusively attributed to Perec himself.

33 I believe that the Oulipo today, **post-Perecquian,** heavily relies on the **Perecquian Oulipo,** as I have described it in the section above. In the after-Perec, it has become automatic, or common practice always to consider both older and newer constraints in light of their potentiality; that is, not only taking into account the relative difficulty involved in producing a certain quantity of texts while respecting a given constraint; nor, for that matter, merely accounting for the relative poetic or narrative value of the results. Instead, speculating about a constraint's potentiality involves discerning the extent to which it is apt to trigger variations and mutations; the extent to which it will naturally and productively participate in families of constraints; and, finally, the extent to which it might evolve over the course of time.

34 I shall close with a remark about the notion of potentiality. The common conception of a **constraint's potentiality** (for the Oulipo) is that of a *potentiality pre-existing the composition* of texts that respect the rule of that constraint. In the *Cent mille milliards de poèmes* (cmmp), once the ten sonnets and their operative rule are given, the rest

is clear. The one hundred trillion are not there, in the published book, but they exist virtually. They are factored to the power of 14. They are potentially there. Their infinity, "for all practical purposes," is revealed and affirmed. What's left is simply actualizing choices in the proposed selection, and a new sonnet reveals itself; new, but one that was already there, waiting to be chosen.

35 The example of the *cmmp* is paradigmatic. All Oulipian constraints provide the same kind of potentiality. This is pure potentiality. Two texts written under the S + 7 constraint will differ if the dictionaries selected to apply the rule differ, but both already exist once we have chosen the two ingredients (the text to be transformed and the tool of its transformation). Speaking more generally, every text resulting from the application of a constraint belongs to the same "possible world of language" (PoWoLa) defined by that constraint, and the boundaries of that world are circumscribed as soon as that constraint is decided.

36 But the potentiality of a constraint harbors yet another aspect. It bears the seeds of
> *variations* and
> *extensions*

that subsequent work on that constraint will ferret out.

> 36 1 We can either imagine that these mutations emerge from a void through the creative activity of this or that Oulipian "*facteur*" (without forgetting the PLANTs); or, we can imagine that they await discovery in a no-man's land, in limbo. I will not pronounce a preference for either of these interpretations:
>> 36 1 1 ancient debate, analogous to the one dividing interpreters of mathematical thought.

37 These two aspects of potentiality necessarily imply a third. A displacement in perspective on a constraint, often brought about through its application and the actualization of certain variations, re-inscribes that constraint into a broader family and that re-inscription in turn generates new variations.

38 In short, *potentiality in actuality* is as critical as predisposed potentiality. The history of the **post-Perecquian** Oulipo
> 38 1 the study of which would include an account of "Oulipian effects" on contemporary literature, as well as the literature of the past

39 is essentially the creative realization of **potentiality in actuality.**

—Translated by Jean-Jacques Poucel

DAPHNÉ SCHNITZER

A Drop in Numbers: Deciphering Georges Perec's Postanalytic Narratives

What do parachute jumping and psychoanalysis have in common? Seemingly, nothing, and therefore it is understandable that Georges Perec was surprised when Clara Malraux once told him that a parachute jump was equivalent to a psychoanalysis. Perec differed, saying "In fact I believe it's not exactly that." To him, the parachute jump meant the capacity for trust—jumping as a leap of faith in life—whereas psychoanalysis brought with it something "entirely different."[1] Indeed the pure emotional energy spent in psychoanalysis seems totally devoid of the life affirming intensity that comes from the physicality of the jump. Yet, upon closer examination, it becomes clear that a parachute jump and a visit to the psychoanalyst's office have more in common than is immediately apparent. For Perec, the parachute jump opened onto a new sense of life, which, when translated into psychoanalytic terms, meant an opening onto writing. That is also why he chose to narrate his parachute jumps and to commit them to writing.

This essay proposes to explore the relationship between jumping and certain narratives related to Perec's analysis. The first section focuses, through a series of intertextual readings, on a specific aspect of Perec's writing techniques, namely the simulating of a syntax of the unconscious, as distinct from alleged autobiographical semi-unconscious, or obsessive forms of writing. In the second section of this essay, the analysis of a chapter from *La vie mode d'emploi*[2] exemplifies the change in Perec's aesthetic orientation. At that juncture, his writing

---

1. Georges Perec, *Je suis né* (Paris: Seuil, 1990), 42 (henceforth *JSN*). All translations from Perec's work are my own here to emphasize the specificity of his poetics in the context of this article.
2. Perec, *La vie mode d'emploi* (Paris: Poche, 1978); henceforth *VME*.

YFS 105, *Pereckonings: Reading Georges Perec*, ed. Warren Motte and Jean-Jacques Poucel, © 2004 by Yale University

becomes distanced from the parental phantasmatic scenario, which acquires—precisely through the act of writing—the status of a personal myth, an artistic credo.

In 1959, during a meeting of the editorial board of the journal *Arguments*, Perec insisted on sharing a personal story. The story, which was recorded on tape, resulted in a written text entitled "The Parachute Jump," and it opens with a symptomatic remark: "It is a very personal experience, I am sharing it because I'm a bit . . . because I've had a bit to drink" (*JSN* 34).

The confession is linked to an inebriated state, reduced inhibitions, a less than perfect control over one's speech, as though, in order to tell the story, Perec had first to get out of his usual frame of mind, and, maybe, jump into the void:

> Attach [the grip of my chute] to the cable, then jump . . . well I could not do it! . . . It is at this exact point that there arises the problem of choice. Precisely the problem of Life itself. . . . On an absolutely individual level, for me, the parachute jump had indisputable bearings: the fact that before 1958 I could not accept myself and that now I can do it constantly, continuously, that I could not define myself and that now I am entirely capable of doing so. [*JSN* 44]

How does the act of jumping encapsulate the problem of "Life itself," beyond the obvious possibility of crashing if the chute does not open? Why does the jump entail unconscious repercussions on oneself? Finally, how does the jump resolve the difficulty of understanding and accepting oneself?

The following passage suggests an answer to these questions:

> The parachute weighs fifteen kilograms, it is a very heavy and extremely hard thing to carry, one is really . . . condemned, one is really . . . minimized! In a word, it is terrible: one cannot carry it, one cannot walk with it. One is forced to bear it. [*JSN* 36–7]

Normally considered a life saving device, which we often conceive of as floating gently in the air, here the parachute appears as a heavy burden to carry, and it can be seen as the metaphor for Perec's past. One need only substitute the word "past" for "parachute" to grasp the difficulty felt by Perec while facing the imminent jump.

Perec's past was heavy to carry in more ways than one: it had been relegated to a preconscious psychic zone, far beyond the reach of memory. His father was killed in 1940 when Perec was four years old, and his mother was deported "in the direction of" Auschwitz in 1942, when he was six.[3] A paternal aunt raised Perec, and he had no memory of his parents. In *W ou le souvenir d'enfance,* he was to write: "I have no childhood memories" (*W* 13).

A highly personal relationship with language also defines the evocation of his "long forgotten" past. Because Perec lost his parents in early childhood, he experiences remembrance as if there were a rift between past and memory, the past partaking of the lost parental universe, and memory, as though emptied of this past, beginning for Perec at age eight, his "birth" year:

> Age eight, fourth grade (like any other child schooled under normal circumstances), a sort of year zero, preceded by I know not what (when in fact did I learn to read, to write, to count?). [*W* 181]

If we pursue our analogy of the parachute and the past, jumping means ridding oneself of this past almost to the point of reaching a *tabula rasa.* It also means a loss of identity and a death warrant, which is why jumping is almost impossible for Perec.

Perec can only respond with an act of faith. He cannot merely jump, but must throw himself, "facing the void, in one movement one must throw oneself [*se jeter*]." Nevertheless, Perec is not content with throwing himself into time just once, rather, he says, "I jumped thirteen times and thirteen times I threw myself" (*JMS* 43). However, jumping 13 times does not erase the previous 13 times. To the contrary, it anchors it in the very gesture that purports to dismiss it: the number thirteen is an anagram of thirty-one, Perec's age when he comes to terms with his fixation on his father, who was killed at thirty-one. This death is itself encrypted into the wordplay *"para-chute/père-chute/chute du père":* (para-chute, father-fall, fall of the father).[4]

---

3. Perec, in his autobiography, is uncertain about the final destination of his mother and aunt: "It is possible that, deported in the direction of Auschwitz, they were directed toward another camp; it is also possible that their entire convoy was gassed upon arrival" (Perec, *W ou le souvenir d'enfance* [Paris: Denoël 1975], 57; subsequently cited as *W*). What seems to be probable, since Perec could not find a trace of them beyond the convoy's number, is that they were never even tattooed, meaning that they never made it alive into a concentration camp.

4. David Bellos notes that Perec's "airborne training started on Monday, 5 May 1958" when "he jumped *six* times in the space of a few days and was promptly awarded his licence, number BP 140602, on Saturday, 10 May 1958" (Bellos, *Georges Perec, A Life in Words* [London: Harvill, 1993], 186–87; my italics). This information, based on Perec's military records, enhances the idiosyncratic meaning of the "thirteen" jumps that Perec recalls at the *Arguments* meeting. Interestingly, one finds in the margin of a letter Perec

That Perec did not accept himself before the jump and that he could do so afterward means that the "before" and the "after," which before the jump did not exist independently—what existed earlier was the nontemporal time of the phantasm—are finally brought into their logical temporal relationship.

Through fear, the jump instigates the reality principle that separates the real act from the phantasm: a parachute jump is but a jump into the void, but, on the phantasmic level, it may also be an agglomerate of existential fears, without the subject's necessarily confusing those two levels. What partakes of a psychological state generally recognized as such is accompanied in Perec's case by an acute consciousness of the phantasmic mechanism that is linked to his parents' deaths and lies at the source of his most profound fears.

In the very act of overcoming his fear, he understands it and transcends it (he throws himself):

> I could read, at the moment of the jump, a deciphered text of this memory: I fell into the void; all the strings were cut; I fell, alone and unsupported. The parachute opened. [W 77]

To which memory is Perec referring? In the text, the only memory that precedes this description is the one left from his childhood: the last goodbye to his mother at the Gare de Lyon in Paris. What Perec reads at the moment of the jump is nothing other than the merging of the past (memory) and the present. The jump causes him to re-experience being abandoned by his mother at the train station.

The severed strings, the controlled fall, are presented as the opposite of what happened at the station, where Perec's mother accompanied him for the last time. There are three variations of this memory in *W*. In the first, Perec sees his mother waving a handkerchief on the platform (*W* 48). In another variation he's wearing a sling on his arm, and in the third he recalls wearing a truss because he has a hernia (*W* 77). His mother, in all cases, buys him an illustrated Charlie Chaplin book, entitled *Charlot parachutiste,* and on the cover Charlie Chaplin, com-

---

wrote to Jacques Lederer during his military service the following series of permutations on the word "parachute" that all leave intact the first syllable: "*Para-tonnerre, Para-vent, Para-pluie, Para-fine, Para-mètre, Para-chute/iste*" (lightning conductor, folding screen, umbrella, paraffin wax, parameter, parachutist) (Lederer, *Cher, très cher, admirable et charmant ami . . . , correspondance Georges Perec-Jacques Lederer 1956–1961* [Paris: Flammarion, 1997], 80; my italics).

plete with his little moustache, his cane, and his soft hat, is attached to a parachute by the suspenders on his trousers.[5]

Perec's choice of words when describing his parachute jump experience isn't altogether innocent. Perec tells us that he is "reading" a deciphered text, which is the one of the memory in the station that readers are simultaneously reading. There is no other memory preexisting the parachute jump, and certainly not the memory of the station.

The trick consists in making us believe that we can find and decipher that nonexistent memory, while in reality it is through this stratagem of inverted reading that Perec ciphers—and creates—at the moment of the parachute jump, the memory at the train station. If the past emerges transformed after the parachute jump, one now understands the meaning of this transformation: for Perec, the past becomes an elaboration constructed on the basis of the present, one that will be presented to the reader in the form of a memory. To quote Perec: "I could read, at the moment of the jump, a deciphered text of this memory."

This existential transformation of Perec's relation to past and present expresses itself on the level of writing through the different emotional charge his words carry. "Before," writing defines itself through the obsessive relation to $mo/r/ts$ (words) whereas their symbolic dimension is glued to the signifier. "After," the symbolic charge moves from the referent to the staging of that referent (into fiction).

Of course, the distinction between before and after isn't due solely to the parachute jumps. Were it that simple, many people would switch from psychoanalysis to parachuting! Perec spent years in and out of analysis, during which he analyzed his relationship to what he wrote and to his writer's vocation. Still, it remains difficult to separate the analysis from the parachuting experience. For example, take this description:

> There was something abstract in that arbitrary time, something that was at the same time reassuring and frightful . . . an immobile time in an improbable space.[6]

---

5. Philippe Lejeune mentions that not only was the *Charlot* book published before Perec's birth, and again after the war (in any case, not at the time of the Gare de Lyon memory), but it was entitled *"Charlot détective,"* with the cover picture sporting a parachute very conventionally tied to Charlie Chaplin (Lejeune, *La mémoire et l'oblique. Georges Perec autobiographe, essai* [Paris: POL, 1991], 82–85). However, Lejeune stops short of asking a fundamental question, namely, why does Perec give so much importance to the parachute jump?

6. Perec, *Penser/Classer* (Paris: Hachette, 1985), 63; subsequently cited as *P/C*.

This description could induce us to mistake the reference for the parachute jump, but what Perec is describing is a familiar place on a familiar street: the psychoanalyst's office.

Writing of his analysis, Perec makes the following comment, which leads us back to the parachute jump:

> My story . . . was given to me, one day . . . like a memory restored to its space, like a gesture, warmth found again. On that day, the analyst heard what I had to tell him, what he had been listening to for four years without hearing it, for the simple reason that I did not tell him, that I did not tell it to myself. [P/C 72]

Did Perec forget to tell the story to the analyst? One can only forget what one knows, and Perec did not know the story. What might pass for a typo—the correct phrasing appearing to be "for the simple reason that I did not tell *it to* him"—is really Perec expressing his own resistance to analysis. The point is not that Perec does not tell the story to the analyst, but rather that Perec *represses* his story (or hides from himself) during the four years of analysis.

But why does he now hide it from the reader? Why is access to what has happened on that "one day" denied to the reader, sending him to look into Perec's other work?

> Of this subterranean place I have nothing to say. I know . . . that, from now on, its trace is inscribed within me and in the texts that I wrote. [P/C 72]

Would Perec's resistance continue even after analysis, perhaps even working against it, posthumously as it were? Or perhaps, and more likely so, the "real" analysis was played out only in the act of writing, which could explain the absence of the story of the unraveling of the analysis (assuming it to be true) in *Les lieux d'une ruse*. "I wanted to put it into writing, it had to be written, I had to find again, in writing, through writing, the trace of what had been said" (P/C 20). What "had" to be done was to regain possession of the memory-trace and to submit it to a by now familiar treatment, hiding it in other texts. The "ruse" could well be in the play of echoes between this text and the book that was written during the analysis:

> I do not know if *I have nothing to say, I know* that I am saying nothing . . . I do not write in order to say that I shall say nothing, I do not write in order to say that *I have nothing to say.* I write . . . *I write* because they have left *in me* their indelible mark and that *its trace* is the

writing . . . buried deep in the depths of the earth, the *subterranean* remnants of a world he will think he had forgotten: piles of gold teeth, wedding rings, spectacles, thousands and thousands of heaped clothes, dusty files, stocks of bad quality soap. [W 58–59][7]

However, psychoanalysis hasn't yet had its last word. Narrating the analysis, by reproducing the unconscious strategy played out in it, could also be, without Perec's realizing it, the only frame where his defenses crumble and where the work of analysis is truly accomplished. Perec, for his part, wrote that "psychoanalysis does not really resemble publicity for bald people: there was no 'before' and 'after'" (P/C 62). To be sure, this was an ongoing story during most of his life, but there still was a "before" and an "after," not in an objective or autobiographical temporality, but in the realm of writing. The work Perec produced after analysis, especially *La vie mode d'emploi* and *Récits d'Ellis Island*,[8] shows that the psychoanalytic thematic (as distinct from the mere obsessions of the writer) became an integrated part of the complex mechanics of Perec's writing.

This postanalytical writing mechanism will be demonstrated here through an analysis of "Altamont, 2," the twenty-fifth chapter of *VME*. Why, specifically, look at this chapter out of the ninety-nine chapters in the novel? Because its structure—typical of the novel's composition, yet unique within the novel—represents, as I demonstrate, a model of Perec's "postanalysis" writing strategies.

Each chapter in the novel contains descriptions of the material contents and of the inhabitants of apartments in the fictitious building number 11, located on Simon-Crubellier Street in Paris. The descriptions encapsulate the biographies of the lodgers or owners of the apartments. These biographies, in turn, are sometimes described in a very concise manner, or narrated at length in several chapters in the novel. The reception given on the occasion of Mr. Altamont's annual return, described at the beginning of Chapter 25, is fragmented

---

7. My italics. Within *W*, the remnants strikingly illustrate the meaningless jumbling together of victims (spectacles, heaped clothes) and perpetrators (dusty files) in personal and cultural memory. However the term "subterranean" can be interpreted very differently in the psychoanalytical context. See Claude Burgelin, *Les parties de dominos chez Monsieur Lefèvre. Perec avec Freud, Perec contre Freud* (Paris: Circé, 1996), 64–72, 170n. Indeed the meaning of Perec's analysis narrative seems to lie precisely in this possibility of withdrawal, created at the intersection between *W* and *Les lieux d'une ruse*.

8. In *Récit d'Ellis Island* (Paris: Éditions du Sorbier, 1980), Perec anchors his personal myth in the American national emigration site of memory, transforming in the process his personal quest into a collective psychoanalysis.

into sections spread among several chapters. Yet the adventure story, which constitutes the heart of Chapter 25, does not appear elsewhere in the novel.

Chapter 25 opens with the description of a dining room in a bourgeois interior, and ends with the brief mention of the owners of the apartment, the Altamont family. These two fragments set in Paris in the year 1975 frame an adventure story that takes place in Indonesia during the thirties. This story involves an expedition led by an ethnographer named Marcel Appenzzell, who is searching for an ancient tribe living in the heart of Sumatra. The tribe has three names: the Andalams, the Orang-Kubus, or Kubus. Appenzzell returns to Paris, and later leaves again for Sumatra in 1939. His mother remains in Paris, narrowly escapes a police roundup, enters into the Resistance, and is killed in 1944.

There are four points worth noting at the outset. First, "Altamont, 2," while being a description of an annual reception, turns out to constitute the pretext for the narration of the story of an ethnographer's quest to find traces of a lost civilization. Second, the protagonist of "Altamont, 2," Marcel Appenzzell, finds himself in the heart of the jungle while searching for signs of the vanished nomadic tribe. Clearly, Indonesia is a signifier, it partakes of a symbolic geography. Third, "Altamont, 2," dated 1975, is written after Perec's psychoanalysis (1971–1975). Again, the difference between the before and the after of analysis is less about a difference of content than about Perec's relation to his writing. His obsessions do not change, but he is capable after analysis of distancing himself from them. They remain, but are expressed and written differently. It is in that sense that we will have to decipher the meaning of "Altamont, 2." Finally, Appenzzell's attempt to find traces of the Kubu civilization brings on their disappearance, as well as his own. In other words, the attempt to reconstruct the past leads to an acute consciousness of absence, of the lack of personal memory, which in Perec's case is the characteristic by which the subject defines himself.

On the thematic level, there is very little in common between the two stories. There is a distant familial connection, which is only mentioned in passing at the end of the chapter: "Mrs. Altamont is a distant second cousin of Mrs. Appenzzell." It turns out that the same apartment at number 22, rue Simon-Crubellier was occupied at different times by those families: the Appenzzell family lived there before the war and the Altamonts after the war, at the beginning of the fifties. The consecutive occupation of a single space—mimicked by the structure of the chapter, which alternates the separate stories taking care to not mix them in any way—seems to be the only point of contact between the two families.

This disjunction is further enhanced from within the Sumatra story by the ambivalent metaphorical dimension of Appenzzell's quest. This quest, which is placed under the auspices of racial persecution—a white man, Appenzzell, relentlessly pursues an almost extinct indigenous tribe—lasts exactly five years and eleven months, the official duration of World War II (September 1939 to August 1945). There is a paradox here. In his single-minded pursuit that leads to the disappearance of the Kubus, Appenzzell symbolizes Nazi savagery. Conversely, his physical appearance after those five years and eleven months is reminiscent of concentration camp survivors: he weighs twenty-nine kilograms, can barely move or eat, and has all but lost the capacity of speech. From this perspective, as long as one identifies with the Kubus, the Sumatra episode reads as a displaced metaphor of the persecution of the Jewish people: the name given to the Kubus, "Orang-Kubus," connotes through homophony Orang-*errant* (wandering), the wandering Jew (*Juif errant*), as well as an anti-Semitic insult of the thirties, Orang-*outang*.

However, this reading, which relies on the ambiguity of Appenzzell's quest, clashes with factual evidence: the Sumatra expedition takes place in the thirties and it ends in 1938, a year before World War II starts. Almost nothing is mentioned in the text about the horrors of the war. Everything happens as if Perec had mistaken the year, and had displaced the elements relating to World War II onto the historical past of Sumatra, so that when one gets to the official opening of the war—1939—there is very little left to say. The description of the war then holds in a tiny paragraph, which leads directly to 1944:

> Mrs. Appenzzell insisted on staying in Paris, even after her name appeared on a list of Jews not wearing the star published in the weekly *Au Pilori*. One evening, a note was slid under her door by a compassionate hand, warning her that she would be arrested on the following day at dawn. She succeeded in reaching Le Mans that same evening, and then crossed over to the free zone, and entered the Resistance. She was killed in June 1944, near Vassieux-en-Vercors. [*VME* 150]

From there one moves straight to the Altamont story.

This temporal disruption is further accentuated by the strangeness of Appenzzell's quest, which seems to regress instead of evolve, and ends with his disappearance. Appenzzell begins by hiring a guide and discovers an authentic Kubu village. Alas, the village—"five houses on wooden piles"—is abandoned. The guide deserts him, Appenzzell continues on alone, and disappears.

Five years and eleven months later he reappears with no explanation. Rescued and sent back to Paris, he is asked to lecture on the Kubus at the Institute of Ethnology. He accepts, but a few days before the conference, he burns all his papers and disappears again, leaving a note for his mother saying that he didn't feel he "had the right" to divulge anything at all about the Orang-Kubus. All that remains is a thin notebook full of half decipherable notes, which escaped the fire. On the basis of those meager traces, a few tenacious students reconstruct the rest of the story, namely that Appenzzell had discovered a second Kubu village, containing not five, but ten houses on wooden piles. For three days, Appenzzell had ample opportunity to observe the Kubus, and noted that their vocabulary was extremely diminished, consisting in fact in no more than a few dozen words:[9]

> [H]e asked himself if like their distant neighbors the Papouas, the Kubus didn't voluntarily impoverish their vocabulary, suppressing a word every time that there was a death in the village. [*VME* 148]

On the fourth day, the Kubus vanished, along with their food and their three goats.

After two months of pursuit, when he finally finds them, the Kubus have further regressed into savagery: they no longer dwell in houses, or even in huts, but in "hastily constructed" shacks, and, of course, they promptly disappear again. For five years Appenzzell doggedly pursues the Kubus:

> No sooner had he succeeded in finding their trace than they fled again, going deeper and deeper into ever more inhospitable regions to reconstruct villages that were more and more precarious. [*VME* 149]

For a while Appenzzell vainly ponders the meaning of the Kubu migratory behavior. It is only much later that he unravels the mystery:

> It was because of me that they abandoned their villages and it was only in order to discourage me, to convince me that my insistence was useless, that they picked out places each time more hostile, imposing upon themselves life conditions more and more terrible. [*VME* 150]

Instead of the quest leading to the discovery and rebuilding of a lost civ-

---

9. In French, "*quelques dizaines de mots*," namely tens and not dozens: Perec's play on the number ten loses its visibility in the translated version.

ilization, the opposite happens: the Kubus disappear, the researcher disappears, and his mother disappears.

More than anything else, it is the systematic dimension of the narrative that undermines its plausibility. A strange numeric logic seems to determine the unraveling of the events: the Kubu village has first five, then ten huts: the Kubu's vocabulary does not exceed tens of words. Appenzzell goes to Sumatra in 1932 when he is twenty-three years old. When he is found six years later (that is, 23 plus 6), he weighs twenty-nine kilograms (six years + 23 years = 29 kilograms). Appenzzell pursues the Kubus for five years; he figures out the truth five months after his second departure. Finally, the time span of the expedition—five years and eleven months—appears in the text in four different forms: five years and eleven months, 71 months (orally said *soixante et onze*, but written 7 and 1), and six years minus one month = 6 minus 1.

The numbers one and six appear in the text with high frequency, and always in proximity to one another. Six years separate the death of Mrs. Appenzzell—killed in 1944—from the apartment's being taken over by the Altamonts, at the beginning of the fifties. Between the number 44 and the age of Mrs. Altamont—45—there is one year. Appenzzell gives himself six months to organize his notes; in the end, only one thin notebook remains. Appenzzell is found 600 kilometers from his departure point; the trip back to Paris lasts one month.

The numbers 7 and 1 appear only twice. First when it is mentioned that Appenzzell kept no document on what had happened during those 71 months, and again when it is mentioned at the end of the chapter that the Altamonts have a seventeen-year-old daughter named Véronique. Much later in the novel, Perec mentions several times that Véronique Altamont is a sixteen-year-old girl. The fictive "seventeen" seems to be the inverse of the number 71, just as Appenzzell's age, 23, is the inverse of the year of his departure to Sumatra (1932).

Finally, the insistence on several incongruous details in the appearance and the behavior of Marcel Appenzzell seems symptomatic:

> His sole piece of clothing was a kind of trousers made of innumerable small pieces of cloth sewn together, attached with yellow suspenders apparently intact, but having lost all their elasticity. [*VME* 145]

Later,

> When his mother entered his room, she would often find him not at his working desk, but sitting erect on the edge of the bed, his hands on his knees, staring vacantly at a wasp bustling about at the window, or fix-

ating as if to find some lost thread at the fringed gray-brown linen towel with the double black-brown border hanging on a nail behind the door. [*VME* 146]

One is struck by the incongruity of Appenzzell's costume, by the contrast between the trousers—innumerable little pieces of cloth sewn together, quilt-like—and the traditional leaves or rags of the jungle survivor. This piece of clothing, which is reminiscent of a clown's costume with its yellow suspenders, acquires an entirely different meaning when a link is established between it and the wasp and towel in the second quotation. If the yellow color connects to the star that Mrs. Appenzzell does not sew on her clothes—"Mrs. Appenzzell insisted on staying in Paris even after her name appeared on a list of Jews not wearing the star" (*VME* 150)—the fringed linen towel with the black-brown border connotes the Jewish prayer shawl, the Talit[10] and, on another associative level, activated by the grayish color and the (wasp's) stripes, the prisoner's outfit. Added to the indication of Appenzzell's weight in the earlier description—"he weighed twenty-nine kilograms"—this double connotation of yellow star and prison builds up a specific context, which has temporarily been suspended during the first metaphorical understanding of the text, namely the concentration camp universe.

It is not irrelevant, given this context, that it is Appenzzell's mother who should discover him staring vacantly at the wasp. One recognizes the neuralgic point of Perec's biography, the disappearance of his mother in a gas chamber when he was six, and the absence of memory of this lost mother. Upon carefully rereading the passage relating the circumstances of Mrs. Appenzzell's death, one finds that 1944 is not the date of Perec's mother's death, but of his father's (1940), added to Perec's age—four—when this death occurred:[11]

---

10. For the reader familiar with the Jewish tradition. A different reading would no doubt link the linen towel to the pseudo-Catholic item found in Perec's *Saint Jerome in his Study:* "On one side of the shelves are fixed two austere hooks, one of which bears an item of clothing that may be an amice or a stole, but is more likely a towel," *Espèces d'espaces* (Paris: Galilée, 1974), 120; *Species of Spaces and Other Pieces*, trans. John Sturrock (London: Penguin, 1999), 87. Subsequently cited as *EE*. This leads to a more mediated relation between Perec and Jewishness. For a detailed study of this text, see Bernard Magné's enlightening "Saint Jérôme mode d'emploi," in *L'oeil d'abord . . . Georges Perec et la peinture, Cahiers Georges Perec* 6 (Paris: Seuil, 1996): 91–112.

11. Because she fails to identify the specific numeric system at play in the chapter, Isabelle Danguy's otherwise extremely attentive reading interprets the lack of any mention of Appenzzell's father as "corresponding" directly to the absence of Perec's own father from his life. See Isabelle Danguy, "La vie mode d'emploi de Georges Perec, Étude du chapitre XXV," in *L'École des lettres* 8 (Paris: L'école des loisirs, 1993): 77.

They would come to arrest her the following day *at dawn*.... She joined the Resistance. She was *killed in June forty-four* near Vassieux-en-Vercors. [*VME* 150; my italics]

The words "killed in June," coupled with the warning on the note "the following day, at dawn," also refer to the description Perec gave in his autobiography of his father's death: killed—at dawn, in the Aube (the name of a department, but also meaning "dawn" in French), the day after the ceasefire, June sixteenth (*W* 53). The sixteenth is the inverted referent to the numbers 6 and 1, and to the six years minus one month, the duration of Appenzzell's expedition.

One should look for Perec's mother elsewhere in the text, not in Vassieux-en-Vercors, France, but on the other side of the world, in the heart of jungle on the island of Sumatra. The text points in this direction through a discreet alliteration: "Like their *distant* neighbors [*voisins*], the papouas . . . , Mrs. Altamont is a *distant* second cou*sin* to Mrs. Appenzzell" (*VME* 148, 150, my italics). The alliteration *voisin-cousin(e)* establishes a syntactic connection between the Kubus, the distant *cousins/voisins* of the Papouas, and Mrs. Appenzzell, who has for a distant cousin Mrs. Altamont. This link leads one to superimpose Appenzzell's mother onto the ghostly inhabitants, the Kubus, and to understand the Sumatra episode as the representation of Perec's desire to join his mother through the act of writing. Desire can be expressed only through the disappearance of the subject. Joining the vanished mother means disappearing into her wake. The narrative stresses the regression Appenzzell experiences: first he is transformed into a savage with monstrous hair growth and reduced to inarticulate cries, then he is plunged into silence, finally returning to Sumatra never to be seen or heard from again.[12]

The entire Kubus episode—their flight, their silence, Appenzzell's dogged pursuit of them—which is implausible from a historical or sociological perspective, is clarified once it is understood as the reflection of a psychic reality, the attempt to restitute what has been exterminated.

This *chassé-croisé*—the description of Mrs. Appenzzell encrypting the circumstances of Perec's father's death, the Kubus episode en-

---

12. Danguy notes the "M(aternal)" muttering surrounding Appenzzell in the text: Marcel Appenzzell, Marcel Mauss, Malinowski, and interprets Appenzzell's regression as "the heritage of a childish position oriented toward a mother figure" (80). In this instance as well, Danguy's overall thematic approach prevents her from interpreting the repetition of the letter "P" in another passage (which she does point out in her reading) as a paternal instance: "il épuisa en pure perte sa petite provision de thé et de tabac").

crypting the disappearance of his mother—is better understood when one reflects on the way *W* joins the incompatible, but impossible to separate, deaths of the father (a soldier's death) and of the mother (in deportation). Reread in this perspective, Chapter 25 becomes a broad commemoration of these deaths. The minutest details echo them, such as Appenzzell's age at the beginning of his expedition—23—which is also the date of Cyrla Perec's incarceration at Drancy (January 23, 1943); the return of the numbers four and three, echoing the year 1943, in the description of the Altamont buffet—*four* wall sections, *three* white silhouettes; *four* barrels, *three* chains—and in the description of the Kubus who vanish on the *fourth* day with their *three* goats.[13]

The reiteration of the numbers four and three—43—brings to the fore a grim detail previously unnoticed in the opening description of the chapter, namely the table made of Pompeii lava, on which is placed a hexagonal piece of smoked glass. The text signifies remnants of extermination—the piece of lava from Pompeii—supporting the mark of Jewishness (the hexagon, the six-pointed star of David, and the smoke). From this perspective, the cheese sticks near the mini pizzas—*pizzas naines*—on the Altamont buffet read as "feu (Mrs.) A*ppenzzell*" (deceased Mrs. (Swiss) cheese).

The text, previously understood as a collage of heterogeneous elements, now holds together as a single entity, whose apparent disruptions are needed to capture an event so obvious and clear-cut as to be inconceivable: a disappearance without a trace. It is this event that informs every element in its enigmatic structure of chapter 25. The spatial and temporal disruption was needed to allow it to emerge, not through the discourse of a survivor, who was reduced to silence in any case, but from what remained and escaped from the flames: the thin notebook partially filled with "often incomprehensible notes," encrypted signs, decipherable to those who know how to read them.

---

13. The 43 is also hidden in the use of octagonal, glazed tiles, and the words "hide" and "double" in the description of the room: "It is an *octagonal* room, its four diagonal wall-sections *hiding* numerous cupboards. The floor is laid with *glazed tiles*, . . . at the rear there is the door to the kitchens, where three white shapes are bustling about. To the right, *double* doors open onto the reception rooms" (*VME*, 143; my italics). Glazed tiles—"*tommettes vernissées*" in the original—are red in color and hexagonal in shape, linking to the "scarlet tongue" on the buffet, and the hexagonal table. Eight (the octagonal room) and six (*les tommettes vernissées*) divided by two (the double doors) are 4 and 3. The "diagonal" wall-sections "hiding" cupboards read like an oblique hint to the textual "storage places" in the text, which the Flaubertian scarlet tongue lying mutely on the Altamont buffet illustrates in an eloquent manner.

Of the event itself—the climb up the black river, the return to origins exterminated a long time ago—nothing can be said or written: it is the universe of the Kubus void of language, of inexpressible savagery. The sole issue offered to Perec consists in reproducing the itinerary leading to this place, and to confirm the improbable survival in the present. The Altamonts are a continuation of the Appenzzells: one learns later in the book that Mr. Altamont's first name is Cyrille, the masculine form of Perec's mother's Yiddish name, Cyrla.

On the last page of Perec's lipogrammatic novel, *La disparition*—320 pages without the letter "e"—one reads the following in red ink:

> The Papous' language is very poor: each tribe has its tongue, and its vocabulary gets impoverished constantly because after each death one suppresses a few words as a sign of mourning.
> E. Baron, *Geography*[14]

Upon comparing the spelling of "Papous" in the above quote to the one in Chapter 25, one finds a small difference: in Chapter 25 it is spelled "Papouas," with an additional "a." These Papouas instantly decompose into *papas-où?* (fathers-where?), pointing to the absence of the only father in this story: Mr. Altamont, "practically always absent from Paris."[15] But is he really absent? And what are we to make of the fact that he bears Perec's mother's name? Is transforming the disappearance accepted as such (after psychoanalysis) into an annual reception—with mini-pizzas!—black humor? Or, better yet, through the principle of repetition is it transformed into a pleasure principle? (One eats well at the Altamont receptions and can have Cyrla and Icek Perec return, so to speak, under the cover of Cyrille Altamont, every year, forever!)

Generally, the identity quest is based on the mnemonic traces of experienced events, and it usually contains three consecutive stages: the event, its trace in memory, and the restitution of the event from its trace. In the case of Perec, the two first stages are missing. The essential event of his biography—the familial extermination in the holocaust—is lacking. There are no traces in memory, or in reality (the mother, the aunt, the grandparents have no tomb). There is only a void, a blank, and just the third stage subsists: the writing, which for Perec becomes the paradoxical reconstitution of an absent trace of

---

14. Perec, *La disparition* (Paris: Denoël, 1969).
15. Clearly the ethnographic tale in Chapter 25 points to the literary dimension, namely Perec's work on language, rather than to the science whose methods of documentation it aptly parodies.

a missing event (let us recall the parachute jump and the analysis narrative).

Essentially, the two first stages, the event and its trace, are subsumed in the third stage, the writing. This process represents the opposite of a typical chronicle, where writing seeks to replace or restitute the event to a referential time and space, which partake of the past. Contrary to the texts of concentration camp survivors, which tend to function as monuments commemorating the memory of the dead, Perec's texts commemorate an absence. The monument—always invisible—is to be found *in* the text. But this is also where its readability touches a limit: when the three contexts—historical, mnemonic, and linguistic—coexist on a single plane, there is both richness and absence. On the one hand, there is only text, a Borgesian universe of texts: hence the multilayered intertextuality, the citation-beneath-citation dimension. On the other hand, the word is at once the absence (of the event, of the memory) and the restitution of that absence. The words are "lacking."

"Altamont, 2," written after psychoanalysis, no longer plays out the phantasm on the thematic level in the narrative. Instead, it displaces it to the planes of structure, through the use of disjointed fragments, and encryption, via word play and numbers. Chapter 25 is the illustration of a writer playing with (and through) psychoanalysis, a writer very much conscious of his obsessions. Knowing that he will not be able to liberate himself from them, Perec opts to make his obsessions material for his fiction. After psychoanalysis, his life truly becomes a "life in words," no longer a life of trauma. The symbolic dimension is transformed into playful ciphers—the father as Mrs. Altamont, the mother displaced to Sumatra, the Kubus staged—with which "identification" is no longer possible. This explains why the choice of a theme, of any thematic material, becomes secondary: almost any story line can work. Perec can now compose *La vie mode d'emploi* from lists of elements—why not?—not only heterogeneous, but without any apparent connection to (his)story.

Numbers as they appear in Chapter 25 ("Altamont, 2") of La vie mode d'emploi *(all emphases are mine)*

5	"During almost *five* years, Appenzzell persistently" (149)
	"The letter Appenzzell sent approximately *five* months after his departure" (149)
	"The village—*five* houses on wooden pillars" (145)
10	"A Kubu village, *ten* huts on wooden pillars" (147)
	"They used a vocabulary which did not exceed a few *dozen* words" (in French—quelques *dizaines* = ten(s))
32 / 23	"in 1932, he was then *twenty three* years old: (144)
23 + 6 = 29	"Appenzzell weighed *twenty nine* kilograms" (145)
5 + 11 = 6 − 1	"Appenzzell reappeared *five* years and *eleven* months later" (145)
+ 6	"She was killed in 1*944* [...] The Altamonts took over her apartment at the beginning of the *fifties*" (150–151)
− 1	"killed in *44* [...] she is today *forty five* years old". (151–152)
6	"He gave himself *six* months" (146)
− 1	"*one* thin notebook escaped the fire" (147)
6(00)	"more than *six hundred* kilometers from his departure point" (145)
− 1	"the return trip took *one* month" (145)
71 = 60 + 11	"what transpired during those *71* months" (146)
71 / 17	"they have a *seventeen*-year-old daughter, Veronica" (151)

JEAN-JACQUES POUCEL

The Arc of Reading in Georges Perec's *La clôture*

When Georges Perec characterized *La vie mode d'emploi* (1978) as a story "one devours flat out on one's bed," he evoked the novel's eminent legibility. He took it as a compliment when readers admitted to having been so engrossed by the novel that they overlooked how the book was written.[1] Such moments were perhaps small triumphs for Perec, proof that his assiduous attention to form had not clouded his lucid prose, and proof, too, that he had managed to pull the wool over his readers' eyes.

For the most part, however, Perec's tendency to dissimulate the intricacies of his poetics is outstripped by the generosity with which he accommodates spaces for readers to enter, and to find their own bearings in his books. Perec builds open space into his work by showing his reader how his books are made, how they fit together. *W ou le souvenir d'enfance* (1975), for example, presents a series of chapters in which two juxtaposed forms of narration alternate—a fictive tale of competitive sport set in a concentration camp, and an autobiographical account of the narrator's childhood. The jarring contrast between the two forces us to pause as we read the seemingly unrelated narratives, it encourages us to consider how both tales relate to each other, and, ultimately, it invites us to understand the novel in its post-Auschwitz context. The gaps in that text situate readers at enough of a distance that they *must* reflect on the form the novel takes, and how that form relates to what is recounted.

---

1. "You pay me a very big compliment in telling me that you did not see how the book was made." Georges Perec, *Entretiens et conférences* (*EC*) Vol. 2, ed. Dominique Bertelli, Mireille Ribière (Paris: Joseph K, 2003), 170. All translations of this and other texts are my own, unless otherwise noted. All page numbers refer to English translations followed by the French.

YFS 105, *Pereckonings: Reading Georges Perec,* ed. Warren Motte and Jean-Jacques Poucel, © 2004 by Yale University

The extent to which a work should reveal its constraint is a perennial question for the Oulipo, the group of experimental writers and mathematicians with which Perec collaborated from 1967 until his early death in 1982. At stake is the question of reading. At what point does the explicit reference to a text's generative constraint cease to enrich its reception and begin to interfere with, or completely obstruct, a naïve reading? And further, what is lost or gained on either side of that boundary? Generally speaking, Oulipians adopt the principle that a constraint should speak of itself in the work, supporting the claim that literary creation is the result of craftsmanship rather than inspiration. But there is no official Oulipian line that incisively responds to the question of degree. In fact, not only do the members of the Oulipo approach the issue differently, individual members respond to it differently at different moments in their career. A case in point might be made around the presentation of Perec's poetry.

In contrast to the novels mentioned above, Perec's poetry can be qualified as comparatively dense and impenetrable. The difficulties arise, in part, as a consequence of the Draconian restraints Perec makes central to his conception of poetry.[2] From as early as *Ulcérations* (1974), through *Alphabets* (1976), *La clôture* (1976), and *Métaux* (1985), Perec elaborated his own strictly condensed poetic economy in a generic poem he called the "heterogram." Consisting of elements adapted from the crossword puzzle, the lipogram, and the anagram (all combinatorial forms of writing in which Perec excelled), the heterogram is a poem written on a square grid using only the letters of a particular series. Perec's series of predilection, in *Ulcérations* for example, consists of the eleven most frequent letters in French—e, s, a, r, t, i, n, u, l, o, c—each of which is used only once in every line of the grid; that is, each line within the grid is the anagram of all the other lines; and, there are generally as many lines as there are letters in the series. In its raw form, then, the heterogram presents a radically defamiliarized text that appears, on paper, as a totemic block of capital letters.

In Perec's practice of the heterogram, the grid, or matrix, is also accompanied by a "translated," or "free verse" transcription of the poem, a text whose setting is naturalized, precisely in order to make it more readable. These versions include standardized punctuation, capitalization, line breaks, and stanza settings. When printed together on the

---

2. See Warren Motte, "Georges Perec on the Grid" (*GG*) *French Review* 57.6 (1984): 820–32.

same page, the two versions inform each other and, effectively, provide clues about how to make sense of the poem in relation to its mode of production. In this case, the matrix poem, the one written in the grid, serves as a kind of user's manual, a *mode d'emploi* for the translated version, which masquerades under the guise of free verse.

From 1974 until 1978, Perec doubled the settings of his heterograms in this fashion, often integrating his poems into more or less explicitly motivated art books. That is, like the juxtaposed narratives in *W*, in the poems' first editions, the typographic contrast between the two settings functioned as an operative aspect of reception (with added visual elements put into play). Since these keys to reading are in fact the forms into which Perec has literally inscribed his poems, in them readers can observe and marvel at the exceptional virtuosity with which he managed to master an extremely difficult form of writing under constraint. However, once Perec began thinking about collecting his poems into a single volume, his approach to printing the heterogram changed. In *La clôture et autres poèmes* (1980), Perec presents only the free verse version of his poems, cutting the reader off from direct access to their mode of production.[3]

Does this decision to hide the constraint indicate that Perec sought to make his poems even more impenetrable? Or, as his comments in various interviews suggest, does it reflect his desire to avoid a certain kind of reading? Discussing his work's critical reception, Perec remarked that, "for *La disparition*, [critics] hardly spoke of the book but rather of its system. It was a book without [the letter] E; and therein, its definition was exhausted" (*EC* 63). Along these lines, Perec's disappointment is all the more acute with regards to his poetry: "In *Alphabets*, readers practically never read the poems as poems, as nursery rhymes (*comptines*), but rather as exploits, and that's very troubling" (*EC* 63). Making constraint explicit, in other words, can also lead to a closure of the text, a closure that Perec figures as a kind of bedazzled blindness, especially when speaking about his poetry: "when one sees the constraint, one sees *nothing but* the constraint" (*EC* 171). To publish free verse settings of heterograms and not provide their matrices, he argues, strategically eschews a form-fascinated reading, and opens the door for the reception of what he so simply and beguilingly calls "a poem."

   3. Perec, *La clôture et autres poèmes* (Paris: Hachette, 1980), 11–27. First privately published as *La clôture* (Paris: Caniel, 1976). Only 100 copies were made of that edition. All citations refer to the individual poems by number as they appear in the Hachette edition. © Hachette 1980. Reprinted with permission.

I recognize that when I publish poems composed according to such complicated systems without giving the key, as I have recently done in *La clôture*, in the end the reader may receive them as a poem. At least, that's what I would like. [EC 171]

This statement is tricky and doubly encoded. In it Perec makes an explicit distinction between the strangeness of his heterograms and the familiarity of the conventional poem, and then he asks us ignore that distinction. However, as readers familiar with *Alphabets* know, if they can be read as "nursery rhymes," Perec's magisterial heterograms would contribute brilliantly to that form (and, more precisely, to the *comptine*'s deictic ends[4]), but only once one manages to make sense of the rather formidable difficulties the heterogram itself poses. Prompted by Perec's invitation, it is in this spirit, in search of a kind of *comptine*, that I provide a preliminary close reading of *La clôture*.

At the outset, let me point out that, like other readings of *La clôture*, this one explicitly evokes its formal constraints, for even when they are masked—indeed, especially because Perec hides them—those constraints contribute to the poem's force.[5] Perec's decision to cut the collection off from its original context should be read as programmatic, for it incites us to come looking for Perec's heterogrammatic writing, and to recreate on our own the sites of the poem's genesis. I will begin that process by describing the original context in which the poem appeared, and pursue this initial break as an intentionally performative move, one that orchestrates our fascination along two equally engrossing lines of inquiry: Perec's autobiographical writing of the self, and his elaboration of a poetics that inscribes meaning into the materiality of language, beginning with its most irreducible character, the letter itself.

RUE VILIN

The month before the first publication of *La clôture*, Perec and his photographer friend, Christine Lipinska, notified their potential patrons that a limited edition deluxe art book would be available in January of 1976. That prospectus explicitly ties the poem to a particular site.

---

4. *Comptine* refers to nursery rhymes used to decide who will play what role in any given game. An equivalent nursery rhyme in English begins: "Eenie, Meenie, Miney, Moe . . ."

5. See Bernard Magné, "Quelques considérations sur les poèmes hétérogrammatiques," (C5) *Cahier Georges Perec* 5 (1992): 27–86.

> I lived on the rue Vilin from my birth, in 1936, to the summer of 1942.
>
> Rue Vilin, in the 20th *arrondissement*, between rue des Courronnes and rue du Piate, has been disappearing for the past few years. One by one the boutiques have been closed, the windows have been blinded, the houses demolished, clearing space for vacant lots and palisades of cement.
>
> Several times over these past years I have returned to the rue Vilin to try to describe both the memories that tie me to this street (my grandparents' house, 1 rue Vilin, and my parents' house and my mother's beauty salon, 24 rue Vilin) and the vestiges, each time more effaced, of what used to be a street. [C5 153]

Readers familiar with Perec's work already know that trauma and memory loss starkly inform much of his writing. The details are minimal. In June of 1940, Perec's father, a recent Polish immigrant, joined the foreign legion and died in battle. Two years later, fearing for her son's safety, Perec's mother sent him to school in the south of France. His mother was arrested and jailed in Paris on 17 January 1943. On 11 February of that year, along with Perec's grandparents and other inhabitants of the rue Vilin, Cyrla Perec was deported to Auschwitz. No subsequent trace of her was ever recovered.

When Perec returned to rue Vilin years later, he had lost virtually all memories of his childhood. Consequently, he possessed no stable knowledge of his parents or his grandparents, save what he could deduce from the slim collections of objects, photographs, and official documents that his aunts had saved for him. Beginning in 1961, Perec would go to the rue Vilin explicitly looking for connections that could grant him access to the past, images that might open the floodgates of his memory. Nothing came. It was thus a doubly raw deal ("*destin cru*" [4]) for him to discover in the early seventies that one of the places most potentially capable of helping him recollect his lost childhood memories was slated for and already undergoing demolition.

Around that period of time (1969), Perec began a curious writing project he called *Les lieux*. That book, which he outlines in *Espèces d'espaces* and *W*, took as its premise the description of twelve Parisian sites over a period of twelve years. Perec would describe in writing each site twice a year; that is, two sites a month, one from memory, and one while he was writing at the site in question. He would then seal each description into an envelope, like a time capsule (sometimes including a photo, a ticket, a receipt, or some other proof of his having been there), not to be reopened until the project was completed. Perec claimed the final product would provide the record of a three-fold aging: the aging of the sites, of his memory, and of his writing.[6] But as an exercise, the project is designed to train the movement of the eye, to jog the memory, and to codify the notation of both activities, looking and remembering.

His incorporation of the street into this descriptive project is of particular interest to me here because in *Les lieux*, as in *La clôture* (which was written as a deviation from and a continuation of that project [*C5* 28 n.3]), Perec appears to have deliberately designed a therapeutic form of writing, in this case obliquely aimed at overcoming his loss of memory. In effect, had it been completed, *Les lieux* would have reproduced dynamics of reading similar to the ones Perec faced when looking at his own family documents, the ones that so hauntingly prove precisely what he can't remember. The envelopes of *Les lieux*, in other words, are analogues of the thin folder where Perec keeps his family-related photographs and documents, with the critical difference that once the journey ended he would have presumably remembered having written what emerged. At that moment, his connection to those places would have been confirmed in a rite of writing/reading that is also a kind of re-enactment.

It is thus no surprise that the rue Vilin is the privileged site of memory in *Les lieux*. There, as well as elsewhere in his *œuvre*, Perec articulates his particular sensitivity to the nostalgia that this street instills in him. And yet, instead of letting that nostalgia turn him away from the trauma that inhabits the street, he transforms his longing into a deliberate process of work, a process of mourning and remembrance that directly draws its working materials from the very things or signs that trigger his nostalgia. As the following excerpt from a remembrance passage suggests, Perec assigns writing the central role in this mourning process.

> What's extraordinary here, what makes of [rue Vilin] a model site is that in simply walking by and seeing things ("things," signs of anchoring [*signes d'ancrage*]), they impose their nostalgia on me (the longing for a native land, for an ancestral dwelling). My own tradition, my only memory, my only place is rhetoric = signs of inking (*signes d'encrage*).[7]

---

6. Perec. *Espèces d'espaces* (*EE*) (Paris: Galilée, 1974); *Species of Spaces and Other Pieces*, trans. John Sturrock (London: Penguin, 1999), 56, 77.

7. From "*Lieux*/ Juillet/ 1970/ La rue Vilin/ Souvenir," cited in *Georges Perec: Images* (*IM*), ed. Jacques Neef and Hans Hartje (Paris: Seuil, 1993), 121.

The homophony in this passage playfully describes a symbolic displacement that Perec had already incorporated into his work. Deprived of a stable relationship to the concrete places of his past, he had decided to take language as his chosen point of reference, as his native land and point of departure. The very notion of stability, then, is in no way a given in Perec's writing of the self, just as it is in constant flux in his poetics of the letter. In both cases, writing is cast as a means of shoring up space.

Throughout his work, Perec explicitly addresses the problems that space presents, not only with regards to describing—anchoring and inking—his sites of memory, but also with regards to marking their disappearance, their slipping into oblivion. On the closing page of *Espèces d'espaces*, for example, Perec explains his relationship to space in terms that emphasize both a writerly conquest of space and the sense that whatever is gained will eventually recede.

> I would like there to exist places that are stable, unmoving, intangible, untouched and almost untouchable. . . . My birthplace, the cradle of my family, the house where I may have been born . . . the attic of my childhood filled with intact memories. . . . Such places don't exist, and it's because they don't exist that space becomes a question. . . . Space is a doubt: I have constantly to mark it, to designate it. It's never mine, never given to me, I have to conquer it.
>
> My spaces are fragile: time is going to wear them away, to destroy them. Nothing will any longer resemble what it was, my memories will betray me, oblivion will infiltrate my memory, I shall look at a few old yellowing photographs with broken edges without recognizing them. (*EE* 91, 122)

If it is the absence of stable places and the corruption of the memories they support that most problematize space for Perec, then it is hard to imagine a site more urgent than his childhood home on the brink of destruction. By its occasion alone, *La clôture* marks a double closure, a two-fold ending at Perec's ground zero of memory. For, as he writes these poems about the rue Vilin, he knows this specific site of loss, this *momento mori*, is also fated to be destroyed.

CLÔTURE

As an art object, *La clôture* is both beautiful and enigmatic. Its first edition consists of seventeen black and white photographs and seventeen heterogrammatic poems, printed on large format paper, sealed inside a handmade box covered in ash-blue cloth and lined with black velvet. The pages and poems are not individually numbered. A separate sheet of paper lists the poems by their first lines. No order, however, is suggested for the photographs, which represent façades of the rue Vilin taken at the time of the poem's composition. On the pages where the poems are printed, the typographic matrices appear on the left, slightly offset from their free verse transcriptions which appear on the right.

One of the elements that makes *La clôture* (and *Métaux*) stand out in Perec's heterogrammatic poetry is precisely how its mode of presentation orients reading in the poem.[8] Presented in a *coffret à l'italienne*, the form itself incites readers to collaborate in the re-assembly and interpretation of its contents. Quite appropriately, Perec begins to draft this collaborative contract by enclosing the textual materials inside a sealed box (which he then wrapped up again in thick brown paper before delivery [*IM* 140]). In fact, the theme of closure is made apparent everywhere in the presentation of the text. It is exhibited in the text's title, in its occasion, and in its packaging. In addition, there are visual parallels between the typographic matrices and the bricked-up doors and windows in the photos, which denote closure, or impenetrability, as well as imminent demolition. But perhaps the most operative closures may be witnessed on the textual level, in the poems themselves.

The liminary poem, for example, speaks of closure along several distinct and interrelated lines. To begin, that poem names two endings, the first being the disappearance of Perec's family ("l'absent lourd" [the heavy absent]), and the second, the final days of Perec's family home before it is razed ("La fin trouble sciant maison" [The end blurs split house]). While both of these referents are implied in the poem's explicit end, to provide a "lecture du clos" (reading of the closed), the roles they play in this particular occasion are different. The "absent," whose heaviness implies an inability to ascend into the "ciel trop nu" (sky too bare), is effectively presented here as that which grants the speaking subject his corporeality. Or, more precisely, it is the absence of Perec's parents, his experience of lack in relation to their vanishing, that gives body to his writing, sound to his poetic voice. The "maison" (house), on the other hand, has a more occasional but nonetheless salient function: it stands in as a symbol for the missing, as an object through which

---

8. In *Alphabets*, on the other hand, Perec did not collaborate with the artist, hence the visual effects there are fortuitous, or not. See Mireille Ribière, "*Alphabets* déchiffré," *Cahier Georges Perec* 5 (1992): 87–150.

Perec mourns. Its imminent destruction provides Perec a symbolic access to the closure for which he may have longed: the opportunity to bury his dead. That kind of closure eluded Perec because, in the case of his mother, no grave, or tomb, or sepulchre was ever concretely established; like many victims of the Shoah, her remains were never recovered, never properly laid to rest.

To these forms of closure we might also add the impenetrability of the language itself, as well as the poem's own hermeneutic encoding. Though certainly not insurmountable as far as poetic difficulties go, the syntax of this poem leaves questions unanswered. Here, to make this point, is the entire first poem, and a tentative literal translation that does not, alas, respect the constraints of the original:

> Tels où m'incarne, ô rictus,
> l'absent lourd à ciel trop nu,
> > si calme,
> > transi ou cloqué,
> > criant secours.
> La fin trouble sciant maison:
> lecture du clos,
> art inscrit à l'enfoui clôturé.
>
> Sang
>
> As where, incarnates me, o rictus,
> the heavy absent in sky too bare,
> > so calm,
> > seized or blistering,
> > crying help.
> The end blurs split house:
> reading of the closed,
> art inscribed to the enclosed buried.
>
> Blood

The parataxis in the first sentence may leave one guessing who or what is "crying help": is it the "absent," or "me," the one implied in the direct object first-person pronoun (which, remarkably, is the only first-person pronoun in the entire sequence)? The potential polyvalence of that phrase heightens the urgency of the poem as an act of reading, and implicitly lends to the next statement its rhetorical force, its moral imperative: art is, or should be, a means of articulating and appeasing that cry.

The hermetic quality of the language here also arises from the specularity involved in reading and writing. The phrase "lecture du clos" (reading of the closed) reminds us that the object of representation is not only closure itself, but also the process of attempting to read what is hidden within its confines. Or, to refer back to his biography, it is the aporia in Perec's remembrance, his gaze upon the yellowing photographs of himself as a child near his parents, that urgently requires our attention. That act of reading as blocked remembering, reenacted in the space of the rue Vilin and in the space of the poem, produces the cry as much as it responds to it. In other words, at the threshold of the poem, we witness another doubling effect, a *mise en abyme*; we are invited to perform a reading of a reading that Perec has enclosed in an art form.

What's more, "art inscrit à l'enfoui cloturé" (art inscribed to the buried enclosed) repeats this almost tautological rationale built around closure. Like the box in which the poem first arrives, art appears as a self-contained, self-referential discourse, dedicated to that which is hidden or buried inside. This sense of double closure, and its artistic ends, is suggested here by the word "transi" (seized, or frozen) which, in its noun form, denotes a genre of medieval and renaissance sculpture. A *transi* (transito) is a recumbent effigy carved from stone or stucco on a sarcophagus. It represents the deceased subject in two states, the perfect living body above, and the decomposing body below. Its function is to ensure the passage of the deceased from one world to the next. While the word "transi" does appear as an adjective in the poem, it resonates with the images of blistering paint and peeling stucco that are "seized" in the photographs. Consequently, this art form gains added relevance in the general context of the poem, especially when one considers that in *Les lieux* Perec devised a means of retracing the mark and the decay of memory.

This sense of hermeneutic closure is further emphasized in the text's use of metapoetic language. Broadly speaking, each poem establishes a discursive game that turns in on itself, a game whose principle object is as much the description of things on the street as it is a performative commentary on what inscription achieves, or fails to achieve. To sustain this metaliterary discourse, Perec often states what he has or has not accomplished, always addressing himself in the second person: "Tu codas l'inertie d'un roc/ la soif creusant . . ./ la constance du sort ligoté" (You've coded the inertia of a stone/ the thirst digging . . ./ the constancy of the snared lot [2]); "tu façonnas/ ce tourbillon, tu rimas/ ce troc inusable" (you've fashioned/ this whirlwind, you've rhymed/ this durable deal [14]); "tu n'as orchestré l'inadouci, le sourd cantique" (you haven't orchestrated the unappeased, the deaf canticle [16]). In addition to describing exactly what his poem seeks to do, Perec also names the result, sometimes pointing to how the inanimate replies: "nul cri" (no cry [2]); sometimes coloring the tenor of his own voicing: "ton cri las" (your slack cry [9]). And finally, to insist on the self-referentiality of the poem as textual space, Perec repeatedly indicates that his poem is concerned with its own inscription of itself *on* itself: "l'arc où . . . tu lias/ la cour indestructible à son glas court nié" (the arc where . . . you tied/ the indestructible court to its curt denied knelling [8]); "inscrit sur le bon cadastre/ où linceul naît corps" (inscribed on the right cadastre/ where shroud is born into body [11]); "nouant le gris où pli scinda ce/ sort lu" (knotting grayness where fold scanned this/ read lot [12]); "l'ossuaire y clôt nue la mort/ inscrite au long scion d'éclat sûr" (the boneyard encloses death naked/ inscribed along the sprig of sure resound [15]). Throughout the poem, this metadiscursive encoding appears in many less direct moments, each of which points to both inscription and decryption.

In the case of the liminary poem, the opening words "Tels où" (As where) direct our attention to method in the space of the poem itself; then the specularity of reading and writing becomes the principle focus, the argument of the entire poem. In a sense, these two words put into motion the apodeictic axis of reading and writing that is sustained across the entire cycle, right to the last word of the last poem, where the notion of art as appeasement is simultaneously articulated and put into question:

> L'accalmie (ton sûr port au silence conquis): l'art?
>
> Quietude (your sure port to silence conquered): art?

In my opinion, this metadiscursivity sets up a double specularity that colors the entire process of reading. While Perec does present a description of space (and that space, as I've noted, is encoded as multilayered, including images of the rue Vilin, but also the attempted remembrance of those who lived there), in the same breath he also questions what, if any, closure his inscription will be able to secure. These metatextual properties animate anxiety in the poem and they force the reader to simultaneously interpret the text on several levels, according to different means of decoding, each of which is at work in the same space. Far from making the production of meaning impervious in *La clôture*, the carefully layered and circumscribed forms of closure that Perec assigns to the poetic space lead to an abundance of interpretive games, the most prominent of which takes the poem itself, its discursive art, as its principle object.

A closing point and a question, before turning to the poetic art of Perec's heterogrammatic practice. The final word of the opening poem, "*Sang*" (Blood), intones that despite all its outward signs of closure, the poem harbors at least one open vein. What's more, by its shape alone in the free verse typographic setting, does this first poem not visually prefigure the question mark that closes the collection, a question mark that would also nearly surround a square-shaped absence?

HETEROGRAM

In Perec's first childhood memory, set on rue Vilin, he recalls that his first conscious gesture was the identification of a Hebrew letter. The scene is described in a key passage of *W*, and has since become a privileged site of reading in Perec's *œuvre*. The critical attention attributed to this memory deals eloquently with the significance of the letter and how the passage illustrates his writing of the self.[9] In "Embellir les lettres," for example, Warren Motte remarks that the episode "figures two apparently contradictory states: alienation (Perec's separation from Yiddish, his mother's tongue), and vocation (Perec's becoming a writer)" (*WM* 111). Claiming that "it is literature that assuages his feeling of exile" (*WM* 123), Motte carefully shows how Perec saturates individual letters with meaning in a singular and deliberate effort to overcome estrangement. Very briefly, I would like to evoke this key passage in order to suggest that Perec's heterogrammatic work in *La clôture* participates in this therapy of the letter.

While I will return to Perec's treatment of the letter itself, for the moment I am interested in the terms of enclosure sketched in the passage.

> I am three. I am sitting in the middle of the room with Yiddish newspapers scattered around me. The family circle surrounds me wholly, but

---

9. See, for example, Marcel Bénabou, "Perec et la judéité," *Cahiers Georges Perec* 1 (1985): 15–30; Magné, "Le puzzle, mode d'emploi," *Texte* 1 (1982): 84–86; Philippe Lejeune, *La mémoire à l'oblique: Georges Perec autobiographe* (*MO*) (Paris: P.O.L., 1991), 210–29; Motte, "Embellir les lettres," (*WM*) *Cahiers Georges Perec* 1 (1985): 110–24; Ribière, "L'autobiographie comme fiction" *Cahiers Georges Perec* 2 (1988): 25–37.

the sensation of encirclement does not cause me any fear or feeling of being smothered; on the contrary, it is warm, protective, loving: all the family—the entirety, the totality of the family—is there, gathered like an impregnable battlement around the child who has just been born (but didn't I say a moment ago that I was three?).

Everyone is in raptures over the fact that I have pointed to a Hebrew character and called it by its name: the sign was supposedly shaped like a square with a gap in its lower left-hand corner, something like,

ㄇ

and its name was apparently gammeth, or gammel.[10]

In this version of the memory, enclosure is protective, and unproblematically equated with an unshakable security of familial love. That protection is amplified by the totality of the family being there and by their delight at the toddler's identification of a letter whose shape nearly sketches the enclosure described in the scene. However, the gap in the lower left-hand corner of this emblematic letter, as well as the various forms of uncertainty that cloud the memory, casts doubt on the imperviousness of the "impregnable battlement" protecting the child. If enclosure in *La clôture* is akin to the encirclement described here—and I think it is—, it is also intrinsically marked by the disappearance of Perec's family members, and correspondingly figured in the radically truncated alphabet of the heterogram.

While most might find little to say using fewer than half the letters of the alphabet, Perec found comfort and extraordinary freedom in this form of poetic expression. In an interview, he once noted that the work of heterogrammatic writing put him at ease: "[t]he intense difficulty posed by this type of composition and the patience necessary to line up, for example, eleven 'verses' of eleven letters each seems nothing to me compared to the terror that freely writing 'some poetry' would represent" (*EC* 99). This terrifying notion of "freely writing 'some poetry'" underscores Perec's critique of inspiration as a source of literary renewal and points, as well, to his deliberate address of grief in his poetry. If, in his words, "[p]oetry is a thing that provokes panic" (*EC* 171), it is the extreme constraints of the heterogram that "constitute for me a type of direct access to the unconscious, far more than any automatic writing" (*C5* 57). Though he may have been drawn to his own degree

10. Perec, *W ou le souvenir d'enfance* (Paris: Denoël, 1975); *W or The Memory of Childhood*, trans. David Bellos (Boston: Godine, 1988), 13, 23.

zero of writing, the so-called freedom of automatic writing bore no appeal for Perec, especially because his creative endeavors led him into digging up and mapping the landscape of the unconscious. Instead, his response to the fears he entertained about the corruption of space or the collapse of memory is the invention of a tight-knit poetic space that imitates, despite its absences, the safe enclosure so central to his first memory.

In addition to a truncated alphabet, Perec turns to the grid as a means of imposing rigor and meaning. Commenting on the coherence of its elaboration throughout Perec's work, Motte posits that the grid is "form in its purest state," adding that it offers Perec, and his readers, "a symmetrical space rigorously obedient to its own laws, in which is pursued the ludic activity of encoding and decoding" (*GG* 832). Furthermore, in his detailed study of Perec's heterogrammatic verse, Bernard Magné outlines the form's operative rules, specifically pinpointing the importance of "sutures" as a generative and hermeneutic device.

The heterogrammatic suture corresponds to enjambment in traditional verse, with the important difference that it is the rule rather than the exception in the grid, and it applies on the level of the word rather than on the level of the phrase. Consider, for example, these heterogrammatic lines, and their free verse transcription, from *La clôture*'s fourth poem:

   ... NISA*RU*
 *PTURE*NISA*CLO*
 *TURE*NILA*CHOS*
 *E*LAMORTNIS*UC*
 CUBELOSRIANT

 ni sa rupture
 ni sa clôture
 ni la chose la mort
 ni succube l'os riant

 nor its rupture
 nor its closure
 nor the thing the dead
 nor the succubus the laughing bone

The first four lines of the matrix break off in the middle of words (ru.pture, clô.ture, chos.e, succ.cube), whereas the fifth one breaks off at the end of a word, exceptionally coinciding with the free verse line break (l'os riant/). Enjambment in the grid thus has a function of tying the poem together, on the level of the line and the word.[11] It holds the entire grid together and, in the extent to which the sutures are maximized, so too is the hermetic seal of the matrix. In addition, enjambment is clearly the site of some considerable play within the confines of the grid; it is a means of cheating the constraint. For example, doubling back permits the inclusion of words containing the same letter twice (*rupture*), or double letters (*succube*). And, as the words "*rupture*" "*clôture*" and "*riant*" suggest, Perec has fun choosing where to break words and lines, and how to sew together the unity of the space.

Pushing the stitch analogy a little further, Magné thematizes the formal function of the suture. Reminding us that Perec often figures symbolic breaks into the presentation of his texts (e.g., by divorcing *La clôture* from its matrices), and that those breaks often refer to lesions, scars, broken bones or, more generally, places that bleed (*Ulcérations*), Magné attributes to the heterogrammatic suture an important unifying function: "In a quasi surgical sense, enjambment is an *operation* intended to reduce fractures. It locally achieves what, in its ensemble, Perecquian writing globally seeks to accomplish: to tie together the scattered elements of a fragmented story" (*C5* 46–47). The consolidation of the scattered fragments of the past into a single durable form is a leitmotif in *La clôture*, and it is the bright threat that unites the poem's metadiscursive commentary. The final poem, for example, straightforwardly states the rationale of consolidation:

> Car plus en toi s'unit l'archéologue
> criant son écart, plus il saigne court.
>
> For the more in you the archeologist unites
> wailing his split, the shorter he bleeds.

This figure of the archeologist identifies two juxtaposed movements, both keys to reading the poem. In order to bring the dismembered fragments of his story together, to knit them into a textile that will symbolically arrest, clot, or constrain the bleeding, the archeologist must dig. This apparent double bind forces one to wonder if Perec digs to bury or to exhume the traces that remain at the rue Vilin. Or, alternatively,

---

11. Judging on the basis of frequency alone, it is clear that enjambment is the dominant practice. Excluding the 17 final lines (where line endings in both settings necessarily coincide), of the 187 lines remaining in the poem's matrix, 29 end between words; of these 29, 14 stand alone inside the matrix (7 of those are first lines), and only 9 coincide with the free verse endings.

turning to the precise practice of inking and anchoring, of filling up space, this contradiction directs our gaze into the blank spaces that Perec incorporates into his practice of building, letter by letter, the matrix text.

JOKERS

One of the elements of *La clôture* that makes it stand apart from Perec's earlier heterogrammatic poems is the incorporation of a clinamen into the form, a clinamen that takes the form of "jokers."[12] Instead of building his poem on an 11 × 11 grid, as he had done in *Ulcérations* and *Alphabets*, in *La clôture* Perec deviates from that model by adding a twelfth letter that functions in the same way as the blank tile in Scrabble. That is, in addition to the truncated alphabet already mentioned—e, s, a, r, t, i, n, u, l, o, c—, in each anagrammatic line Perec recuperates one of the twenty-five letters that he had amputated from the dominant series (those letters are, in essence, his *disjecti membra poetae*). If this loosening in the difficulty of the constraint makes the language of *La clôture* more closely resemble normative language (*GG* 828), it also presents another window for reading the text. Because the jokers are visually marked in the typographic matrices, all of them masked behind the same typographic character, the section marker (§), they help elaborate the visual axis of reading I've already mentioned with respect to the photographs and the speculative inscription of reading ("lecture du clos"). However, granted that the jokers also provide for the return of the repressed, the apparition of the missing letters, their inscription into the closed space of the grid also points to a deeper, more rooted form of structural encryption. A simple example of this encryption is articulated in the fact that all twenty-five missing letters re-appear at least once in the body of *La clôture*, with the crucial exception of Z. If we examine a little more closely how these visual and letter-based codes intersect, it becomes clear that the poem orchestrates an internal friction or rift that is equally operative, thus resonant in form-motivated readings and in thematic, or autobiographic readings.

The fourteenth poem in *La clôture* presents an exceptionally interesting example of how Perec plays with the various codes of the form. Here, to begin, is the typographic matrix as it was printed in its first edition:

12. See Motte, "Clinamen Redux," *Comparative Literature Studies* 23/4 (1986): 263–81.

LATRIC§ENOUS
CAL§EUTRIONS
LA§RICETOSNU
ETLOINARCS§U
ERILSTU§ACON
NASCETOUR§IL
LONTURI§ASCE
TROCINUSA§LE
ECRISTULA§ON
IE§UNARTLOSC
ULATION§ESCR
E§ISCROULANT

At first glance, what catches the eye in this block of letters is the joker, or the section mark that simultaneously signals and covers up the spectral letters, or *revenentes*. To enter the matrix, our first gesture is to decrypt the jokers, like an archeologist who digs for artifacts. In keeping with his ethic of generosity toward his reader, Perec makes that step for us by transcribing the jokers—H, F, B, P, F, B, M, B, G, D, D, P—into the "translation." The ease of retracing this first step, I would suggest, prompts readers to enter deeper into the joker code, or to begin looking more carefully at places where the text provides for gaps. In the case of the individual poems of *La clôture*, Perec makes space for those openings by juxtaposing what the poems say to how the poems say it, by articulating movement in the interplay between the form and its contents.

La triche: nous
    calfeutrions l'abri,
    cet os nu et loin
(arcs puérils: tu façonnas
    ce tourbillon, tu rimas
    ce troc inusable)
Ecris-tu l'agonie d'un art,
    l'osculation des crépis croulant?

Trickery: we
    occlude the shelter
    this naked and distant bone
(puerile arcs: you've fashioned
    this whirlwind, you've rhymed
    the durable deal)
Do you write the agony of an art,
    the osculation of peeling roughcast?

To the extent that this particular poem describes a scene from the street, it focuses on the closure of space, and redirects the eye to the photographs of "blinded façades" with their doors and windows bricked and boarded up: "nous/ calfeutrions l'abri" (we/ occlude the shelter). The verb *calfeutrer* literally means to stop-up the open passageways in a window or a door, to hermetically seal spaces that are normally open and used for passing through. But split in two, *calfeutrer* reminds us of two particularly Perecquian procedures: tying together and the process of inking and anchoring. *Cal*, a word that appears in a similar context in the third poem ("Crois le ciment, sa lourdeur, son cal titanique" [Believe in cement, its weight, its titanic callus]), refers to the knitting together of bones, or the ossification of a split; *feutrer*, in its verb form, literally refers to the creation of the fabric felt, a procedure that entails tightly rolling and pressing together various materials (hair, wool, fur, fibers, thread); and *feutre* denotes a felt-tip pen. Each of these words thus communicates the sense of closure visible in the pictures and marked by the typographic matrix.

And yet, upon closer inspection, taking into account suturing as the central heterogrammatic textual "operation," the matrix text shows telling signs of leaks. The first three lines all stand alone, precisely not sutured to the others, each pointing to breaks that we might associate with "nous," "calfeutrions," and "os nu."[13]

LATRIC§ENOUS
CAL§EUTRIONS
LA§RICETOSNU

What's more, even inside the parentheses of the second stanza (and *parent*heses reinforce Perec's insistence on closure), we find the fourth stand-alone matrix verse (of which there are only 14 in the entire sequence of poems): TROCINUSA§LE (everlasting exchange). These stand-alone grid verses point to places where the matrix is crumbling,

---

13. In what he terms "the story of the bear" in Perec's dual bilingualism (the first drawing on Perec's French-English bilingual poetry, the second evoking the crisscrossing reading directions of French and Hebrew), Magné convincingly demonstrates how the bear, "*l'ours*," the most common animal in Perec's heterograms, is a deeply encoded figure (C5 78–85). Drawing on a Perecquian dictionary of out-of-the-way definitions, Magné manages to link "*oursins*" (cubs) to the word "*règles*" (rules, but also a French word denoting the menstrual cycle, hence a link to bleeding), and to Perec's insistent remembrance of his family. In that reading *oursons* becomes the English OUR SONS. Adding to this system of bilingual reading, one might also read into the words "*os*" (bone) the English homophone "us," which is so often figured as broken apart in Perec's work.

or peeling apart. In effect, as in the transito (*transi*), they point to the representation of the deceased in a more advanced state of decay. And, given the sites of their occurrences, I am persuaded that Perec strategically unstitched certain matrix lines to fashion signifying gaps in the texture of his poem. In this case (14), the poem most richly marked with this kind of decrepitude, the detached verses contribute force to the final question, and they perform the agony and decay that are described in the closing lines.

Another important site of this kind of detachment helps figure the poem's title, and reminds us, once again, of the object of Perec's mourning. The eleventh poem, in its first printing, marks its difference with respect to the other texts in that, on that page, the typographic matrix is printed slightly *below* and to the left of the free verse transcription (*IM* 140). The first lines of that poem read: CLOTURESAŞIN; "Clôture./ Sa fin." (Closure./ Her end.), and they mark the entire collection as a gravesite—or, more precisely, as a tomb intended for the memory of Perec's mother whose *acte de disparition* anchors her official death to a place, but only to a place in time: 11 February 1943.[14]

FOSSOYEUR

In some respects, constraint fosters restraint. And restraint, when its ends are focused, can also produce abundance. These two principles underscore how Perec maximizes his pared down alphabet to produce precisely calculated poetic effects. On the one hand, the elimination of twenty-five letters from his vocabulary forces him to mine the dictionary for jewels with which to coin his poetic lexicon. The felicity with which he had already accomplished this extraction in *Ulcérations* and *Alphabets* is, of course, enriched by the manner in which his poetry illuminates his other writings, and vice versa. On the other hand, despite the sometimes tortuously sinuous paths that these constraints impose on modes of expression, in *La clôture* Perec steadfastly understates the appeasement to which elegiac writing might aspire. That is, if Perec is testing the resourcefulness of language by recourse to anagrammatic and lipogrammatic constraints, he also appeals to conventional lyrical tropes, but in a muted and reduced, though sometimes oneiric, mode. And, once more, in keeping with his practice of re-collecting the material traces that evoke longing in him, it is in objects themselves, in this case words, that he invests immanence.

14. See Magné, "Pour une lecture réticulée," *Cahiers Georges Perec* 4 (1990): 159.

Illustrating the minimalist adage that less is more, the lexical field of *La clôture* is paradoxically impoverished and enriched by its radically reduced alphabet. While the constraint does not seem to adversely affect the variety of verbal forms Perec uses (there are more than sixty in the poem), it does impede syntax and thereby solicits strategies designed to optimize textual economy. Perec negotiates this syntactical restraint through aggressive punctuation, frequently interceding parentheses, and spare use of subject markers (*elle* and *une*, for example, are not used).

What's more, the confines of the letter series necessarily force the repetition of certain sounds, though relatively rarely does Perec resort to the repetition of the same word (except in cases like *"sort"* [to exit, fate], where wordplay is overt). There are, as a result, palpable sonorous effects created as similar, lightly varying words build in consonance, echoing one another from poem to poem. Two short lists elucidate this point. The first signals the central theme: *clos, clore, clôture, clotiner, cloquer, clouer, cloporte, clowns, clamer, clandestine* (shut, closure, drudging, blister, nail, book lice, clowns, clamor, clandestine); the second obliquely reflects the metapoetic thread: *secours, court, cour, courroux, coursant, discourant, corsant* (help, courtyard, short, rage, chasing after, discoursing, giving body to). Cast together in such proximity, each of these terms soaks up extra lyrical dye.

In addition to the effects produced by resonance, Perec structures his lexical archeology around linking techniques, investing particular importance in words that hold space together. Very briefly, I will index two families of words that participate in this general program of holding things together. The first is formally motivated and draws on the words that perform sutures inside the grid. The second is more thematic and draws on the act of gazing, or reading, as it is presented in the poem.

As I've already indicated, suture words are of particular interest when reading in the grid. Among them, two subclasses are particularly marked: words that emphatically state enclosure by incorporating the same letter twice, and, in the case of *La clôture*, words that explore the new lexical possibilities opened up by the incorporation of jokers into the heretofore closed heterogrammatic series. Within each genus we can identify various levels of optimization. For example, *"cour.roux"* (rage [12]) stands out because it contains three repetitions. Likewise, *"in*destructible*"* (8), *"**B**rocélian.de"* (13), and *"**b**rouil.lard*"* (fog [16]) come to our attention because they incorporate two jokers each, and at a distance of eight interceding letters in each case. Following the logic of the form, it is clear that since the jokers signal openings in the series and therefore in the lexical terrain, the distance between jokers within the same word is an additional means of marking their optimization. Similarly, in double letter words like "*os.suaire*" (boneyard [15]) the proximity of the letters underscores closure, or a tight stitch. These two forms of encoding are independent, thus not mutually exclusive, and there are varying degrees of marking, since there are varying degrees of separation.

However, if we analyze the two most marked species of suture words, those that inscribe double letters right next to each other, and those that include two jokers, we discover that there are ten double letter sutures and sixteen double joker sutures, totaling twenty-six especially marked stitches. This number suggests a recuperated alphabet whose amplitude is achieved on the level of formal constraint. Furthermore, if we cross the two categories we find that some words are marked several times over. For example, "*archéo.logue*" (archeologist [17]) binds three letters in the same word, including the jokers; or "*indestr.uctible*" which incorporates four letters, including the jokers. Finally, I would like to point to two similar, but perhaps a bit more arcane examples, both of which also bear the trace of multiple markings: "*brouil.lard*" and "*fos.soyeur*" (fog, gravedigger [16, 6]). If, as I've suggested, the lexical archeology of *La clôture* takes its initiative from words that hold space together, we might suggest that both of these words evoke Perec's insistent and contradictory desire simultaneously to hide and dig up things that fall apart with age.

Similarly, words that label the hardened or cohesive building materials mentioned in the poems (glass, cement, stucco, glaze, roughcast) also contribute to this general program of filling up and breaking apart species of spaces. Again, here I am looking at repeated instances of the same genre of phenomena. In this case, the encoding is more thematic, directly referring to what is pictured in the photographs, or things that are seen in the street. And yet their naming also obliquely elaborates the metapoetic discourse funded by reading and inscription. Here's how: the poem frequently takes surface textures as its visual referents, captures them in brief objective statements that then serve as anchors, as points of departure, or as points of contact from which the poetic subjectivity tries to pry new information. These "suture points" are critical loci in an extendable and telescopic axis of metonymic specularity at work in the poem, *qua* poem. That is, Perec's eye/I, indirectly implied and incarnate in both the poems and the photographs, invites us to gaze not only at what he describes in the rue Vilin, but also, simultaneously, to infer from the present traces what we can—indeed, what he can—about the past. Mostly, this attempt at reading into the space simply fails. But the experience is not a lost one.[15] For failure to elicit any new discovery provides the template for two forms of witnessing.

The first gives voice to this insistent digging impulse, and its tendency constantly to qualify or cast doubt on the value of the connections made. On these occasions, the poet directs our eye to an opening—for example, to "l'osculation des crépis croulant" (the osculation of the crumbling roughcast [14])—and then he overshadows the very premise for looking in, calling it both puerile and futile ("placet futile" [10], "arçon futile" [12], "arcs puérils" [14]). Such moments also give him pause to reflect on the deep rooted impulse, the id—"ça si trouble" (id so misty [12])—that drives him onward in his work: "Lors,/ clame construite pulsion:/ racine (tu l'as), corps forçant lieu" (Then,/ clamors constructed impulse:/ root (you've got it), body forcing space [3]).

The second makes space for the unknown, the unheard, the unseen inside the texture of the poem. This is done by simply naming what is out of reach: "l'absent," "glas nié," "hier clos," "clos pays," "cet insu oculaire," "l'inadouci" (the absent, denied knelling, yesterday enclosed, closed country, that unknown sight, the unappeased [1, 8, 8, 9, 16, 16]); or by the use of laconic, ungrammatical constructions: "ça si lent/ ça si trouble" (it so slow/ it so misty [12]); or, more visually, through typographical settings, as I've suggested with regards to the first poem, and the joker code. Both forms of witnessing are independent, thus not mutually exclusive; the rhetoric of anxiety itself produces the openings for what's missing, and in return, that rhetoric is generated by the recognition of an absence, by the recursive confrontation of aporia in memory. In short, it is in the interplay between impermeable surfaces in the space and the drive of his (our) probing gaze that we witness once again the scriptive drama at the core of the poem: the alternating impulses of digging and covering up, of piercing through and of enclosing.

A brief example, from the sixth poem, illustrates the protocols of these suturing procedures. That poem begins with a purely descriptive

---

15. In *Espèces d'espaces* Perec tries and fails to imagine "A Space Without a Use." In reflecting on that failure he remarks that "[t]he effort itself seemed to produce something that might be a statute of the inhabitable" (*EE* 35, 49). That comment points to the passages about "Uninhabitable Spaces" (*EE* 89, 120) which evoke the rue Vilin, the parsimonious space of private property, and concentration camp landscapes.

utterance: "Traces du lointain, rues cloportes" (Traces of the distant, booklice streets). This literal translation does not account for the fact that in French *"cloporte"* connotes someone who remains confined behind closed doors, and, by extension, a repugnant, vile individual, like a "louse" in English. These secondary, largely associative meanings shore up the text's connection to the rue Vilin, whose name also connotes vileness. They are refractory reminders that the inhabitants of that neighborhood were treated like pests, deported and exterminated in WWII; reminders, too, that in the early seventies when Perec returned to the street, the inhabitants who had managed to settle there, many of them Arab and Portuguese immigrants, were again uprooted and evicted in the name of urban renewal. The first meaning of the word, however, develops the poem's theme of interpretation, figuring the act of reading as a means of anchoring to and feeding from a single point of reference, as booklice do.

> Traces du lointain, rues cloportes.
> Fil à nu croisant ce flux (l'as-tu?)
> Incoercibles outrances gourant l'inarticulé
>   fossoyeur
> liant ce corps à l'inutile mourant scoriant muscle

> Traces of the distant, booklice streets.
> Bare thread crossing this flux (have you got it?)
> Incoercible outrages mistaking the inarticulate
>   gravedigger
> binding this body to the useless dying scoriaceous muscle

There is a marked difference here between the legibility of the first line, and what follows. It is as if framing the "traces" is itself enough to elicit the verbal commentary on what could remain. Above all, what this lexical display does communicate, however, is an unbendable will to cross what's in flux and to bind "this body," or the space of the text itself, to another. On two separate occasions Perec mentions "threads" (6, 10). The word is key because it recalls the opening of W ("I don't know where the break is in the threads that tie me to my childhood" [W 13, 21]), and because it participates in both gestures of reading as a metaphorical suturing, the piercing and the drawing together. In this case, the thread traverses a chaotic space, characterized by the determination and shortcomings that Perec may have experienced with relation to what he could not recognize, what he could not read. And, it links to an equally sordid place that is associated with uselessness, death, and slag, to a body that can be discarded. The tone here recalls Perec's sense of imprisonment within the writing of memory, his sense that enunciation itself constitutes a dead-end in mining memory: "[A]ll I shall ever find in my very reiteration is the final refraction of a voice that is absent from writing, the scandal of their silence and of mine" (*W* 42, 58). But there is also something to be said for what this poem does not say. It does not overdetermine the traces it reads, only notes their character. It does not say that Perec has fixed his (our) gaze on nothingness, nor that he recognizes what arises from the inarticulate. Nor, for that matter, does it invest hope in the implied metallurgical purification hidden underneath "scoraceous."

His is a visual scansion of space, a measured and methodical glancing at and taking note of small things. If his gaze takes its initiative from the desire to make unnamable stories speak, it does not lead to scripting those stories. In effect, while unnamable spaces may not be as tactile as the pane of glass (3), the cracked stucco walls (15), and the cement packed windows (14), in *La clôture* they are overtly constructed by what is not said, by leaving space for the unnamable, through understatement. Indeed, how does one write about gentle moments where the gaze itself unhinges words from within clogged up surfaces: "Un mot sec, mort au silence, sort câlin du stuc" (A dry word, dead to silence, leaves the stucco caressed [5])? Moments where what is listened to, what is marked textually, is precisely the silence that continues to inhabit bricked-up passageways, muted within the materials that seal them? What remains here signifies in lieu of what's missing. What is left is also left to speak of its isolation.

ARCHEOLOGY OF LETTERS

Perec founds his poetic language on letter-based constraints, but constraints alone are not what he writes. His ambitions for the letter, for the entire alphabet, are nothing if not maximal: "[O]ne of the things I am attempting is precisely to inscribe the entire world into the alphabet. All that we know of the world, we know it through words and all of these words are forged in letters" (*EC* 305–06). Alluding to the Mallarméan notion that the world was made to culminate in a book, for Perec, literary space is simultaneously small and vast, inscribed into language's most irreducible and combinatorial character. More than metanarratives, more than generic forms, more perhaps even than words themselves, letters animate Perec's imaginary universe. For in them, he invests an emblematic symbolism that connects and arches over the variegated works of his œuvre.

Sustained research into Perec's letter-centered poetics has progressively unearthed a deeply personal mythology of letters, an abstract and independent infra-universe encoded in starkly personal terms. The E in *La disparition*, for example, signals the novel's central formal and thematic disappearances while also simultaneously evoking the *eux* (them) to whom the novel is dedicated. Or W, in the novel by that name, emblazons Perec's feeling of exile into the form of a letter, one that is little used in French, if only for foreign words. Along these same lines, a second letter that also connotes foreignness, K, the eleventh letter of the alphabet, is at the very root of Perec's heterogrammatic practice. There are eleven letters in every line of *Ulcérations* and *Alphabets*, and it is not by coincidence, for Cyrla Perec was deported on 11 February 1943. Because Perec designs the deep structures of his texts on the basis of givens from his personal history, certain letters and their corresponding numbers become encoded sites of trauma, or sites of work and play where the writer negotiates the "destin cru" (raw lot [4]) that history made his. What interests me here, in closing, is how this infra-inscription reveals itself in *La clôture*, how Perec uses these codes to designate the object of his mourning and—perhaps more decisively for the question of reading—how they inscribe his signature deep within the poem's framework.

Granted its difficulty, the heterogram offers Perec a peculiarly reliable conquest of space. While writing, his progress through the series is certain, as much as it is incremental. In fact, the form seems custom tailored for the work of mourning, for the arduousness of the constraint itself gives body to the difficulty of confronting grief over and over again. As Magné has pointed out, the inscription of the letter directly into the grid recursively reproduces a reenactment of the trauma's source: not only does the heterogram impose loss on the alphabet as a whole, it also imposes loss in the progression of the series, as it is written (*C5* 33). In this respect, each line reopens a wound, first by recalling the absent letters, and then by imposing a one-by-one elimination of those that are left. It is a dark vision of the form, but entirely in keeping with the reenactment procedures I pointed to in *Les lieux*, as well as in Perec's estranging *La clôture* from its sites of origin. Working through heterogrammatic constraint as a means of voicing grief generously provides for a therapy of the letter, one that is both arduous enough to grant the work of mourning a stable and strong space, but dynamic enough to shelter the extreme doubts, helplessness, and anger that are sometimes occasioned by that work.

But inscription into heterogrammatic space also takes on a more abstract, emblematic character if, as Perec suggests, we approach the poems as nursery rhymes, or *comptines*. *Comptines*, moreover, refers to a specific species of nursery rhymes, those that are intended to designate the roles individuals play in a game. In effect they perform a means of naming by method and fancy, and most of all by modes of counting. Consequently, let me review some of the numerical structures at work in *La clôture*. There are $12 \times 12 \times 17 = 2,448$ letters in the poem which suggests a pattern built around the number 12 (12/24/48). These numbers designate the house where Perec spent the first six years of his life, 24 rue Vilin. In this respect, they anchor the text to its urban referent. But the individual numbers also impart clues to reading structure in the text.

"Poetry used to entail counting to twelve on one's fingers. Since this is no longer done so innocently . . . I have decided to call 'poetry' texts that are engendered according to difficult constraints" (*EC* 98). Until the publication of *La clôture*, Perec had avoided associating the numerical substructure of his poetry to canonical numbers. Nonetheless, his texts evince deliberate and lucid numerical structures. *Alphabets*, for example, consists of one-hundred and seventy-six *onzains* (heterograms based on an 11×11 grid), or, 1,936 anagrams written in the primary series: Georges Perec was born in 1936. But in *La clôture* and after, Perec seems to orient the numerical structures of his poetry toward more commonly used poetic numbers. This is certainly apparent in *Métaux*, a later collection that consists of seven heterograms based on a 14×14 grid, a form Perec christened "sonnets hétérogrammatiques." Yet in *La clôture*, Perec's foundational poetic number, 11, is still present and highlighted as the principle series, and it is the addition of the joker, the blank character, that pulls the form toward a more normative numerology, one that obliquely implies the alexandrine verse form. But perhaps more than conventional forms, in his numerology, Perec seeks his own degree zero of writing.

Indeed, to read the joker numerically is to associate it with the creation of empty space on the surface of the text (§), to associate it with the "nul cri " (no cry [2]) that Perec attends to in the rue Vilin, and to count it as a cipher for nothingness within the substructure of each anagram. That is, there are 204 matrix lines in *La clôture*. Or, to insist on the creation of a potential space, one that Perec anchors to the center of his childhood address, we might say the text consists of 2§4 anagrams.

Once again, this typographic section mark (§) figures open spaces that incite the reader to enter, and to make connections. Like the absent E of *La disparition*, or the parenthetical ellipsis—(. . .)—that separates the two halves of *W* (61, 85), it is central in the poem's emblematic inscription. Normally, the character itself signals the beginning of a given section, and thus the end of what precedes; that is, it denotes a break in the text. On a more figurative level, the shape of the symbol resembles two slightly off-set and superimposed S-shaped letters. This observation is suggested by the manner in which Perec mapped his street according to the shape of that letter. In that passage from *L'infra-ordinaire*, he is describing two bends in the rue Vilin: "This gives the street the shape of a very elongated S (like the high tension symbol [§§]" (*EE* 215).[16] The slightly off-set superimposition of the letters might also suggest a parallel with the two slightly off-set verse settings that appear on each page of the poem; indeed, strictly speaking, the verse forms of those two figures only really coincide, or touch, at the beginning and end of each text.

What is most telling about the joker code, though, comes into relief by accounting for the letters it reintroduces into Perec's poetic language. Of the fifteen estranged letters, only fourteen return (Z, the sign of closure, is the final missing letter). The fourteenth poem, as I've indicated, is the most strongly marked by matrix verse decay, and thus may also begin to sketch Perec's drift toward conventional poetic numbers. But scanning the frequency of letters more closely reveals that two marked pairs of letters, the two most frequent and the two least frequent to appear (D-P, K-W, respectively) are each twelve letters apart in the alphabet. This spacing technique echoes the analogous gesture in a suture word like "*indestr.uctible*" and it is overtly addressed when Perec writes "L'é-cart,/ dis-nous l'écart" (the split,/ tell us the split [7]), or else "l'archéo-logue/ criant son écart" (the archeologist/ wailing his split [17]). What's more, the only two letters to appear exactly seventeen times in the text (G-H) are right next to each other in the alphabet, and, like the double letters that mark a tight stitch in suture words like "*fos.soyeur*," they formally articulate the principle of tying together. In other words, on the level of the alphabet, in its most irreducible form, the joker code in *La clôture* also stages the knitting up and holding apart of spaces.

16. Perec, "La rue Vilin," in *L'infra-ordinaire* (Paris: Seuil, 1989), 21. See also *W* 77, 106.

Furthermore, the careful attention Perec pays to the space between objects, lines, words, and letters may also have been operative in his numerological choices for *La clôture*. I am persuaded that the text is not so much marked by an emblematic inscription of the letters corresponding to its two constituent numbers (12 = L, 17 = Q), but rather that it is considerably more marked by the letter that corresponds to their difference (5 = E). The letter E, because of its role in prosody, marks silence—especially for the author of *La disparition*. Likewise, the letters to appear only once, K (11) and W (23), are both particularly saturated letters in Perec's corpus. Both take information about Perec's mother as points of departure: eleven marks the date of her deportation (11 February 1943), and twenty-three is the date stamped on the very item in Perec's possession he knows his mother last held (23 September 1942). It will come as no surprise then to learn that $144 = 12 \times 12$ days elapsed between the two dates. That is, the very structure of the text designates an arch over the span of time between Cyrla Perec's last known act and the date of her official death.

The circumstances surrounding the official record of that date were undoubtedly a source of some discomfort to Perec.

> My mother has no grave. It was only on 13 October 1958 that she was officially declared to have died on 11 February 1943 at Drancy (France). A subsequent decree dated 17 November 1959 stipulated that "had she been of French nationality" she would have been entitled to the citation "Died for France." [*W* 41, 57–58]

I read his mention of the Mallarmé sonnet "Placet Futile" in the tenth poem as an allusion to this second decree, for in emblematically inscribing the details of his mother's absence, he also registers an official complaint for what he sees as a clear injustice. That second decree, in a sense, is salt in his wounds. This begins to explain why its date is doubly incorporated into the text's structure, first in the quantity of poems, and then in the date of the text's publication. That is, there is a seventeen year span between the date of this second decree (1959) and the date of text's first publication (1976).

But the number seventeen also flags two other motivating factors: Perec's mother was arrested on 17 February 1943; and, in the last item he knows she touched, the number seventeen points directly back to Perec, and his nationality. As is often the case in Perec's writing of the self, this episode is fraught with contradiction. This is especially so in *W*, when Perec is quick to associate his recollected letter to the G of his name, a telling association that quickly falls apart. In a note intended to rectify a mistake he made describing how his father named him the week of his birth, the narrator of *W* recounts that "the declaration . . . was entered by my father a few months later, on 17 August 1936 to be precise" (*W* 20, 32). In a sense then, the number seventeen is where Perec and his mother coincide, or touch at the extremities; for her it marks the day of her arrest, the day of her official "expulsion" (11) from the "bon cadastre" (the right cadaster [11]); for him, it marks the day his birth is officially noted, the beginning of his "ronce sublime" (sublime barb [7]), and the point to which we might affix his "Halo incrusté" (Encrusted halo [7]).

Finally, in his study of Perec's heterogrammatic writing, Bernard Magné traces an evolution away from a poetry invested in personal mourning toward a more occasional, public writing where the strictures of the form are perhaps a little less elegantly negotiated. To stake this claim, Magné points to the decline of sutures in the later poems (*C5* 29). The implication is that Perec was able to break through the form, and that it then ceased to maintain so much charge for his personal writing. Yet, the recursive doubt underlying *La clôture* betrays Perec's continued tentativeness with regards to what remains irrecoverable in his past. One continues to sense that the void into which Perec so arduously labored had not stopped eating away at him.

But *La clôture* is also a poem that marks a kind of arrival in Perec's poetic production, for in it he grafts a new, a mature, and a radically reformulated concept of poetry to the contemporary landscape. Indeed, Perec treats the heterogram with the mastery of a great poet manipulating traditional verse form. And his invention harbors the potential for at least as much virtuosity. In his hands, heterogrammatic verse reveals its own semiotic system in ways that inscribe human consciousness and pathos, without blockading them behind an opaque artifice or casting them in the dilapidated vestiges of rhetorical convention. Casting his experience into bold new forms in lieu of risking them to worn out convention, Perec enfranchises his readers and provides them with new avenues by which to question literature, space, and the means by which memory traverses them.

RENÉE RIESE HUBERT AND
JUDD D. HUBERT

Georges Perec's and Paolo Boni's *Métaux*

Georges Perec became close friends with the Italian sculptor Paolo Boni and his American wife, the photographer Cuchi White, when they resided in the same neighborhood in Paris. They traveled together in southern France and Italy. Perec collaborated with White on a limited edition book, *Trompe l'œil*, and prefaced a volume of colored photographs entitled *L'œil ébloui*.[1] In *Métaux*, an artist's book of epic proportions published by the master printer Robert Dutrou, seven "sonnets hétérogrammatiques" by Perec accompany Boni's "graphisculptures." An often-reproduced snapshot taken by White early in 1977 shows the three collaborators examining *Métaux* well on its way to completion.[2] Unfortunately, the book did not appear until 1985, three years after Perec's death. While belonging in the "livres de peintres" category—limited editions featuring original graphics—*Métaux* displays the innovative qualities indispensable in artists' books where bookwork plays a preponderant part. In this respect, it

---

1. Born in Tuscany in 1926, Paolo Boni has had numerous one-person shows not only in France and Italy, but also in Canada and the United States, of his sculptures, paintings, and "graphisculptures," a technique he invented more than forty years ago. For Perec's relationship with Paolo Boni and Cuchi White and all aspects of his life and works see David Bellos's illuminating study *Georges Perec. A Life in Words* (Boston: Godine, 1993). Professor Bellos has suggested several subtle interpretations of Perec's poems in *Métaux*. White's photographs in the privately published *Trompe l'œil* (Paris: 1978) accompany Perec's homographic poems in which the same graphemes result in texts that make sense in both French and English without ever having the same meaning. Perec prefaced White's *L'œil ébloui* (Paris: Chêne/Hachette, 1981).

2. *Métaux* consists of seven poems by Perec accompanied by seven colored and two uninked graphisculptures by Boni. Dutrou printed both the text and the engravings. All illustrations in this article are from *Métaux*. Reprinted with permission. Four of the poems from *Métaux* (B, C, G, V) reprinted here also appeared in *La clôture et autres poèmes* (Paris: Hachette, 1980). Reprinted with permission. © Hachette 1980.

continues a tradition that started with Sonia Delaunay and Blaise Cendrars's famous *La prose du Transsibérien et de la petite Jehanne de France* (1913).[3]

Métaux marks a radical departure from other artists' books. Boni's graphisculptures have little in common from the standpoint of technique with Hungarian sculptor Etienne Hajdu's embossed but uninked plates that accompany Pierre Lecuire's *Règnes* or with surrealist Jacques Hérold's numerous relief aquatints.[4] In his youth, Boni had earned his living in metallurgy. Instead of working on rectangular copper sheets, he rivets various odd shaped metal plates, etches, inserts found objects and clichés, carefully inks them, and finally produces an embossed multicolored engraving. Instead of the rectangular frame of conventional engravings, we see, in relief, the margins of the irregularly shaped plates. We become aware of a constant interplay between the white paper and the invading or retreating colored imprint. As a result, the graphisculptures can remind the viewer of Henry Moore's dynamic use of negative space. In perfecting these unusual techniques, Boni became aware that the same ink produces different shades according to the metal selected. As a result, his low-relief sculptures produce stunning painterly effects.[5]

Before composing the seven "heterogrammatic sonnets" that accompany Boni's graphisculptures, Perec had published *Alphabets*, limiting himself to the ten most frequent letters in French—**ESARTIN-ULO**—to which he systematically added one of the remaining sixteen letters called "jokers," as in a card game—each one making its presence felt in exactly eleven of the 176 texts.[6] The painter Felic Dado provided

---

3. Published by Blaise Cendrars in his privately owned Éditions des Hommes Nouveaux in 1913, this accordion fold volume that is two meters high has little in common with earlier "artist's books." See, in this connection, Yves Peyré, *Peinture et poésie. Le dialogue par le livre* (Paris: Gallimard, 2001); and Renée Riese and Judd D. Hubert, "La prose du Transsiberien et de la petite Jehanne de France" in *The Dialogue between Painting and Poetry*, ed. Jean Khalfa (Cambridge: Black Apollo Press, Catalogue of the book exhibit at the Fitzwilliam Museum, 2001).

4. In Pierre Lecuire's *Règnes* (Paris: Lecuire, 1961), Hajdu limited himself to deep, uncolored embossing. Hérold produced his brightly colored embossed aquatints from rectangular plates, for instance in Michel Butor's *Dialogues des règnes* (Paris: Brunidor, 1967).

5. Philippe Lepeut has explained Boni's technical innovations in *Graphisculpture. A Technical Study* (New York: Italian Cultural Institute, n.d.). See also Gayzag Zakarian, *Boni "Graphisculptures." Œuvre gravé (1957–70)* (Paris: Zakarian, 1970).

6. The joker functions as a sort of "clinamen" in Perec's poetry by introducing a disturbance in an established system capable of inducing change. See, in this connection, Warren Motte, "Clinamen Redux," *Comparative Literature Studies* 23/4 (1986): 263–81.

illustrations for *Alphabets*, but without bothering to study the poems, many of them decipherable.[7]

In *Métaux*, Perec followed a different but no less constraining formula. Each of the seven poems consists, like conventional sonnets, of fourteen lines. But as one would expect, adherence to tradition stops there, for each line invariably consists of fourteen letters ($14 \times 14 = 196$ letters per poem). In order to prevent giant folio pages from overwhelming these brief texts, Robert Dutrou printed them twice, first as small capitals forming an elegant square in the top left corner and then as a more readable free verse rendition in larger characters. At the bottom of each page, he noted in exiguous lettering the date and place of composition of the poem. The restrictions chosen for the seven texts of *Métaux* resemble those of *Alphabets*. Twelve letters: the vowels **a, e, i, o, u** and seven consonants **d, l, m, n, r, s, t** appear exactly fourteen times in each heterogrammatic sonnet. An additional letter—the joker—**b, c, f, g, h, p, v,** placed in alphabetical order, materializes fourteen times in a single poem. Featured in the only sonnet to which it lends its name, each of these letters emerges sporadically in the other six poems together with the rarely recurring letters **j, q, x, y, z.** Perhaps Perec's most difficult constraint consists in observing throughout the defining rule of the heterogram: he never repeats a letter in any of the ninety-eight lines of the seven poems. Moreover, he further reduced his choice by excluding **k**, the eleventh letter of the alphabet, and **w**, featured in the title of his *W ou le souvenir d'enfance.* Thanks to the exclusion of **k**, the **w** would have become the twenty-second letter in the alphabet. Bernard Magné has pointed out the function of **k** in several of Perec's works (65), and has shown the crucial importance for the author of 11 February 1943, the day the Nazis deported his mother to Auschwitz and the official date of her death.[8] Thus, the exclusion of **k** and **w** reveals once again the orphaned writer's obsession with disappearance and absence particularly because the circumstances and exact date of his mother's death remained a mystery.

---

7. Dado nonetheless produced innumerable drawings for *Alphabets* (Paris: Galilée, 1976). For the meanings of Perec's texts, see Mireille Ribière's "*Alphabets* déchiffré," in *Cahiers Georges Perec* 5 (Paris: Editions du Limon, 1992). We have found her remarkable interpretive study of these anagrammatic poems most helpful. In "Quelques considérations sur les poèmes hétérogrammatiques," also in *Cahiers Georges Perec* 5, Bernard Magné has provided indispensable commentaries on the technical aspects of these texts and shown how they relate to Perec's other works. He has also pointed out the connection between words referring to metals and Boni's "métaux rivés," 52.

8. In *Georges Perec* (Paris: Nathan, 1999), 65, Magné has also stressed Perec's frequent recourse to squares not only in his poetry but also in *La vie mode d'emploi* (75ff).

As though he had not imposed enough constraints, Perec added two more. All fourteen lines in the **V** poem start with the letter **v** while in the **F** sonnet the letters **m** and **u** cross the poem diagonally so as to form a large **X** or Saint Andrew's cross. Finally, he refrains from using the verb "to be." We have adopted the latter constraint, by far the easiest, in writing our essay. Unfortunately, we have had to limit ourselves to a tentative rather than an "Oulipian" translation of Perec's hermetic verse.

The arduous constraints under which Perec labored create difficulties for readers eager to appreciate the poems. Indeed, the texts definitely require collaboration on the part of consenting consumers. But before venturing into Perec's semantic minefields, we had better take into account the phonetic and typographical benefits of these restrictions. By including fourteen times thirteen letters with their attendant sonorities in a 196-letter heterogrammmatic poem, the author inevitably produces unusual sound effects. And it will hardly surprise anyone that Perec in relying chiefly on five vowels and seven consonants had knowledge of serial or twelve-tone music.[9] His "sonnets hétérogrammatiques" sound far less like Racine's flowing alexandrines than, let us say, Gerald Manley Hopkins's sprung rhythm. From a musical standpoint, his verse shows far greater affinities with Alban Berg than with Lully. Not that all seven poems sound the same: the multiple presence of the so-called joker letter—**b, c, f, g, h, p,** or **v** in a poem—does indeed give each text an individual sound track. In any case, constraints automatically assure the phonetic peculiarity and originality of each of the texts.

Starting with the large red design decorating the front cover of the beige box in which he presented them, Robert Dutrou skillfully made the texts and their constraints not only legible but also visually compelling. The design's contorted shape prefigures the graphisculptures while functioning as a readable text by prominently displaying the six letters of the title: M-É-T-A-U-X, and the acute accent on the E. The same design reappears within a dry printed graphisculpture on the enveloping cover page made of thick paper imitating the rough linen texture of the box. Small capital letters disport themselves like dancers on a second dry printed graphisculpture. The reader soon realizes that these seventeen letters form a readable text: "pour accompagner . . . de," preceding "Sept sonnets hétérogrammatiques de Georges Perec"

---

9. Magné, *Georges Perec*, 33–34.

and "Sept graphisculptures de Paolo Boni" printed at the top and bottom of the facing page.

The dancing letters actually function as a preliminary to the astonishing typographical fireworks that follow. We see at first small black capital letters scattered all over the page and, in the middle, a large violet capital **B**. On closer examination, we find that the seemingly disordered letters obligingly fit into fourteen groups: fourteen **a**s, **d**s, **e**s, **i**s, **l**s, **m**s, **n**s, **o**s, **r**s, **s**s, and **b**s—the designated joker—and fourteen disparate letters. Close scrutiny reveals that Dutrou arranged the groups so as to repeat the first line of the poem. The large violet **B** foretells the dominant color of the graphisculpture on the facing page and even its shape. Moreover, the groups of surrounding letters, each one differing ever so slightly from the others, prefigure, but more vaguely than the featured **B**, the shape of the corresponding graphisculpture (Fig. 1). With **C**, **F**, **G**, **H**, **P**, and **V**, Dutrou repeats the same maneuver. In the **F** section, however, **m** and **u** replace their usual scattered formation with two diagonal lines while in the **V** section the **v** forms a straight vertical line. As though to increase the difficulty of his task, Dutrou printed the **m**s in violet, the **u**s and **v**s in green. Clearly, the typographer did everything in his power to transform the text into a visual but nonetheless readable artifact. In fact, he engineered the progression leading by stages from the twice-printed poem to the graphisculpture. Moving in the opposite direction, Boni included legible words and numbers in all but one of the seven colored plates.

Perec's heterogrammatic sonnets lend themselves to interpretation more readily than the anagrammatic texts of *Alphabets*. Without ever becoming lyrical, they allude to the plates, referred to as "métaux rivés," to writing, and to personal experiences. Metals of all sorts abound in the **B** poem:

>Instar du plomb et du bronze
>Sa limpide brûlant somnambule
>>tris d'oxydes
>>laiton (brumes)
>>angström du billon
>>stries du Cambrien
>
>Tombacs d'ultime jour dans blindages
>
>>mort lubrique
>>blond mastoc
>>lambris net
>>dur tocsin déambulant
>>>Rhum d'œils

In keeping with lead and bronze
its limpid burning sleep walker
      sorting oxides
      brass (mists)
      angstrom of copper coins
      Cambrian striae

Armor plated tombacs of the ultimate day

      lewd death
      blond oaf
      spotless paneling
  tough sauntering tocsin

            Rhumb of typographical faces

The sudden appearance of a Swedish name ("angström") referring to subatomic measures produces a striking phonetic and semantic effect. A number of metals or metallic objects connect the text to the plates that Boni rivets together: "lead," "bronze," "billon," "tombacs," "armor plating," "tocsin," "œils," while "burning" refers to the heat generated in riveting or soldering and "oxides" to the chemistry involved in colored etchings. While this poem alludes more often and more directly to Boni's complex enterprise than do the following texts, it so happens that the artist has included in his first graphisculpture more found objects and readable clichés than elswehere in the book as though to reduce even further the gap between text and image. Of course, we can regard the metallic display in the initial poem as relevant to all seven of the colored images. Both "stries" and "billon," an ambiguous word referring to "copper coins" and to "furrow," relate to the numerous scratches Boni has etched into the plates and the ridges produced by their overlapping. Finally, the typographical meaning of "œils" hardly precludes an allusion to the small eye-shaped circles that decorate several of the engravings.

    The **B** poem and the accompanying graphisculpture interweave in more specific ways. As though generated by all the metals, chemicals, fire, subatomic physics, and disproportions such as "angström du billon," "stries du cambrien" and "rhum d'œils," a diminished and somewhat ridiculous human presence disports itself in the poem. The oxymoron "mort lubrique," suggesting a debased love-death relationship, the oafish "blond mastoc," and the uncertain tread of "somnambule" sound a disparaging note consonant with base metals such as lead, brass, and copper coins. Manifested earlier in the poem by the pun on "tombacs" and "ultime jour," threatening death personified as a noisy and metallic "sauntering tocsin" mockingly performs a triumphant dance in this end of the world *danse macabre*.

Far more anthropomorphic than the following plates, the **B** graphisculpture evokes by its shape and violent colors an aggressive and defiant dancer bent on expressing hostility. More than in the following engravings, the colored plates give the distinct impression of invading the surrounding white space. The creature expresses mockery in every gesture as well as in the numerous readable clichés displayed in every part of its body. Nonetheless, this brightly colored graphisculpture impresses the viewer with its Dionysian beauty.

In the **C** poem, Perec continues to evoke Boni's technique not only by referring to metals and acids—"bitten"—but also to the wires embedded in the metal plates and creating linear networks in the engraving:

>Le zinc mordu sature climats d'onyx:
>>Sacre du limon
>>tamis lent du corps
>>chemin du rat
>
>>lorsque - dit-on - macle du cristal
>>n'ombre plus mica dont cobalt s'indure,
>>modulant crispements:
>
>>>l'or du mâchicoulis d'argent
>>>mot armé d'un schlich
>>>solide
>>>murant

>Bitten zinc saturates onyx climates
>>Alluvial anointment
>>slow body sieve
>>the rat's pathway
>
>>when—they say—macle of the crystal
>>no longer shadows cobalt-hardening mica
>>modulating crispations:
>
>>>the gold of silvered machicolation
>>>word armed with a slick
>>>solid
>>>walling

In addition to several terms pertinent to engraving, Perec alludes to his own verbal performance: "they say" and "word" as well as to mu-

Figure 1. Paolo Boni, "Semi de lettres, B"

sic: "modulating." By means of burial, death makes its presence felt in "alluvial annointment" and "slow body sieve." Imprisonment—"walling"—adds to the negative impact of this poem in which onyx, mica, cobalt, gold, and silver scintillate in harmony with the bright colors of the corresponding graphisculpture. The expression "Sacre du limon" alludes also to the creation of Adam and to Prometheus's multifarious production of human beings while evoking the crowning of kings. In keeping with the idea of royalty, "machicolation" leads us back to the middle ages while emphasizing the verbal: "they say" transforms into a sort of Gothic novel, a fatal anointment combined with incarceration in the secret and rat-infested dungeons of a keep. Combined with this return to a distant past, the stress on chemistry and metals, particularly on gold, transforms the poem into a sort of verbal alchemy. The **C** poem develops even more intensely than the previous text the theme of death and a return to the past. Indeed, the **B** poem contained only one antiquarian term: "tocsin," an archaic warning system.

The accompanying image conveys a perhaps misleading sense of stability and calm. (Fig. 2) Instead of the frenzied anthropomorphic figure of the first illustration, we see a brightly colored and monumental landscape whose shape vaguely suggests a castle. The relationship between the colored imprint and its white support has changed. Instead of invading the white paper, the self-containing colored section seems to float above it. Even though a peaceful harmony has replaced warring colors, an inescapable feeling of immobility and imprisonment hardly marks an improvement over the menacing gesture of the first engraving. Fewer in number than in the previous image, the clichés have become more legible. Boni has added manuscript letters that blend in with the linear networks produced by wires. The resulting movement within the graphisculpture gives an impression of continuous creativity. Finally, groups of exiguous **xs** or white crosses evoke at one and the same time a medieval coat of arms and a cemetery. All in all, Perec's poem has privileged the somber rather than the bright side of this Apollonian graphisculpture. In that outstanding modernist artist's book, *La prose du transsibérien et de la petite Jehanne de France,* Sonia Delaunay had moved in the opposite direction by bringing out the sunny aspects of Blaise Cendrars's consistently somber poem.[10]

As we have already noted, Perec's constraints peak in the **F** poem:

> Métal gris fondu
>   ambre
> Flot
>   si d'un simple rond tu affirmes
>   vol du tant promis feu
>   Landes
>   film d'outrances
> Flot mû
>   brin d'ail
>   parfum dont s'éprend us à mi-
> flot
> L'an fait d'ombres refusant d'ombilic un
> flot
>   drames hurlant défis
>   mou frein d'Alsthom

> Gray melted metal
>   amber
> Flow
>   if from a simple rotundity you assert
>   theft of the promised fire

---

10. See *La prose du transsibérien et de la petite Jehanne de France,* 59–82.

Figure 2. Paolo Boni, "Semi de lettres, C"

> moors
> film at bitter ends
> Flow in motion
> garlic shoot
> perfume infatuating usage in mid-
> flow
> The year flees shadows rejecting the umbillicus of a
> flow
> dramas shouting defiance
> Alsthom's false brake

Perhaps because of the added restriction, this poem demands even greater efforts on the part of the reader than the preceding texts. In one way or another everything in this sonnet springs into movement as though influenced by the capital **F** that lets fly two arrows from its standing position. The "gray metal" melts down; "Flow" flows along while directly referring to Prometheus' theft: "vol," which means both "theft" and "flight" takes wing; "fire" spreads; "moors" extend beyond the horizon; "film" turns and moves beyond; "perfume" evaporates; "the year" speeds toward the years ahead. At the end, "dramas" transform this general flight into defiant shouts while "Alsthom," a giant corporation, attempts to slow down this irresistible rush so willingly accepted by humankind. Indeed, the affirmative "rotundity" rolls along with all the rest while shaping and formulating an approving **OUI**. This text in which metaphors of flowing predominate may very well refer to Perec's childhood when, fleeing the Nazis, he found relative safety in the Vercors region. In fact, the small lettering at the bottom of the pages indicates that he wrote the seven poems in conjunction with his return to Villard-de-Lans, the mountain village where he had spent his childhood. Boni provides some confirmation of this interpretation by inserting in the corresponding graphisculpture two Pétainist medals with the slogan: "Patrie, Travail, Famille," "Country, Work, Family."

No less than the poem, the graphisculpture conveys, by its centrifugal movement, a need to escape. (Fig. 3) Instead of forming a cohesive mass as in the second engraving, the various plates seem to fly apart even though the artist must have riveted them together. Boni has inserted a number of round objects such as medals and coins. One of them contains a date, 1967, perhaps the source of the fleeting year in the poem. Provided we can trust our imagination, we can perceive in the engraving a lurking sea monster and birds of prey. But because that menacing green arch also looks like an innocent telephone, it can relate to the commercial clichés clearly visible in the engraving and to the "Alsthom" corporation in the text. Moreover, the green arch adds circularity to the fleeting motion so prevalent in the engraving. Finally, the letters **m** and **u** forming an **X** meet in "mû," a word indicating movement while referring, like "angstrom," to a subatomic measure.[11] Indeed, science plays a part in this thoroughly "Oulipian" text.

In the **F** and **G** poems, metals continue to interweave, though less conspicuously than before, in both the texts and the graphics. But in **G,** Perec introduces painting and, more indirectly, music in addition to using terms relevant to writing: "mot" (word) and "pli" (fold), indicating the paper on which Dutrou printed both the texts and the graphics.

> Monde si brut:
> la gangue tord simple granit s'y modulant gris
>
> Doux mélange du pli Stromboli:
>   Sang
>   Dur temps du métal groin

---

11. For the implications of X, see *Cahiers Georges Perec* 5, 24.

Figure 3. Paolo Boni, "Semi de lettres, F"

    Crime du sanglot d'argent mis où flacon
    Gel du Mistral
    "String"

d'où embringue plat d'osmose,
    mi-glu d'anthrax,
     mot lu d'Ingres

So crude a world
the gangue twists simple granite self-modulating grayness

Sweet mixture of the Stromboli fold
  Blood
  Hard time of the metal snout
  Crime of the silvery sob set by the flask
  The Mistral's frost
  "String"

thereby involving dish of osmosis
    carbuncular half paste
    a reading from Ingres

More violent than the other texts, the **G** poem contrasts morbid viscosity, softness, and liquefaction with a hardness conducive to artistic constraint. The poem might even provide an appreciation of Boni who from crudeness and a contorted "gangue" has fashioned a work of art. Conversely, a "gangue," such as a volcano or a carbuncle, can cause, if not death, an eruption of burning lava or flows of blood, tears, and pus—"half paste." On the side of hardness, we find "granite," the purifying "Mistral's frost" and Ingres, famous for the rigorous precision of his drawings and for his fiddling. Indeed, this violin-playing master relates directly to "modulating" and "String." Hard metal finally comes to grips with organic viscosity in "metal snout." The "so crude a world," "gangue," "Stromboli," "anthrax," "flask," and "dish" function as containers ready to spew out their multifarious contents, including on rare occasions an artifact or a poem that has somehow escaped the general corruption. We can regard the text itself as a container yielding its constrained meanings to the patient reader. The English word "String" requires special attention. In spite of all the containers, it probably has nothing to do with the material used in packaging even though Boni embeds metal strings into his plates. Rather, it refers to "string theory" in keeping with other terms borrowed from physics such as "angström" and "mû." But because "string theory" derives its name from a comparison with the vibrating strings of a violin, Ingres's notorious violin becomes quite relevant. In any case, subatomic measures and the biological transformations of osmosis interweave metaphorically with the more subdued interrelationships of poetry, painting, and music.

The poem may have derived its complexity and its intensity from the power and complicated structure of the accompanying graphisculpture, the most spectacular in the book. (Fig. 4) Consisting of fragments of larger objects, the clichés fail to provide readable texts with the exception of part of a railroad timetable. As we have already noted, Perec wrote the poems in conjunction with his return to Villard-de-Lans and perhaps to commemorate the years he spent in this mountain retreat. Actually, he composed one of the sonnets on the train, no doubt on the capitalized "Mistral," functioning both as a powerful wind and perennially as one of the SNCF's crack performers. The Mistral stops at Valence where you have a connection to the Vercors. As David Bellos suggested to us in a conversation, the French railroad system emerges elsewhere in the texts, notably in "Alsthom," which supplies it with locomotives as well as brakes. And some of the lines in the engraving evoke a train in motion. More important still, the graphisculpture re-

Figure 4. Paolo Boni, "Semi de lettres, G"

sembles a "gangue" whose contortion sets off an overwhelming array of shapes and colors. In short, it functions as a potentially explosive container, even though the plates, notably those in the dominant red color, show greater uniformity than in the preceding images.

In the **H** poem, a legal terminology seemingly justifies drastic and definitive punishments:

>   Droit
>   Nuls mâchefers—lot humain d'un Méphisto
>   lardant dol mûri—sphériques
>   dont malheurs y liant d'hommes d'intox hurlant
>
>   Mais le jourd'hui manchot
>   les drachmes d'or
>   un lit très chaud, loin
>
>   Morphines
>   Talmud
>
>   Trahison d'emplumé hors l'indu bât

Law
        No clinkers—human lot of a Mephistopheles
inflicting ripened fraud—spherical
          Whose misfortunes tying in men of shouting propaganda

    But the armless today
        gold drachmas
    a very hot bed, far off

        Morphine
        Talmud

Betrayal of the feathered creature outside
Unwonted drudgery

By the inclusion of "gold," "drachmas," and "clinkers," metals continue to play a major part in this poem. In addition, "drachmas," ancient Greek coins featuring engraved effigies and words, relate to Dutrou's and Boni's crafts while metatextually involving writing, present also in "Talmud" and, somewhat derisively, in "feathered" ("emplumé"). The latter term can designate a writer holding a pen, a bird, for instance Prometheus's vulture, and "Mephisto," flying over Paris in Delacroix's famous lithograph. An opposition between fullness and lack also plays an important part as "Law," "ripened," and "spherical" give way to a truncated word: "intox" and to "armless." In the last line, the unwarranted imposition of "unwanted drudgery" contrasts with Perec's freely chosen constraints. We might also regard "Law" and "Talmud" as legal and religious curtailments of freedom. Goethe's and Delacroix's devil together with "a very hot bed, far off" suggest that tricksters, traitors, and perhaps even drug dealers might end up in Hell. But because "intox" (propaganda) has little to do with intoxication, while morphine induces sleep rather than hallucinations, belief in eternal retribution may arise from propaganda, from "intox." Similar in this respect to Goya's famous etching, "El Sueño de la razon produce monstros," this poem sounds like a wakeup call for humanity, victimized by religious restrictions of all descriptions and by various kinds of fraud. Perec, who often included English words in his texts, may have associated **H** with Hell.

Because the corresponding graphisculpture appears more symmet-

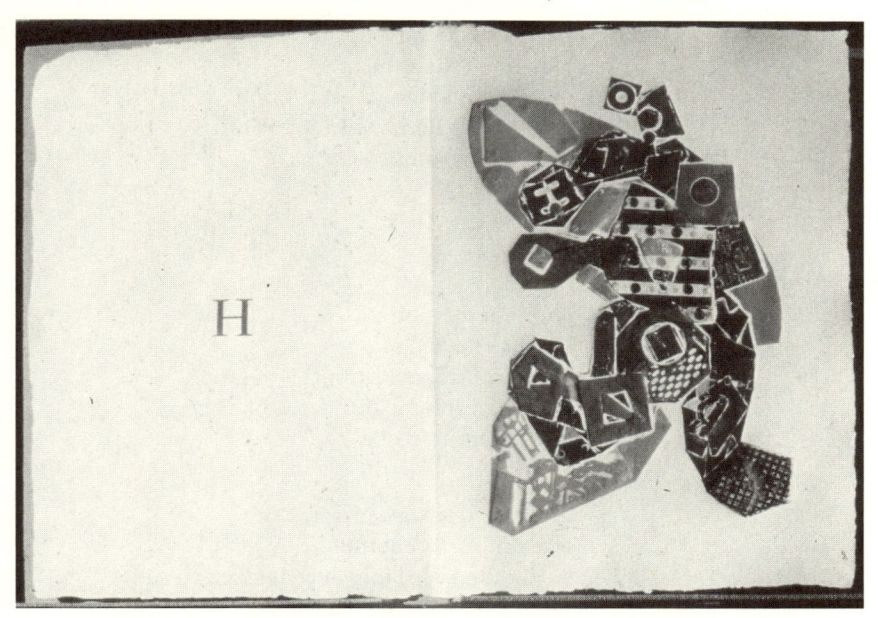

Figure 5. Paolo Boni, "Semi de lettres, H"

rically balanced than the others, Perec may have transformed "Droit" in the geometrical sense—meaning "straight"—into "Droit" in the legal meaning of the term ("Law"). (Fig. 5) Moreover, the various colored plates produce more decorative effects than usual. Toward the bottom of the page, we can see what looks very much like a stained glass window in a Gothic church. Scrutinized from the right, this purportedly abstract engraving reveals the threatening presence of a devil.

Surprisingly, the **P** poem does not contain any allusions to metals apart from the etymology of "surplombant," which means "overhanging" but whose root contains the word *"plomb,"* "lead." This term might describe the position of an observer looking at a graphisculpture from above. Though attributed to Prometheus, "biting the white fold" applies more readily to his vulture. It also describes the various operations required in preparing and printing a graphisculpture. Involvement with writing limits itself to a single term: "dits" ("sentences"), and music returns one again in "modulating." Nor has the author left out the idea of measuring: "empan" ("span"), a term as archaic as "machicoulis" and "tocsin."

Larcin su dompté
d'un sali Prometheus
mordant pli blanc d'esprit mou
défiant lors Puma, piment d'Horus
(lard), félin somptueux:

                Sprint modal

Humant d'espoir
l'empan sorti du flanc
trous de l'impavide mort
plus ne surplombant
dits du milan probe

Theft well thwarted
of a sullied Prometheus
biting the white fold of a yielding mind
then defying Puma, Horus' hot spice
(bacon) sumptuous feline:

                Modal sprint

Sniffing with hope
the span removed from the side
holes of fearless death
no longer overhanging
the honest kite's sentences

Reversal characterizes this poem in which aggression, transgression, defeat, and humiliation predominate. Prometheus, the persecuted Titan who had brought life and fire to humans, becomes "a sullied Prometheus," a thief who deserves the punishment inflicted by the gods, whereas his voracious vulture has metamorphosed into an "honest kite." Described as "fearless," death has usurped the role of hero, a role belonging by rights to an unsullied Prometheus. Transgressors such as the large felines and raptors who prey on and subdue others ironically function also as consumers of spicy food. And Horus, the sun god often represented as a falcon, joins forces with the honest kite. We may also detect irony in Perec's dwelling on, and exchanging roles with, Prometheus in several of the poems. He may have seen in this mythical figure a symbol of constraint, whether imposed by outside forces or freely chosen.

Figure 6. Paolo Boni, "Semi de lettres, P"

Boni did not include any readable clichés in the accompanying engraving. (Fig. 6) Although the plates extend more than usual, their trompe l'œil overlapping gives the impression that each one attempts to upstage the others. Far from creating anarchy and confusion, the artist has produced perfectly calculated entanglements where trompe l'œil arises from systematic reversals between the metal matrix and the colored imprint. Toward the bottom of the graphisculpture, vague animal shapes may have suggested the felines in the poem. And we can identify an anthropomorphic and somewhat diabolical form at the top with a criminal Prometheus.

In spite of all the usual constraints including the additional problem of starting each line with the letter **v**, Perec succeeded in including an obvious pastiche of one of Mallarmé's most famous lines from "Le vierge, le vivace et le bel aujourd'hui": "givrant d'oubli mes vols"—"frosting with oblivion my flights"—parodies "des vols qui n'ont pas fui" ["flights that did not take wing"] of the icebound swan. And he vastly increases the humor of his plagiarism by a play on words: "vol" once again means both flight and theft.

            Vides   (mot nul)
            Gravure
                                     (mots)
                   Plan d'ivoire
                   Lys d'un mât
            Vint l'arc des mouvances
Mort du livide lu sombrant vers fil dont mauve satin mord
    glu vile
Morts d'un havre quand mots livrent l'omis du javelot
         dans mur givrant d'oubli mes vols

                            (brandi, muet)

            Voids   (word of no account)
            Engraving
                                     (words)
                   Ivory plan
                   Lily of a mast
            Came the cry of motions
Death of livid reading sinking toward the thread whose mauve satin bites
    base bird-lime
Deaths of a harbor when words surrender the javelin's omission
         in a wall frosting with oblivion my flights

                            (brandished, mute)

The clever borrowing from Mallarmé adds a final touch to a poem in which writing plays the major part: "mot" (word) appears three times and "lu" (read) completes the picture. In addition, "lily of a mast" and "ivory plan" may indicate the color and flatness of paper needed in printing words and images. As in the previous texts, we can discern a spotty narrative involving a maritime adventure, as suggested by the presence of a sail, a mast, and a harbor. And we cannot ignore the perils involved in sailing as expressed in the negative terms "*nul*," "livid," and especially "sinking." The mention of "arc," "javelin," and "brandished" seems to increase the danger. But because these medieval weapons, no less archaic than "mouvances," indicating feudal dependence while suggesting motion, function at present only in athletic events, we can dismiss these perils as illusory. And the "glu vile," in the sense of bird-lime rather than glue, threatens only small birds. But it may also entrap the poet by stopping his creative flow. Stressing the

Figure 7. Paolo Boni, "Semi de lettres, V"

opposition between creative intent and resulting sterility, "brandished, mute" in the final line repeats Mallarmé's fear of failure. Perec's masterly irony may express in the guise of a sea voyage his failed attempts to recapture the past, a task made all the more difficult by self-imposed restrictions. And this poem contains even more terms indicating a lack than the preceding texts. According to Bernard Magné, these words correspond to missing letters in the alphabet. Moreover, Perec's interest in disappearances and voids has thus carried over from his novel *La disparition.*[12]

The corresponding engraving features even greater luminosity than the poem that darkens toward the middle (Fig. 7). To catch the resemblance between the green **V** and the image, we have to turn the engraving upside down. Ironically, fertility appears everywhere, particularly in the oversized cliché resembling a cornucopia and advertising a variety of fruits, vegetables, and dairy products for a Niçois enterprise.

12. Magné sees a connection between these negative terms and Perec's use of a lacunary alphabet (*Georges Perec,* 36). The murder of "e" in *La disparition* (Paris: Denoël, 1969) encouraged Gilbert Adair to perpetrate a similar alphabetic assassination in *A Void* (London: Harvill Press, 1994), his translation of *La disparition.*

In the lower part of the engraving, a cartwheel that might serve to steer a boat alludes to abundant crops and to seafaring. Moreover, this graphisculpture may complete the dialogue by commemorating the time when the poet and the two artists vacationed together on the Riviera. In this way, the book ends on a happy note after a succession of encounters with violence and death.

Although the seven poems resemble one another phonetically because of the constraints they share, the narratives they propose have little in common. They do form, however, a progression insofar as the emphasis on metals and on other aspects of Boni's accompaniment gives way to more literary and personal preoccupations. The fact that in all seven texts nouns far outstrip verbs results in an unusual number of juxtapositions, many of them producing astonishing effects similar in some respects to those produced by Lautréamont's famous metaphor: "Beautiful as the chance encounter on a dissecting table of an umbrella and a sewing machine." Actually, we can define the strange verbal encounters in Perec as epiphors insofar as the juxtaposed concepts usually clash and thus induce the reader to discover or imagine suitable contexts. It will suffice to mention the following encounters: "angström du billon," "Sacre du limon," "mou frein d'Alsthom," "métal groin," "jourd'hui manchot," "milan probe," "satin mord." The distances separating suddenly juxtaposed contexts set off verbal shock waves capable of increasing the violence evoked in the narratives. Abetted by the presence of death and a plethora of negatives, this violence might very well stem from Perec's frightening childhood experiences culminating in his mother's disappearance. The mad flight in the F poem and the Pétain medals in the engraving confirm his preoccupation with past events. Perec, however, involves more than his personal past insofar as myths, particularly the persecution of Prometheus, and references to the middle ages recur in the poems.

Although all seven graphisculptures show the vertical uplift of monumental sculptures, they differ from one another by their coloring and especially by the harmonious or conflicting relationships among the dovetailing plates. In some of the engravings, anthropomorphism predominates while others resemble landscapes. At times, a centripetal force gives a massive cohesion to the various parts while at others, a centrifugal movement sets off a helter-skelter flight. However greatly the imbrications of the plates vary from one engraving to the next, they always feature trompe l'œil effects, particularly because, as viewers, we cannot easily determine how the plates overlay or underlie each other. Perec, who had written a long introduction to a book of trompe l'œil photographs by Cuchi White, stresses Boni's use of this essential procedure in connection with an exhibition in Granada in April 1973, of the latter's paintings and engravings.[13] While Perec and the other members of the Oulipo imposed restrictions on the writing of poetry at a time when free verse and prose poems had replaced classical forms such as the sonnet, Boni and Dutrou greatly increased the difficulties of illustrating and printing books. A graphisculpture requires far more material effort and inventiveness on the part of an artist than etching or lithography. Boni gave up the traditional flatness of copper plates with their well defined margins in favor of a variety of unevenly surfaced metals riveted together to form a suitable matrix. And he had to insert all sorts of found objects, clichés, and wires in such a manner that they would enhance, rather than detract from, the engraving. With the help of embossing, he succeeded in transforming paper into low-relief sculpture. An artist who took such pains in obtaining results previously considered impossible would fully appreciate Perec's strange search for the most arduous of constraints and engage with him in a productive adventure.

---

13. White, Boni, and Perec—notably in *Un cabinet d'amateur* (Paris: Balland, 1979)—share an uncommon interest in trompe l'œil and other kinds of illusion. Perec prefaced an exhibition catalogue of Boni's works: *Paolo Boni, Mecanico de lo imaginario* (Granada: Banco di Granada, April, 1979) in which he insists on trompe l'œil in his friend's art.

JACQUES ROUBAUD

Les 17 expériences extrêmes de Perec

1. Perec déclame l'Erec de Chrétien de Troyes sur la montagne Pelée
2. Perec déplore la perte de son armoire normande en bois de teck
3. Perec, forcé de lire les discours du Général Peron s'exclame: "Mais qu'il est con"
4. Perec, forcé de lire les œuvres de Delly à Péronne s'exclame: "Mais qu'elle est conne !"
5. Perec opère des transformations oulipiennes sur les œuvres d'Eco
6. Perec récupère un chèque tombé dans la Seine avec une perche
7. Perec constate: "le nouvel ordre mondial signifie la perte de mon dialecte"
8. Perec se rend compte qu'il lui faut sans cesse récrire ou périr
9. Perec contemple l'écran où rampèrent ses phrases
10. Perec se souvient de celles qui le vampèrent devant une reproduction de Van Eyck
11. Perec éprouve un sentiment de paix rare à la lecture de maître Eckhart
12. Perec payerait bien mille écus pour une rencontre avec Isabelle Huppert
13. Perec regrette les rosées d'antan qui perlèrent sous les éclairs
14. Perec troufion envisage d'aller passer la perme à La Mecque
14. Perec admire les exploits de Persée mais sans excès
15. Perec enchâsse dans un écrin une médaille ayant appartenu à Jean Perrin
16. Perec pour une salade broie du persil avec un silex
17. Perec s'efforce d'évaluer l'horizontalité du boulevard Pereire avec une équerre

Perec's 17 Extreme Experiences

1 Perec declaiming Erec by Chrétien de Troyes on Mount Peleus
2 Perec deploring the perdition of his antique wardrobe now a wreck
3 Perec, forced to read General Peron's speeches, crying out: "Heck what a twot!"
4 Perec, forced to read the works of Delly in Péronne, crying out: "Heck what a twot!"
5 Perec operating Oulipian transformations on the work of Eco
6 Perec fishing up a cheque from the Seine in the mouth of a perch
7 Perec remarking: "the new world order means my dialect can't perdure
8 Perec realising he must constantly express himself or perish
9 Perec perusing the screen exhibiting his words
10 Perec remembering those which perforated him with love before a reproduction of Van Eyck
11 Perec calmly appreciating the performance of master Eckhart
12 Perec wanting to pay a thousand ecus for a date with Isabelle Huppert
13 Perec regretting yesterday's roses' perfume as thunder echoes
14 Perec cheekily asking for permission to go to Mecca
14 Perec's modest admiration for the exploits of Perseus
15 Perec putting into a casket a necklace belonging to Jeanne Perrin
16 Perec chopping aperitif olives with some silex
17 Perec carefully evaluating the area of Boulevard Pereire in hectares

—Translated by Ian Monk

Pierre Getzler, "G.P. reading a chapter of *Life a User's Manual* at the Pompidou Center, 1979," 1979. Courtesy of the artist.

Contributors

MARCEL BÉNABOU is a scholar of Roman history, a novelist, and, since 1970, the Definitively Provisional Secretary of the Oulipo. His first and latest books are *La résistance africaine à la romanisation* (1976) and *Écrire sur Tamara* (2002). Three of his novels have been published in English by the University of Nebraska Press: *Why I Have Not Written Any of My Books* (1996), *Dump This Book While You Still Can!* (2001), and, winner of the National Jewish Book Award, *Jacob, Menahem, and Mimoun: A Family Epic* (1998).

CLAUDE BURGELIN is a Professor Emeritus of French Literature at the Université Lumière-Lyon 2. His publications include *Georges Perec* (1988) and *Les parties de dominos chez Monsieur Lefèvre, Perec avec Freud, Perec contre Freud* (1996).

PETER CONSENSTEIN is Professor of French at the Borough of Manhattan Community College of the City University of New York. He is the author of *Literary Memory, Consciousness and the Group Oulipo* (2002) and the editor of a casebook on Jacques Roubaud's *The Great Fire of London* (www.centerforbookculture.org/casebooks). He is currently translating Dominique Fourcade's *IL*, writing an article on George Perec's *A Man Asleep*, and studying contemporary French poetry.

PIERRE GETZLER is a painter who lives and works in Bagnolet, near Paris. His paintings, drawings, watercolors, and etchings have appeared in conjunction with writings by H. Deluy, J. Jouet, G. Perec, J. Roubaud, and P. L. Rossi. He has written on Perec's *Species of Spaces and Other Pieces* and collaborated with Roubaud on *Le sonnet en France des origines à 1630* (1998) as well as *Sonnet en France 1631/1800* (2002). His work has been exhibited broadly.

RENÉE RIESE HUBERT, Professor Emerita, University of California at Irvine, is the author of *Surrealism and the Book* (1988) and *Magnifying Mirrors: Women, Surrealism and Partnership* (1994). JUDD D. HUBERT, Professor Emeritus, University of California at Irvine, is the author of *Metatheater: The Example of Shakespeare* (1991) and *Corneille's Performative Metaphors* (1997). Together they have written *The Cutting Edge of Reading: Artists' Books* (1999).

JACQUES JOUET is a poet, novelist, playwright, and essayist. He joined the Oulipo in 1983. His recent novels include *Mon bel autocar* (2003), *La république de Mek-Ouyes* (2001), *Une réunion pour le nettoiement* (2001) and *Fins* (1999). His poetic works include *Poèmes avec partenaires* (2002), *Poèmes de métro* (2000), and *Navet, linge, œil-de-vieux* (1998). He is the author of the play *Vanghel* (2003). A special edition of the journal *SubStance* (number 96, 2001) is devoted to his work and an English translation of his second novel, *Mountain R,* appeared in 2004.

SYDNEY LÉVY is Professor of French and Comparative Literature at the University of California, Santa Barbara. He has written on twentieth-century poetry and on Balzac, Poe, Queneau, and Perec. He has translated contemporary American poetry, and has co-founded and co-edited the journal *SubStance: A Review of Theory and Literary Criticism.* His latest book is *Francis Ponge. De la connaissance en poésie* (1999).

JOSEPH MAI is Visiting Assistant Professor of French at Tulane University. His dissertation, recently completed at Yale University, examines repercussions of secularization in literary and cinematic form.

BERNARD MAGNÉ is Professor Emeritus at the University of Toulouse Le Mirail. He has published numerous studies of Georges Perec, including *Perecollages* (1982), *Tentative d'inventaire pas trop approximatif des écrits de Georges Perec* (1993), *Georges Perec, Cahier des charges de* La vie mode d'emploi (1993), *Georges Perec* (1999). He also edited and presented *Pochothèque, Georges Perec, romans et récits* (2002).

IAN MONK is a poet who writes in both English and French, and a translator of the work of Georges Perec, Daniel Pennac, and Raymond Roussel, among others. He has been a member of the Oulipo since 1998.

WARREN MOTTE is Professor of French and Comparative Literature at the University of Colorado. His most recent book is *Fables of the Novel: French Fiction Since 1990* (2003).

JEAN-JACQUES POUCEL is Assistant Professor of French at Yale University. He is currently completing a study of the works of Jacques Roubaud.

GERALD PRINCE is Professor of Romance Languages at the University of Pennsylvania. The author of several books, including *Guide du roman de langue française (1901–1950)* (2002), he is currently working on a postcolonial narratology.

BRIAN J. REILLY is a graduate student in French at Yale University.

JACQUES ROUBAUD is a poet and has been a member of the Oulipo since 1966. Now retired, he has been a Professor of Mathematics at the University of Paris X Nanterre, and a Professor of Poetics at the École des Hautes Études en Sciences Sociales. His books include: ∈ (1967), *Quelque chose noir* (1986), *'Le grand incendie de Londres'* (1989), *La Boucle* (1993), *Poésie, etcetera: ménage* (1995), and *La forme d'une ville change plus vite hélas que le coeur des humains* (1999).

DAPHNÉ SCHNITZER is Assistant Professor of French at Tel-Aviv University. She has written on the autobiographical works of Georges Perec. She is currently completing a study on *Georges Perec. Une écriture oulipo-juive de la Shoah*.

ALYSON WATERS is the Managing Editor of Yale French Studies and a translator. She received a National Endowment for the Arts Translation Fellowship in 2004. Her most recent book translation is Réda Bensmaïa's *Experimental Nations or, the Invention of the Maghreb* (2003). She teaches in the French Department at Yale University.

The following issues are available through **Yale University Press,** Customer Service Department, P.O. Box 209040, New Haven, CT 06520-9040. Tel. 1-800-405-1619. yalebooks.com

69 The Lesson of Paul de Man (1985) $17.00
73 Everyday Life (1987) $17.00
75 The Politics of Tradition: Placing Women in French Literature (1988) $17.00
Special Issue: After the Age of Suspicion: The French Novel Today (1989) $17.00
76 Autour de Racine: Studies in Intertextuality (1989) $17.00
77 Reading the Archive: On Texts and Institutions (1990) $17.00
78 On Bataille (1990) $17.00
79 Literature and the Ethical Question (1991) $17.00
Special Issue: Contexts: Style and Value in Medieval Art and Literature (1991) $17.00
80 Baroque Topographies: Literature/History/ Philosophy (1992) $17.00
81 On Leiris (1992) $17.00
82 Post/Colonial Conditions Vol. 1 (1993) $17.00

83 Post/Colonial Conditions Vol. 2 (1993) $17.00
84 Boundaries: Writing and Drawing (1993) $17.00
85 Discourses of Jewish Identity in 20th-Century France (1994) $17.00
86 Corps Mystique, Corps Sacré (1994) $17.00
87 Another Look, Another Woman (1995) $17.00
88 Depositions: Althusser, Balibar, Macherey (1995) $17.00
89 Drafts (1996) $17.00
90 Same Sex / Different Text? Gay and Lesbian Writing in French (1996) $17.00
91 Genet: In the Language of the Enemy (1997) $17.00
92 Exploring the Conversible World (1997) $17.00
93 The Place of Maurice Blanchot (1998) $17.00
94 Libertinage and Modernity (1999) $17.00

95 Rereading Allegory: Essays in Memory of Daniel Poirion (1999) $17.00
96 50 Years of *Yale French Studies*, Part I: 1948-1979 (1999) $17.00
97 50 Years of *Yale French Studies,* Part 2: 1980-1998 (2000) $17.00
98 The French Fifties (2000) $17.00
99 Jean-François Lyotard: Time and Judgment (2001) $17.00
100 FRANCE/USA: The Cultural Wars (2001) $17.00
101 Fragments of Revolution (2002) $17.00
102 Belgian Memories (2002) $17.00
103 French and Francophone: the Challenge of Expanding Horizons (2003) $17.00
104 Encounters with Levinas (2003) $17.00

ORDER FORM   Yale University Press, P.O. Box 209040, New Haven, CT 06520-9040
I would like to purchase the following individual issues:
_____
_____

For individual issues, please add postage and handling:
Single issue, United States $2.75   Each additional issue $.50
Single issue, foreign countries $5.00   Each additional issue $1.00
Connecticut residents please add sales tax of 6%.

Payment of $_____ is enclosed (including sales tax if applicable).

MasterCard no. _____ Expiration date _____

VISA no. _____ Expiration date _____

Signature _____
SHIP TO _____
_____

See the next page for ordering other back issues. Yale French Studies is also available through Xerox University Microfilms, 300 North Zeeb Road, Ann Arbor, MI 48106.

The following issues are still available through the **Yale French Studies Office**, P.O. Box 208251, New Haven, CT 06520-8251.

19/20 Contemporary Art $3.50	42 Zola $5.00	54 Mallarmé $5.00
33 Shakespeare $3.50	43 The Child's Part $5.00	61 Toward a Theory of Description $6.00
35 Sade $3.50	45 Language as Action $5.00	
39 Literature and Revolution $3.50	46 From Stage to Street $3.50	
	52 Graphesis $5.00	

Add for postage & handling

Single issue, United States $3.00 (Priority Mail)   Each additional issue $1.25
Single issue, United States $1.80 (Third Class)   Each additional issue $ .50
Single issue, foreign countries $2.50 (Book Rate)   Each additional issue $1.50

YALE FRENCH STUDIES, P.O. Box 208251, New Haven, Connecticut 06520-8251
A check made payable to YFS is enclosed. Please send me the following issue(s):

Issue no.   Title   Price
_____
_____

                                               Postage & handling _____
                                                            Total _____

Name _____

Number/Street _____

City _____ State _____ Zip _____

The following issues are now available through Periodicals Service Company, 11 Main Street, Germantown, N.Y. 12526, Phone: (518) 537-4700. Fax: (518) 537-5899.

1 Critical Bibliography of Existentialism
2 Modern Poets
3 Criticism & Creation
4 Literature & Ideas
5 The Modern Theatre
6 France and World Literature
7 André Gide
8 What's Novel in the Novel
9 Symbolism
10 French-American Literature Relationships
11 Eros, Variations...
12 God & the Writer
13 Romanticism Revisited
14 Motley: Today's French Theater
15 Social & Political France
16 Foray through Existentialism
17 The Art of the Cinema
18 Passion & the Intellect, or Malraux
19/20 Contemporary Art
21 Poetry Since the Liberation
22 French Education
23 Humor
24 Midnight Novelists
25 Albert Camus
26 The Myth of Napoleon
27 Women Writers
28 Rousseau
29 The New Dramatists
30 Sartre
31 Surrealism
32 Paris in Literature
33 Shakespeare in France
34 Proust
48 French Freud
51 Approaches to Medieval Romance

36/37 Structuralism has been reprinted by Doubleday as an Anchor Book.
55/56 Literature and Psychoanalysis has been reprinted by Johns Hopkins University Press, and can be ordered through Customer Service, Johns Hopkins University Press, Baltimore, MD 21218.